THE REBELS

THE REBELS

A STUDY OF
POST-WAR INSURRECTIONS

BRIAN CROZIER

Beacon Press   Boston

©1960 by Brian Crozier

Library of Congress catalog card number: 60-11735

First published in Great Britain in 1960 by Chatto & Windus, Ltd.

First published in the United States in 1960 by the Beacon Press

Printed in the United States of America

Third printing, October 1964

CONTENTS

Part V: Repression

Postlude: A Glimpse of Sanity

From Author to Reader

I FIRST became rebel-conscious in Indonesia, Malaya and Indo-China in 1952. Since then I have taken every opportunity of meeting rebel leaders and studying rebellions, either by direct observation or by reading. A first, tentative presentation of the subject was my article "The Anatomy of Rebellion", which appeared in *The Twentieth Century* (London) in November, 1958. This book is not, however, an expansion of that article, for in writing it I have modified some of my earlier judgments.

It may be helpful if I explain other things which this book does not pretend to be. It is not, for instance, an encyclopædia of rebellions: many well-deserving insurrections have not even been mentioned. Nor is it a history of the rebellions that *are* dealt with, for you cannot write a history of events that are still in progress. Nor, on the other hand, is it an 'I was there' book; from time to time I bring myself in, but usually only to quote what some of the personages of this book have said to me.

The Rebels does attempt, however, to present an inquiry into the origins and causes of the major armed insurrections since the end of the second world war; to introduce the major rebel leaders; and to describe certain techniques of rebellion and repression. Here and there, and particularly in the Postlude, I try to suggest alternative courses of action which might have averted the violent outbreaks I have described, thus depriving me of the subject-matter of this book.

You will notice that all the insurrections or terrorist movements I have dealt with were launched against superior odds, nearly all by civilians turned soldier. I have not attempted to deal with successful *coups d'état*, such as those that killed off the Fourth Republic in France, deprived Perón of his power in Argentina or turned Egypt and Iraq into republics. This does not mean that I regard these *coups d'état* as unimportant; merely that the line I have drawn excludes the overthrow of institutions by the legitimate armed forces.

It remains for me to thank the staff of the Royal Institute of International Affairs for their unfailing courtesy and help; the Editor of *The Economist*, Donald Tyerman, for his indulgence; and my wife for keeping me at it and never complaining during a seven-days-a-week routine that lasted eight months.

BRIAN CROZIER

London,
  November, 1958*–June,* 1959

PRELUDE
THE ANATOMY OF REBELLION

IT has been said, rather unkindly, that history is made by historians. In a much truer sense, rebellions are made by rebels. This proposition is not as self-evident as it seems. Marxists would have us believe that historical movements result only from economic conditions and pressures. I do not doubt that such pressures play a part, sometimes an important part, in the upheavals I call rebellions; but many other elements come into play. And in any event, men do not necessarily rebel merely because their conditions of life are intolerable: it takes a rebel to rebel.

Look at it another way: some men or groups of men will tolerate more than others. If one describes conditions of life as intolerable, one begs the question: "To whom?" Millions in India are passive in conditions that would indeed be intolerable if suddenly imposed on people used to greater comfort and a higher intake of calories. Therein lies part of the secret of rebellion: hunger may spur a man to rebel, but not if it is a hunger so acute and constant that he is robbed of energy and the will to fight.

In another sense also, "intolerable" conditions of life are not by themselves enough to cause rebellion. Another factor must be present: the potential rebel must believe that by rebelling he will improve his lot. This implies that there must be somebody, or some recognisable group, to blame for his misfortune: something to rebel against. I do not suggest that this rule is without exceptions, for history provides many examples of blind and self-destructive acts of rebellion, induced by despair and inevitably defeated. But leaderless acts of this nature are hardly different in kind from mob rioting; unless they are exploited by "real" rebels and turned into real rebellions, they peter out. I shall not devote much space to them.

Inevitably, I am brought back to the rebels, the men who make rebellions. To rebel, a man needs will, courage, purpose and a fanatical concentration on essentials. A purpose is provided by external circumstances: it is what a man fights for and what he fights against. To the born rebel, the second is usually easier to identify than the first: it was clear from the start that the Algerian rebels were fighting *against* the French; what they were fighting *for*, beyond recognition of an "Algerian personality" or "independence", was less clear. On the other hand, it was clear from the start that Colonel Grivas in Cyprus was fighting not only *against* the British but also *for* the union of Greece and Cyprus (*enosis*).

The "for" and "against" constitute the purpose. The will, the courage and the concentration on essentials, unlike the purpose, do not derive from external circumstances. They are human qualities. A man may be born with them; but an aspiring rebel will need to cultivate them, probably for years, before they become serviceable and reliable instruments of rebellion. It follows that the proposition "rebellions are made by rebels" is true in the deeper sense of time as well as in the sense of human impulses. The rebel comes first, the rebellion second. Let me give some examples. Ho Chi Minh, the almost legendary Vietnamese communist leader, was already a rebel in the 1920s; but his major rebellion against the French did not begin till the end of 1946. Colonel Grivas, the leader of the Eoka terrorists in Cyprus, was already a rebel, in a different cause, in the first years after the second world war in Greece. His clandestine organisation "X" (or *Khi*) was an apprenticeship in terrorism in 1944 and 1945. But the Eoka rebellion in Cyrpus did not begin till 1955. Similarly, Belkacem Krim, the military leader of the Algerian National Liberation Front (FLN), was a militant rebel from 1945. But the great Algerian insurrection did not begin till November, 1954.

This factor ought to be of great importance. An administration given long and ample warning that a rebellion is brewing ought to be able to prevent it. In practice, few administrations seem able to prevent insurrections, however long the warning. It is not that they do not act, but that they take the wrong kind of action. When the blow comes, it takes them by surprise, for the successful insurgent always preserves secrecy just before striking.

It is not hard to find reasons for this administrative failure. Plain repression is the easiest, though in the long run the costliest, way to deal with a rebellion. Prevention requires more than the zeal of the policeman or the skill of the commander: it requires political initiative. Unfortunately, few administrators have the imagination to think of the right measures in time. Of those that have, fewer still have the time to initiate the right courses of action, in the midst of daily preoccupations, often of a routine but time-consuming nature. And where they are the local representatives of a colonial nation, their power to initiate major reforms or changes of policy is limited. The approval of a government has to be sought. But few governments can spare the time they are forced to devote to current crises for the prevention of crises to come. Emergency action seems easier than enlightened planning. Moreover, the information on which enlightened policies might be based is often of the slightly offensive kind known as "intelligence". It tends to reach police forces and security services in the first instance. At that level, repression is normal routine. And the repression goes on, perhaps for years, before the major rebellion has even begun. That plain repression is ineffectual is indeed shown by the fact that major rebellions still break out, even after years of repressive measures against the rebel leaders. Those are the years that might be used to recommend, initiate and implement preventive policies. They are usually wasted years.

This book is mainly, but not exclusively, concerned with those wasted years. It is an exercise that bears some resemblance to the nursery rhyme about the house that Jack built. I shall attempt to describe the conditions that authority permitted, that caused the frustrations that threw up the rebels who laid the conspiracies that led to rebellions. This is the prosaic jingle of insurrection. Having traced the tragic sequence, I shall try to describe certain

techniques of rebellion and of repression. I shall attempt, for instance, to assess the returns of terrorism, and to pinpoint the stage
at which they tend to become *diminishing* returns. I shall try to
show that terroristic methods are successful, in the long run, only
when the objective for which the terrorists are fighting enjoys
popular support, as in Palestine when the British were being
driven out; and that they tend to fail when the terrorists devote
their main efforts to bringing their own side to heel, as in Cyprus
or Algeria.

When dealing with repression, we shall find that pure repression is not necessarily obsolete, but that it has definite
limitations. It is, I think, true that pure repression never *solves*
political problems; suppressed today, a rebellion will break out
again tomorrow. But "tomorrow" may be ten or twenty years
ahead. And this is important: a government without a policy may
gain the time needed to think of one by resorting to pure repression. The trouble is that the very fact of repressing a rebellion in the first place makes it all the harder to initiate an enlightened policy, for violence troubles the calm which alone
enables the voice of reason to be heard. There are, moreover,
other limiting factors. The experience of the post-war years suggests that pure repression has become virtually impossible for
democratic governments, exposed as they are to the shafts of
parliamentary debate and an unfettered press. Pure repression
may succeed, but only if it takes place in remote places of little
concern to other powers; or, alternatively, if news of the repression is suppressed along with the rebellion itself. Since the
war, France has suppressed several rebellions, with great loss of
life to the rebels and virtual immunity to outside pressure. Examples are the 1947 insurrection in Madagascar, which attracted
little attention outside France, and the 1945 outbreak at Sétif in
Algeria, news of which was almost totally stifled. In both cases,
rebel losses ran into thousands, perhaps tens of thousands. Yet
the French governments of the day got away with it.

What a democratic government can accomplish, given favourable circumstances, a totalitarian government can do, even in the

full glare of world publicity, given overwhelming power on the spot. Thus Russian tanks crushed the uprising of German workers in east Berlin in June, 1953, and the revolt of an entire people in Hungary in November, 1956. Both these operations involved some risk to the Soviet Government, for if the North Atlantic Treaty powers had intervened in either world war might have ensued. In both cases, however, the Soviet leaders balanced the possibility of Western intervention against the certainty of losing their satellite empire if they did not suppress the rebellions, and rightly decided that the West would not intervene. They could afford to ignore the opinion of the overwhelming majority of nations, because their own people were denied access to any version of the facts beyond the official account. So they, too, got away with it.

But "getting away with it", when all is said and done, is a clumsy and barbarous substitute for statesmanship. If one compares the relative merits of repression and political accommodation, one is bound to notice the superior merits of the latter. In politics, as in medicine, prevention is better than cure, and finding remedies for grievances, before they explode into violence, does not necessarily constitute appeasement. Official delay breeds rebel fanaticism and intransigence. The British Labour Government grasped this essential truth after the war, when it transformed the old white Commonwealth into a new Commonwealth of many hues. So did the enlightened but short-lived administrations of MM. Mendès-France and Edgar Faure in their dealings with Morocco and Tunisia. On their side, some rebels—like Gandhi before and during the war—have understood the drawbacks of violence. I shall end, therefore, by exploring alternative courses: non-violence for rebels, statesmanship for those in authority. And, in so doing, I shall try to suggest what might have been done to prevent some of the major post-war insurrections.

PART I
REBEL FRUSTRATIONS

I
The Raw Material of Rebellion

FRUSTRATION is the one element common to all rebels, whatever their aims, political ideas or social backgrounds. It does not matter whether the rebel is a highly intelligent communist like Vo Nguyen Giap of Vietnam, a primitive politician like Jomo Kenyatta of Kenya, a sober banker like Sjafruddin Prawiranegara of Indonesia or a non-commissioned officer of limited attainments like Belkacem Krim: frustration unites them in a brotherhood of rebellion. The nature of their frustrations varies enormously, as one would expect from the variety of their origins: a Colonel George Theodorus Grivas in post-war Athens will have different reasons for feeling frustrated from those of a Dr Fidel Castro of Cuba in the 'fifties. We, the public, may feel that the reasons of the first are more—or less—valid than those of the second. This is important but—for the purposes of this inquiry—not for ethical reasons. The important thing is to find out whether our rebels grew up or worked in conditions likely to lead to frustration, for often such conditions are avoidable. The exercise is far from academic: where such conditions continue, rebellion is bound to break out afresh; where a newly independent country allows similar conditions to develop, it is asking for rebellion against its own authority.

In another sense also, the nature of a frustration is worth determining. Where its origins are purely personal and psychological, it is hardly within the power of the authorities to relieve it. There are men, and women, who are by nature rebels. This disposition does not necessarily incline them to violence. But give such a person, particularly among the half-educated, a real or fancied grievance and he may well turn to violence. Such violence may be anarchic, anti-social and apolitical; in that event, it rates as delinquency and need not concern us here. But if violence is directed towards political ends, it may be anything but anarchic; terrorists, if they aim at success, must be highly organised or they will be betrayed and defeated. This kind of frustration, erupting in violence for political ends, is the basic subject-matter of this book.

What, then, is frustration? For my purpose, it is simply the inability to do something one badly wants to do, through circumstances beyond one's control. It does not help at all to adopt a high moral tone about frustrations, and to pronounce one frustrated desire to be more worthy of sympathy than another. It does not matter whether an ambition is laudable; what matters is that it exists. What matters even more is to discover it.

This quest is, however, far from easy. Most true rebels— leaders of violent uprisings—are not easily accessible while their struggle lasts. After it is over, they become less interesting: the revolutionary of yesterday is the conservative of tomorrow. Those who do seek publicity may be physically remote from normal communications, like Fidel Castro. Some may be less communicative than others, even if they are disposed to receive visitors. Those who are disposed to talk may tend to exaggerate their own exploits or difficulties.

I have met a number of rebels, including some of the central figures of this book. I have, for instance, interviewed Ho Chi Minh of Vietnam, Ferhat Abbas of Algeria and Sumitro of Indonesia; Sjafruddin, who became Prime Minister of the Indonesian revolutionary Government, I met at a cocktail party in Jakarta in 1952. But among these, only Sumitro and Abbas were in context, that is in rebellion. Ho had driven the French from his domain two and a half years earlier; Sjafruddin was still Governor of the Bank Indonesia, far in thought, I feel certain, from planning dissidence. I have also met a host of minor rebels, from whom I learned something of the mentality of rebels, of their toughness, their courage, above all their intransigence. The true rebel does not compromise, though often the practical politician fighting in the same cause will compromise above his head: Menachem Beigin, leader of the terrorist group Irgun Zvai Leumi, never accepted the *de facto* frontiers of Israel; the statesman Ben Gurion reached an understanding with reality.

In the end, one is driven to the few scraps of documents left or strewn abroad by rebels, to recorded statements or anecdotes: to the captured diaries of Grivas, the trial of Jomo Kenyatta, the reminiscences of people who had dealings with Giap, the occasional newspaper interview vouchsafed by an insurgent. One's appreciation of characters is bound to be tentative, and I should be the last to claim conclusiveness. On the other hand, no such restraints need hamper our evaluation of the circumstances—the *ambiance*—of our rebellions. It will be clear, I think, that certain circumstances are bound to provoke rebellions. In a forcing ground like Vietnam or Algeria, it is really accidental whether the leader is Ho or Benbella, or others. *Somebody* was bound to rebel some time.

The pattern of this narrative is, inevitably, complex; the strands that compose it come from many countries and were a manufactured in widely varying conditions. I shall try to help the reader disentangle them and keep the pattern in focus. My principal examples are drawn from Indo-China, Malaya and the Philippines; from Kenya, Cyprus and Algeria; from Hungary, too, for the spontaneous uprising of a whole people cannot be ignored. Palestine and the Suez Canal Zone provide interesting examples of terrorism in action. Cuba is a classic of rebellion and claims our attention. Burma provides two competing communist rebellions and a host of separatist ones that deserve a passing mention. Indonesia provides so many rebellions that the only embarrassment lies in the choice; two of them are dealt with in this book. The feudal or sectarian dissensions of Indo-China have a bizarre attraction, but are of little significance compared to the full-scale war between the French and the Vietnamese communists; they do not deserve more than a glance. Finally, in describing methods of repression, the anti-French rebellions in Madagascar in 1947 and in Algeria in 1945 will be cited in a later chapter; so must the rebellion against Chinese communist rule in Tibet.

The central figures are few and not always those most prominently in the public eye. A front man is a convenience to those who prefer to wield power in obscurity, as the almost forgotten General Nagib was to Colonel Nasser. In Vietnam, the real rebel was Giap rather than Ho Chi Minh; in Algeria, the men who plotted the insurrection were Mohammed Benbella and Belkacem Krim, not Ferhat Abbas, who became the first "Prime Minister" of the provisional Algerian Government. In Cyprus, the division of labour between Grivas and Archbishop Makarios was clearer than the division of responsibility for the outbreak. In the anti-Sukarno rebellion in Indonesia, the leadership was indeterminate, which helps to account for its initial failures. But in most of the other rebellions there was no ambiguity about the Number One: Castro of Cuba, Chin Peng of Malaya, Luis Taruc of the "Huks" in the Philippines were unchallenged.

2

Against French Rule

IN Tunis, in February, 1958, I vainly sought an interview with Belkacem Krim who, at that time, was not in to journalists. A more fortunate colleague, Stanley Karnow of *Time* magazine, found himself sitting next to him in an airliner some months later. When Krim realised that he was not talking to a Frenchman, he became communicative. Karnow's account of this conversation, which appeared in *Time* of July 7th, 1958, is a revealing and important document. Krim is a Berber, a member of the autochthonous race of the Maghreb. He was born near Dra el-Mizan in Kabylia, in a wild and inhospitable area of eastern Algeria. He is a natural rebel, almost a prototype. His first rebellion, says Karnow, was against his father, a *garde champêtre* who wanted him to stay with the clan and mould his life according to Berber traditions. But Krim had heard of the European way of life; to taste it, he ran away to Algiers, where he learned to read and speak

French. This, he may have thought, would be the key to life in the European style. That it was not was the basis of his enduring frustration. He joined the army—Marshal Pétain's army—in 1942, and served until his discharge in 1945. He had reached the modest rank of *caporal-chef*, and his frustration had deepened.

"Wherever I turned", he told Karnow, "there was injustice. There were always differences between us, the Moslem inferiors and the superior Europeans. I was a clerk and I had to fill out forms for new recruits. For Moslems the forms were filled out in red ink, for the French in blue ink. That doesn't seem important, does it? It was important to me."

Frustration . . . and a capacity for violence. The frustration was written in red ink. The capacity for violence was there, too. Shortly after his discharge, Krim was an outlaw: because he had killed a man whose job he coveted, said the French; because of nationalist agitation, said Krim. But whether or not he had served an apprenticeship in murder, Belkacem Krim was ready to use terrorism against the Algerian Moslems when the rebellion began in November, 1954. "I tried to avoid it at first because it isn't efficient," he told Karnow (much as a French security chief in Vietnam had told me that he was against torture because it didn't bring results: "*Ce n'est pas payant*," he had remarked). "You cannot hold a population by terror, and we need the population on our side. But we have traitors among us. And we had to answer French repressions, too—massacres, tortures, bombardments. This is a hard war, but perhaps that is a good thing. We are building a nation, and we want no gifts. For nothing you get nothing."

The real leader of the rebellion, Mohammed Benbella, has been even less free with his confidences. The arch-plotter and mastermind, his natural medium was clandestinity. In the beginning, he had chosen silence; from October 22nd, 1956, silence was forced upon him. In an incident that aroused much passion and intellectual controversy, the DC-3 aircraft in which he and four other rebel leaders were travelling between Morocco and Tunisia landed at Algiers instead of Tunis. The French pilot had obeyed

radio instructions to bring the aircraft down. In so doing he condemned Benbella to the obscurity of imprisonment.

It was always plain, however, that Benbella and Belkacem Krim
were men of the same mould. They shared the same frustrations
and were of one mind in their choice of violence to achieve their
aims. Both belonged to the younger wing of militant Algerian
nationalists formed by the war; their militancy grew naturally out
of military experience, their desire to strike out of the demonstration of French incapacity and weakness in 1940 and out of the
growing conviction that the French would not keep their promises to the Algerian Moslems. Like Krim, Benbella had been a
"non-com", but Krim was only 17 when the war broke out;
nearly six years older, Benbella had correspondingly greater
opportunities for a display of merit. Discharged in 1945 as a
reserve warrant officer, he had been mentioned four times in
dispatches and had won the Médaille Militaire. Unlike Krim, he
did give orthodox politics a try. Returning to his home town of
Marnia, in Oranie, he was elected as a municipal councillor of the
MTLD, the legal party of the veteran nationalist Messali Hadj.
This was in 1946. Later he became assistant to the mayor and
local chairman of the MTLD's proscribed militant counterpart,
the *Parti Populaire Algérien*. His flirtation with orthodoxy had
been short-lived. By 1948, he was a member of the general staff
of the MTLD's terrorist secret society, the *Organisation Spéciale*
(OS). And a year after that, he was head of the OS, which, by
then, had grown to 1,800 dedicated members. Dedicated, of
course, to violent solutions.

If Benbella, like Krim, is a prototype rebel, Ferhat Abbas,
first Prime Minister of the "Provisional Government of the
Algerian Republic", is a man of very different stamp. One is
tempted to describe him as "the Tunku Abdul Rahman of
Algeria". Only, unlike the Tunku, this sensible and moderate
man was never allowed to reach power by electoral processes. It
was a tragedy, for France and Algeria, that he also came to feel
that the alternatives to violence were sterile.

It is informative and fascinating to compare a man like Abbas with men like Benbella or Krim. All three started from the same frustrations, but reached, at first, two conflicting conclusions. All three started from the premise: "The French are privileged. We Algerian Moslems are underprivileged." The conclusion drawn by Benbella and Krim was: "Therefore we must have independence." For many years, Ferhat Abbas stood by a quite different conclusion: "Therefore we must become true Frenchmen, with the rights and living standards of European Algerians." Those were the years when Abbas, as he said, was searching for the Algerian nation and failing to find it.

Ferhat Abbas was born on October 24th, 1899, and is thus seventeen years older than Benbella and twenty-three years older than Belkacem Krim. His father, a *caïd* or local chief in the Constantinois village of Chahna, was unshakeably loyal to the French. Ferhat himself went through the French *lycée* in Philippeville and graduated in pharmacy at the University of Algiers. He thereupon opened a drug store at Sétif which, in 1945, was the scene of a violent Moslem uprising, the precursor of the insurrection of 1954.

In his student days, Abbas used to say that legal equality of Moslem and European Algerians was all that was necessary to transform Algeria from a colony into a province of France. Note that the transformation into a French province was the aim in view, not independence. Abbas's loyalty to France was total, for it even survived the French defeat of 1940. A nationalist in search of independence would have exploited France's difficulties. Instead, in a report to Marshal Pétain, the father-figure of the Vichy régime, on August 10th, 1941, Abbas wrote:

> Since June, 1940, France has been unhappy. She has never been dearer to (Moslems') hearts. Rich or poor, she remains for them France, that is to say the nation of generous traditions which, for generations, has sacrificed herself for the respect of the individual and human dignity in the world.

It is a far cry from these sentiments to the life of an insurgent leader who was to become the first Prime Minister of the "Provisional Government of the Algerian Republic" that was proclaimed in Cairo in September, 1958. What accounts for this change of view? The answer lies in a gradual disillusionment with French promises which deepened Abbas's frustrations to the point where he felt that he had been wrong and Benbella right. At this point, national independence came to seem the right goal and war the right way of reaching it.

In his report to Pétain, Abbas declared that all Algerian Moslems would continue to agitate until all in Algeria were equal before the law and until all privileges were abolished. He translated this general aim into specific demands in his famous "Manifesto of the Algerian People", which he presented to the Governor-General, Peyrouton, on March 31st, 1943, after the allied landings in North Africa. The manifesto called for an Algerian constitution, guaranteeing the freedom and equality of all inhabitants, irrespective of race or religion, the recognition of Arabic as an official language, agrarian reform, freedom of the press and of association, free and compulsory education for both sexes, and freedom of worship.

These were evolutionary, not revolutionary, demands. To further them, Ferhat Abbas founded the Union Démocratique du Manifeste Algerien (UDMA). Its members were known as the "Friends of the Manifesto", and on at least two famous occasions they must have thought that they were well on the way to achieving their aims. The crux of the difficulty was the "personal Koranic status" of Algerian Moslems—that is, their right to practise Islamic customs such as plural marriage. Most French lawyers held that the retention of the personal Koranic status was incompatible with the rights and obligations of French citizens. Algerian Moslems were therefore required to abandon their Koranic status before applying for French citizenship. These objections were, however, waived by the French National Liberation Committee under General de Gaulle. The Committee, which sat in Algiers, decided on December 11th, 1943—less than a year after the publication of the manifesto—to confer French citizenship on the Moslem "élites" forthwith and without abandonment of the Koranic status. This decision, which ought to have been epoch-making, was given the force of law under the Ordinance of March 7th, 1944, again promulgated by General de Gaulle. It aroused fierce resentment among the Europeans of Algeria, not merely on legal grounds but mainly because it seemed to pave the way to *political* domination by the Moslems. This argument was not without force. The European settlers considered their privileged position to be safe only so long as the principle of the "double college" was preserved. The Europeans constituted one electoral college, the Moslems another. This system ensured that the Moslem majority of the country could not gain a majority in elected bodies. By throwing French citizenship open to educated Moslems, the 1944 Ordinance did undermine the principle of the dual college. Indeed, as Jacques Chevallier, former Mayor of Algiers, pointed out in his admirable book *Nous, Algériens . . .*:

> This system opened the door to a progressive invasion of the first college [the European college] and led inevitably, in time, to the single college of which it was, in one sense, a forerunner.

The new principle was, nevertheless, reaffirmed in the Statute of Algeria of September 20th, 1947. This elaborate document went even farther than the Ordinance of 1944, and met many of the demands of Ferhat Abbas's manifesto. Indeed, Abbas himself was elected to the Algerian Assembly (still under the dual college), and continued, as his speeches showed, to believe in the long-term possibility of equality through evolution.

The disillusionment of Abbas and others like him was due to the gradual realisation that the settlers were determined that no ordinance or statute, however liberal, should prevent them from retaining intact their privileges and their political ascendancy. Even with the advantages of the dual college, the Algerian administration considered it necessary to fake the elections of 1947 and the partial elections of 1951; by the second of these dates, the preparations for the insurrection were well advanced. Packed with a majority of Europeans and selected Moslems, the Algerian Assembly was the pliant instrument of the Administration. In the

end, membership of the Assembly was but a further frustration to
Ferhat Abbas and other moderate politicians. It did not fulfil
their aspirations; rather did it underline their incapacity to influence the course of events.

Yet neither the still-birth of the 1947 statute nor the fraud of
the 1951 elections was sufficient to complete the disillusionment
of Abbas and other moderates. Even after the outbreak of the
rebellion, he retained, in some degree, his ultimate faith in French
good-will. The final disillusionment bears a date: February 6th,
1956. On that day the new Prime Minister of France, M. Guy
Mollet, visited Algiers and was greeted by rowdyism and a shower
of rotten tomatoes. This, as previous and later occasions have
shown, is the standard greeting Algiers reserves for representatives of the central power, irrespective of their politics. Nevertheless, February 6th, 1956, is a fateful date. It was not, however,
a turning-point, but the reverse; the date that was intended to be
a turning-point marked the continuation of a sterile policy of
pure repression. M. Mollet's Socialists, in alliance with M.
Mendès-France's Radicals under the banner of the Republican
Front, had won the elections of January, 1956, on a platform of
reforms in Algeria. During the campaign, M. Mendès-France had
been to the right of M. Mollet, for M. Mendès-France was merely
advocating autonomy for Algeria and M. Mollet envisaged
independence. After February 6th, the positions were reversed;
M. Mollet returned to Paris bent on a policy of pure repression,
and sent a "strong man", M. Lacoste, to Algeria as Minister-
Resident with orders to implement it; M. Mendès-France, by
continuing to advocate reforms leading to autonomy, began to
look, in comparison, like a left-wing extremist. And indeed M.
Mollet treated him as such, until he resigned in May, 1956. About
the time M. Mendès-France resigned, and for the same reasons,
Ferhat Abbas finally decided that there was no alternative to
violence. He dissolved the UDMA, flew to Cairo and announced:
"There is only the FLN." By a more devious emotional and
intellectual route, Ferhat Abbas had reached the point where a
short-cut had taken Benbella and Belkacem Krim.

The frustrations of the Algerian rebels were similar in kind to those of other colonial people, differing from others only in circumstantial detail. In sum, however, the legal impediments of colonial people may be less important than a sense of inferiority in personal relations. To be treated as inferiors, to be humiliated by members of another race, these are, in the final analysis, the deepest causes of frustration. These discriminations are often called "the colour bar", but they transcend the barriers of race. There is basically no difference between the humiliations of Indians under British rule and those of tribalised Liberians under a ruling caste descended from American slaves. The Karens of Burma have complained of being treated as inferiors by the Burmese; the Turkic-speaking Uighurs of China have made similar complaints about the Han Chinese. The discrimination between rulers and ruled may be due to colour; or to fancied differences of intellectual level; or to cultural distinctions. The resulting frustrations are equally real.

Because the Algerian case is typical, I shall quote from a little-known circular sent to local administrators by the former Governor-General of Algeria, M. Jacques Soustelle. This circular, dated April 5th, 1955, shows, incidentally, how wrong it is to generalise about a man who has been called "the settlers' champion". In it, Soustelle noted that it was already less fashionable than formerly to despise the natives; that the automatic *tutoiement* of Moslems was tending to disappear; and that mutual prejudices were fading. He added:

> A big effort is still needed for courtesy to become normal practice. One still occasionally notices, on the part of people whose culture leaves something to be desired, offhanded, or even ill-bred, words or gestures, towards Moslem Frenchmen.
>
> Such attitudes might have passed, long ago, as the expression of a certain rough good nature. Today and more and more, as our language and concepts spread, the "native" wishes to be treated as politely as anybody else. He is attached, legitimately, to his human dignity.
>
> Wounds of self-respect, in a naturally proud people imbued with

the rules of oriental courtesy, are always the longest to heal. A big step will be accomplished the day when all inhabitants of this country respect each other and behave accordingly, whatever their race, their religion and their social situation.

It is not necessary to add that the representatives of authority must, in this domain, set the example.

In brief, if the "Algerian problem" is of an economic, social and political character, it is also, and perhaps even more, a problem of human relations.

How right was Soustelle. But how impotent is mere legislation in this intangible realm of human relations. On the other hand, if the legislator cannot force white people to take darker people into their homes, he can remove the legal basis for the superiority of a ruling caste. But he has seldom done so.

M. Soustelle's remarks would have been applicable, and with even greater intensity, in French-administered Vietnam, scene of the other major rebellion of the post-war years. It is impossible, in a book that ranges over so many countries, to do justice to a situation as infinitely complex as that of Vietnam in the formative years of the rebellion. But in a chapter devoted to rebel frustrations, it is at least possible to isolate the major causes of frustration. They were both economic and political, but of the two the political causes strike me as far the more important. True, the economy of Vietnam under the French was a typical colonial economy: it was exploited for the benefit of the colonising country. It exported rice, rubber, coal, cement, and imported manufactured articles, mainly from France or other parts of the French colonial empire. French Indo-China (which comprised the kingdoms of Laos and Cambodia as well as Vietnam) was enclosed in the French tariff wall, denying its inhabitants the benefit of cheaper imports from, say, Japan. On the other side, the French built roads, railways and hospitals and created a rubber industry from nothing. Moreover, if Vietnam was exploited by the French, the exploitation benefited only a few thousand Frenchmen concerned in trade or production in the country; and the Vietnamese themselves were at least as efficient as the French in exploiting their own countrymen. Paul Bernard, a French authority on Indo-Chinese economic problems of the 'thirties, established that, in 1931, the annual income per head in Vietnam was as follows for various social groups: European civilians, 5,000 piastres; European servicemen, 600; indigenous upper class, 6,000; indigenous middle class, 168; and indigenous lower class, 49. The same expert pointed out, again in 1931, that the middle and upper classes (including the European civilians), though numbering less than 10 per cent of the population, absorbed 49 per cent of all imports. He concluded: "The greater part of imported products does not reach the mass of the consumers."

In at least one direction, however—that of usury—the French reduced the exploitation of Vietnamese by Vietnamese: as Philippe Devillers pointed out, in his admirable *Histoire du Vietnam de* 1940 *à* 1952, interest rates on loans to peasants often reached 75 per cent *per month* when the French conquest began in the 1860s; by 1939, the legal ceiling was 8 per cent per year— although monthly rates of 8 to 10 per cent were often charged even then.

To say that the primary causes of Vietnamese frustration were political, not economic, is not to say that the economic condition of Vietnam was beyond criticism. But the essential fact is that the Vietnamese insurrection—at least in its origins—had nationalist and political aims, rather than social ones. The important communist element on the rebel side aimed, of course, at overthrowing the traditional Vietnamese social structure; but the basis of their common cause with the non-communist nationalists was the projected overthrow of French rule, not a programme of social change.

Nevertheless, socially as well as politically, the Vietnamese suffered apparently irremediable injustices. He was, in the fullest sense, a second-class citizen. He could not form a political party in the protectorates of Annam and Tonking; in the colony of Cochin-China he could do so only if he first acquired French citizenship. He could not form trade unions; he needed special permission to travel among the three regions of his own country;

he needed a police visa to go to France. Freedom of the press was almost non-existent; the judicial system was weighted in favour of the French; suffrage was restricted to a few thousand people. There was a Colonial Council in Cochin-China, but ten of its twenty-four members were French and elected by universal suffrage, while its ten Vietnamese members were elected by restricted suffrage; the remaining four members were nominated by the Chambers of Commerce and Agriculture. Though a very small minority benefited from French education, either in Vietnam or in France, this served merely to increase their frustration. For, on the one hand, French education stirred their minds with the revolutionary fervours of 1789, and, on the other, they were denied the outlet of *égalité* in their own country. Ellen J. Hammer, the American authority on French Indo-China, put this frustration in these words in *The Struggle for Indo-China*:

> What future could the educated Vietnamese find in colonial Indo-China? During his student days, if he were one of the fortunate few who were permitted to study in France, he encountered Western democracy in action . . .; but back in Indo-China, it was rapidly borne in upon him that he belonged to a subject race. He was a second-class citizen. Socially, he was treated as an inferior by the French; he found important jobs in the colony closed to him; and he received a much lower salary for those he did get than Frenchmen in similar positions.

As Devillers put it, the European society of Vietnam was "imbued with a complex of racial superiority". This was the Vietnam in which the rebel leaders Ho Chi Minh and Vo Nguyen Giap grew to maturity: a country economically and politically exploited, in which the indigenous people were denied freedom and justice, as these terms were understood in France, the ruling country; economic rewards commensurate with their abilities; and an outlet for their political energies. This, moreover, was a country of high and ancient civilisation, and a most tenacious national spirit, which had survived a thousand years of Chinese occupation, breaking out time and again in rebellion.

Ho and his followers were not the first Vietnamese anti-French leaders. In the 1920s a large number of nationalist parties had been founded. They bore pretentious names which the feebleness of their membership and resources did not justify: "Restoration of Annam", "Renovation of Annam", "Revolutionary Party of Vietnam", "Revolutionary Party of the New Vietnam" and so forth. But the first serious challenge to French authority came from the Vietnamese National Party or VNQDD (Viet-Nam Quoc Dan Dang), founded in Hanoi at the beginning of 1927 by a young schoolteacher called Nguyen Thai Hoc. The VNQDD, which enjoyed Chinese (Nationalist) backing, was modelled on the Kuomintang, then at the height of its revolutionary drive. It aimed at the expulsion of the French with Chinese help and the establishment of a "democratic republic". Its methods included terrorism. Informers handed over some of its secrets to the Sûreté; it was thus in a weakened state when Hoc decided to launch a rebellion in February, 1930. After short-lived successes, ruthless repression stamped out the uprising; Hoc himself was captured and guillotined. An official terror, in which Vietnamese nationalists of many opinions lost their lives, reigned unchecked through 1930 and 1931. These were, however, the years in which Ho Chi Minh laid his plans for the future and founded the instrument that was to realise them: the Communist Party of Indo-China.

By any standards, Ho is a great revolutionary leader and a great Asian leader. It is idle to speculate what course his life might have taken if he had not been drawn so early into the communist network. The experience of the VNQDD and lesser nationalist parties is there to show that there were *no* outlets for normal political opposition; on empirical grounds alone, Ho would find it easy to justify his view that only a world-wide organisation like the international communist movement could provide the framework of revolutionary success.

Ho Chi Minh was born in 1892, or thereabouts, in the village of Kim Lien, in the old kingdom of Annam. Kim Lien is in Nghe An province, where many Vietnamese revolutionaries were born. This tradition is still alive: it was in this province, in November,

1956, that there took place a spontaneous peasant uprising against Ho Chi Minh's communist régime.

Ho's original name was Nguyen Tat Thanh; Ho Chi Minh ("the Enlightened One") is only the last of many aliases: the name by which he was best known during his secret revolutionary life was Nguyen Ai Quoc ("Nguyen the Patriot"). His father was a government official who had been dismissed for political activity. He was brought up in full consciousness of Vietnam's humiliations. At 19, in 1911, he left Vietnam as a cabin-boy in a French merchant ship, and after some years of wandering settled in Paris during the first world war. There he earned a meagre living as a photographer's retoucher, devoting the major part of his energies to politics. He joined the French Socialist Party and the League for the Rights of Man, and contributed to *Le Populaire*. He made news for the first time in 1919, during the Peace Conference, when he sent the Big Four a memorandum calling for the application of Woodrow Wilson's principles to Vietnam. The Big Four, who had other preoccupations, did not take cognisance of this document. It is interesting to note, however, that it did not constitute a demand for independence; but its list of claims reads like a catalogue of Vietnamese frustrations:

General amnesty for all Vietnamese sentenced for political offences.

Reform of Indo-Chinese justice by according to the indigenous population the same judicial safeguards as enjoyed by Europeans.

Final and complete suppression of the *tribunaux d'exception*, which are the instruments of terrorism and oppression against the most honest portion of the Annamite (Vietnamese) people.

Freedom of the press and opinion, freedom of association and assembly, freedom of immigration and travel abroad, freedom of education.

Replacement of the régime of decrees by that of laws.

Permanent delegation of the indigenous population to the French parliament, to inform it of the desiderata of the indigenous population.

In May, 1920, Ho attended the famous congress of the French Socialist Party at Tours at which the party split into socialist and communist wings; he was among those who voted in favour of breaking from the Socialist Party and founding the French Communist Party. Two years later, he wrote a short book called *French Colonisation on Trial* which, in smuggled copies, became a rallying cry for revolutionary-minded students. He became the editor of a newspaper called *Le Paria* (*The Outcast*), which attacked French colonial policy. In his activities up till then, there was nothing of which liberal-minded persons could reasonably disapprove. French colonial policy, particularly perhaps in Indo-China, seemed almost designed for the emergence of revolutionaries; normal political activity being impossible, revolutionary courses were inevitable. It would be idle to pretend that Ho Chi Minh is not a true communist. But it is plain, on the record of the early years, that he was a nationalist first and a communist second; or, alternatively, that he turned to Marxism as a patriot.

Whatever the sequence, he was soon deeply enmeshed in the international machine of the communist movement, from which he has never emerged. In October, 1923, he turns up in Moscow, for the first time, as delegate of the French Communist Party to the congress of the Peasant International (Krestintern). There he stays more than a year, studying Marxism and revolutionary techniques, under the name of Song Man Tcho. In 1925, he goes to southern China under the name of Ly Thuy, officially as interpreter to Borodin, the Soviet adviser to the Kuomintang, but in reality as a propagandist for the Chinese Communist Party. He does not neglect the opportunities for proselytising among Vietnamese exiles in Canton. Gathering them around him, he founds the "Association of Revolutionary Vietnamese Youth" and turns out a duplicated clandestine news-sheet called *Youth*. Perfectly aware, as Devillers points out, of the irrelevance of Marxism to Vietnam, he concentrates on patriotic themes, introducing Marxist terms and concepts only gradually and sparingly.

In 1928, Nguyen Ai Quoc turns up in Siam to organise the Vietnamese minority in that country on Marxist lines. There, late in 1929, an urgent message reaches him from the ruling committee of the Revolutionary Youth Association which, in his absence, has split, the members within Vietnam having decided to form an Indo-Chinese Communist Party. In Hong Kong, Ho summons all his followers, and in March, 1930, talks them all into unity. The new party is to be known as the Communist Party of Indo-China—thus covering Laos and Cambodia as well as Vietnam—and shortly afterwards gains recognition from the Comintern.

Ho Chi Minh had founded his instrument of revolution. How did he use it? At first, by exploiting and canalising peasant unrest. There was at that time a terrible famine in north Annam and, simultaneously, the great repression that followed the arrest of the VNQDD leaders was in full swing. In three provinces of Annam, including Ho's native province of Nghe An, the communists organised great peasant demonstrations, culminating in a march of 6,000 on the port of Vinh, on September 12th, 1930. Landlords were attacked and the peasants attempted to break up large estates, but no attacks on Frenchmen were recorded. Nevertheless, French repression was swift and ruthless. The party apparatus was smashed and hundreds of militants were arrested. Most of them were executed. Ho, still in Hong Kong, was arrested—on June 6th, 1931—in deference to French wishes, by the British police, and held for two years.

There is no need to follow the remainder of Ho Chi Minh's career in detail—and, indeed, there is a great blank of clan-destinity over the next seven years. But a few more dates ought to be mentioned, for they clarify the circumstances in which the great insurrection later took place. In 1940, France was overrun by the Nazis and Tonking by the Japanese, who, however, left the administration in French hands, in return for the use of the airfields and naval bases. A section of the Communist Party saw in these circumstances the ideal occasion to strike. Against Ho's opposition, they launched revolts in all three regions of Vietnam. The Japanese stood aside and allowed the French to suppress them with their customary ruthlessness. New instructions arrived from the Comintern: the Communist Party was to form "national liberation fronts" with non-communist parties, and launch a general movement against "Fascist imperialism". At the beginning of 1941, Ho went to south China, where he secured the co-operation of the authorities in Kwangsi and Yunnan provinces. In May, 1941, he convened a congress of Vietnamese nationalists of which the hard core was the Communist Party. The congress met at Tsin Tsi, in Kwangsi province about sixty miles from the Tonking border, and created the *Viet*nam Doc Lap Dong *Minh* Hoi or League for the Independence of Vietnam, usually shortened to Vietminh. It was the Vietminh, always under communist direction, which master-minded the war against the French. Its programme, to which it adhered undeviatingly, comprised three main points: to drive out the French and Japanese Fascists; to make Vietnam independent; and to build a democratic republic of Vietnam. Although other parties then or later adopted the Vietminh programme, in fact the third of these aims was peculiar to the Communist Party; the other nationalists had no programme beyond the expulsion of the French and Japanese.

One of the Vietnamese communists who attended the Vietminh congress was Vo Nguyen Giap, whose career assumes ever greater importance from that point forward. Giap[1] is twenty years younger than Ho; he was born in 1912 in Quang Binh province (north Annam) and was the son of a peasant. His great intelligence and dynamic energy were revealed at an early age. At 14, in 1926, he joined the small revolutionary party of Vietnam and four years later was gaoled at Hué, the ancient imperial capital of Annam. As soon as he left prison, he joined the Communist Party. He earned a living by teaching at a private school run by an old nationalist, Huynh Thuc Khang, while studying at Hanoi university. In 1937 he obtained a licence in law and a doctorate in political economy. Two years later he and other communists went to Kwangsi. His companions included Pham Van Dong, later Prime Minister of the Democratic Republic of Vietnam, and Dang Xuan Khu who, under the name of Truong Chinh, later became known as the principal Vietnamese communist theorist.

---

[1] Ho seems to be an exception to the general rule that Vietnamese are known by the last particle of their names.

Over and above the standard causes of frustration, Giap had additional reasons for resentment against the French. When he went to Kwangsi, he left his wife and child at Vinh. Like him, his wife was a militant communist. She was arrested by the French Sûreté in May, 1941, and sentenced to fifteen years' hard labour. She died in gaol in 1943. His sister-in-law, also a militant communist, was executed about the same time in Saigon.

The newly formed Vietminh entrusted Giap with the formation of a clandestine organisation in the mountainous region of Tonking. For the next four years, living a life of adventure and secrecy, the young rebel organised a network of informants, rallied followers and converted new ones, planted agents in villages and bought friendships by bribes or persuasion. By 1943, he had organised units of guerrillas and was ready, where necessary, to terrorise the timid or unwilling. These, however, were few in numbers: the great majority of the population supported the Vietminh. By 1945, Giap had 10,000 men under arms. At some stage—probably in 1942—he appears to have spent some time at Yenan, the operational headquarters of the Chinese communists, from whom Giap apparently learned the principles of guerrilla war and peasant revolution. He was an apt pupil, as events were to show.

I have suggested that it was Giap, rather than Ho, who was the real rebel in Indo-China. This bald statement needs qualification. The major rôle in the Vietnamese revolution was undoubtedly Ho's. It was Ho's long and patient work that laid the foundations; Ho Chi Minh was, in the fullest sense of the word, a "revolutionary", and as a life-long Marxist he could not, on principle, have been opposed to violence where necessary. But there is fairly strong evidence that he would have preferred to avoid violence. In contrast, Giap was by nature inclined to prefer violent courses. Ho's behaviour in the year that preceded the rebellion was at least consistent with that of a man bent on finding a peaceful solution; Giap's suggested that of a man who, from the outset, had decided that a pacific approach would be futile.

The most interesting testimony about the rôle played by these two men is that of Jean Sainteny, former Commissioner of the French Republic in Tonking and north Annam, in his book *Histoire d'une Paix Manquée (Story of a Peace that Failed)*. M. Sainteny landed in Hanoi in August, 1945, in a grudgingly offered American aircraft. A provisional Vietnamese government had already been established; the Japanese, though defeated, were still there; the Chinese Nationalists, under the Potsdam Agreement, were about to occupy Indo-China north of the 16th parallel. In the face of these difficulties, Sainteny, almost single-handed, re-established the French "presence" in Tonking. He played an important, though never a determining, rôle in the protracted and abortive Franco-Vietminh negotiations which failed to avert the insurrection. From the start, he established cordial, and indeed intimate, relations with Ho Chï Minh. There is no doubt that he fell under the charm of Ho's extraordinary personality. He became convinced that Ho, although aiming at independence, was content to reach it in easy stages, and that he desired to maintain links of some kind with France. In Sainteny's view, Ho felt that an independent Vietnam would need the protection of a great power; and that, although he was a communist, he would prefer France to Soviet Russia—which he knew too well—as a protector. As for China, it was not, at that time, a communist country; as a Vietnamese patriot, Ho would have preferred to avoid the protection of the hereditary enemy on Vietnam's doorstep. Despite the disillusioning experiences of the intervening years, Sainteny still held these views when I first met him in London in 1955, and even when I saw him again, eighteen months later, in Hanoi. Yet at our second meeting, Hanoi was the capital of Ho Chi Minh's Democratic Republic of Vietnam, and Sainteny was merely Delegate-General of the special French mission to that minor communist state.

Patriotic sentiment must have played a part in M. Sainteny's views about Ho's innermost desires, and I do not share those views; but I am sure he was right in his assessment of the relative rôles played by Ho and Giap in the months before the rebellion.

Giap, then Minister of the Interior, was the first Vietminh leader he met. He gave Sainteny the impression of "a man of decision, extraordinarily hard, cunning and intelligent". The interview was cordial and "I was very far from realising that this Giap, whom I was meeting for the first time, was to become within a few months one of our fiercest adversaries and that it would be he who, turning to profit the excessively prolonged absence of Ho Chi Minh in France, would set Vietnam on a more and more vicious path, with no other issue possible than a trial of strength."

In his account of that "prolonged absence", Sainteny quotes Ho as saying, time and again: "Don't let me go back empty-handed." Ho had arrived in France in June, 1946, and left in September. During most of that time, frustrating negotiations between the French and Vietnamese went on at Fontainebleau. In Hanoi, Giap was organising anti-French demonstrations, incidents and meetings, at which Ho Chi Minh was freely described as a *Viêt-giân* or traitor. When the Vietnamese delegation set sail for home in August, convinced that the talks were leading nowhere, Ho stayed on in France, apparently determined to make a last effort. On September 2nd, he had even sent a telegram to his government in Hanoi appealing to it to refrain from giving an anti-French character to the proposed independence day celebrations. Finally, on September 14th, he signed the inadequate *modus vivendi* agreement—a mouse of a pact which even the elephantine labours of Fontainebleau had failed to produce, for it had been hastily drafted in Sainteny's office as a last resort to enable Ho to say that he had not gone back empty-handed. Earlier, at dinner with Sainteny and Marius Moutet, Minister for France Overseas, Ho had remarked: "Don't let me go back like this. Give me a weapon against those who are trying to go faster than I. You won't have cause to regret it."

Ho Chi Minh had been away from Vietnam more than four months, having returned by sea. By the time he arrived, the situation had deteriorated beyond repair. The responsibility for this deterioration was at least as great in Paris as in Hanoi. But there is little doubt that Giap had done everything he could, during Ho's absence, to bring events to the point of no return. Sainteny's verdict on Giap was:

> He is the man of extreme solutions, and it is probable that he carries the responsibility for setting off the *coup de force* of December 19th, 1946, as he was also the promoter of the tactic of scorched earth, which he enforced without weakness.

Ho, then, was the long-term revolutionary planner, but Giap was the real insurgent.

3
Communist Rebels

THE other post-war communist insurrections in Asia were less important—and less interesting—than Vietnam's. In their strictly communist aspects, they are dealt with in a later chapter. All of them broke out in 1948. They resulted from a communist conspiracy, and were of little or no relevance to the needs or aspirations of the inhabitants of the countries in which they took place. It is, however, relevant to this chapter to ask why two of them in particular developed into major insurrections. Was there a soil of frustration in which the seeds planted by communist agents in Malaya and the Philippines could take root? The answer is that there was, particularly in the Philippines.

The Philippine insurrection was the work of the Hukbalahaps, or "Huks" for short. Hukbalahap is itself an abbreviation of five words in Tagalog, the language of the Filipinos, meaning "People's Anti-Japanese Resistance Army". At the time of the insurrection in 1948, the Huks were firmly under the control of the communists, led by Luis Taruc. As the insurrection gained strength, more and more of the insurgents were indoctrinated in "Stalin University", a mobile outfit organised by an American communist, William J. Pomeroy. Married to a Filipino girl, Pomeroy had served in the Philippines in the American Army during the war. Although the insurgents continued to be known as the Huks, they had given their organisation a new name: the People's Liberation Army, or HMB. The 1948 insurrection was, however, the second Huk uprising. The first, which began in 1942 during the Japanese occupation, was—as the name Hukbalahap indicated—an anti-Japanese movement aimed at securing the independence of the Philippines. It was also, and perhaps even more importantly, an anti-landlord movement. Although Luis Taruc organised the Huks from the start, he did not reveal himself as a communist during the occupation period; for at the outset the Huks were not all communists: the elements of an insurrection were there and all Taruc had to do was to canalise and organise them.

Landlordism was the curse of the Philippine Islands. It was a curse under the Spaniards, and it remained an undiminished curse under the Americans. Very late in the day—in 1952—an American Mutual Security Agency report, known as the Hardie Report or by its full title of "Philippine Land Tenure Reform, Analysis and Recommendations", gave some startling statistics. The crux of the problem was the high percentage of farms operated by tenants. The global figure of 35 per cent was hardly impressive; but this figure was as misleading as an average can be: in the Candaba Swamp area of Luzon, some 2 per cent of the people owned 98 per cent of the land, and 70 per cent of the farmers were tenants. In four of the provinces of Luzon, at least 60 per cent of the farms were worked by tenants, and those provinces were the real strongholds of the Huks. There existed estates of 80,000 acres, and some landlords employed up to 30,000 tenants apiece. Next to the giants were the small estates of ten to thirty acres, purchased by absentee landlords as an investment. Their business sense was admirable, for returns of 20 to 22 per cent per annum were common. Much of the capital that might have been used for industrialisation or other development schemes was thus tied up unprofitably—for the people—in the land.

As elsewhere in Asia, absentee landlordism brought its concomitant curse: moneylending. Sugar-cane tenant families had an average gross income of only $160 a year. The rice tenants fared marginally better with $180. With incomes at those levels, tenant families were faced with average yearly living costs of $313. Inevitably, they turned to the moneylender who, in the Philippines, is usually a Chinese. Once caught in the clutches of the usurer, the tenant farmer never emerged; with interest rates of 100 and even 200 per cent a year, repayment of principal was out of the question. Yet these, as the American writer William O. Douglas pointed out in *North from Malaya*, were only a few of the tenant farmer's troubles:

> The absence of all-weather roads puts many farmers out of contact with the markets at critical periods. The absence of adequate and economic storage space for farm produce forces the farmer to sell in a low and to buy in a high market. The absence of co-operative marketing and buying facilities puts the farmer at the mercy of the Chinese middleman. There are very few co-operative rice-mills. The Chinese capitalist or the landlord takes his toll there, too. And there is no such thing in the Philippines as a floor under farm prices.

These were, in brief, the conditions in which the doctrines implanted by Taruc and Pomeroy flourished. And it was among the 1½ million farming families below the subsistence level that they found their recruits. Taruc's biography deserves less space than Ho's or Giap's. Like Giap, he had a taste and capacity for violence and a talent for organisation. During the war, he mustered 100,000 followers, and his Huks caused the deaths of many Japanese and collaborators. During the second rebellion, his armed following was not more than 25,000 men and women; but his potential of reserves numbered perhaps two million. In some areas—notably in Zambales province in western Luzon—he controlled the towns as well as the countryside and levied taxes. Although his movement had a strong basis of popular support, he did not hesitate to resort to terror where support was lukewarm. His favourite method of gaining control of a town was to have one of its prominent citizens murdered and leave his body in the street with the tag: "He resisted the Huks." Another device was to have a man torn in two by horses galloping in opposite directions. He plotted to murder President Magsaysay. Yet in the end that remarkable man defeated him, by energetic and imaginative methods that belong to a later chapter. On May 17th, 1954, utterly demoralised, Luis Taruc surrendered alone to Manuel Manahan, a newspaper publisher and head of Magsaysay's Complaints and Action Commission, and to Benigno Aquino, a reporter on the *Manila Times*. He was forty and had a price of £18,000 on his head. Eighteen years earlier, he had joined Pedro Santos's Socialist Party, which had a programme of agrarian reform. Two years later, with Taruc as its Secretary-General, the socialists were absorbed into the Communist Party. Already he was set on the path of revolution. Even now his career may not be over, for by a curious leniency of justice he escaped a capital sentence; instead, he was fined $10,000 and gaoled for twelve years.

The Malayan insurrection had some points in common with the Philippine one. As in the Philippines, it originated as a resistance movement against the Japanese. The name of the Malayan resistance organisation was almost the same as that of its Philippine counterpart: the Malayan People's Anti-Japanese Army, or MPAJA. Like the Hukbalahaps, the MPAJA was led by communists. Both armies sheltered in the jungles; both launched their insurrections on orders from Moscow. There, however, the resemblance abruptly ends. The Huks were a popular mass movement—until their communist leaders showed their hands too clearly. They found their strength in a deep-seated peasant discontent arising from genuine grievances. In contrast, the Malayan insurrection, even at the outset, was a minority movement. The frustrations on which it thrived for a while were temporary and largely accidental.

These frustrations were predominantly of economic, rather than political, origin. Malaya emerged from the Japanese occupation and defeat into an administrative vacuum and an economic chaos. Epidemics were breaking out among an undernourished population. The rubber and tin industries were at a standstill and their labour force had vanished: no more than 10,000 starving Malayans returned, out of more than 100,000—mainly Chinese and Indians—press-ganged by the Japanese to work on the notorious Burma–Siam railway. Retreating down the peninsula, between December, 1941, and February, 1942, the British military authorities, with the co-operation of rubber-estate and tin-mine owners, had scorched the Malayan earth. Mines had been dynamited and rubber smoke-houses burned down; bridges had been blown up. Allied bombing later completed the devastation to communications.

All three of Malaya's major communities—the indigenous Malays, the Chinese and the Indians—had suffered, in varying degrees, from the brutality or callousness of the Japanese. Partly for that reason, partly because the pre-war days had been a time of order, progress and relative plenty, the British were given a warming welcome after the Japanese defeat. For various reasons, however, the warmth did not last long. As in other countries emerging from Japanese occupation, Malaya was not effectively reoccupied by the British for several weeks. During those weeks, the communist resistance force emerged from the jungle and instituted a short but impressive reign of terror. The people were the more ready to greet the returning British. On the personal plane, they were soon disappointed; and on the economic plane, the conquering *tuans* failed to bring back the carefree plenty of the good old days.

The personal disappointment in the returning British sprang from a number of causes. In the first place, they were not the same British as before. As J. B. Perry Robinson put it in *Transformation in Malaya*:

As individuals, many of them were strange. For the first seven months (September, 1945, to April, 1946) they were the British Military Administration, staffed mostly by men who had never seen Malaya before and manned by soldiers of the types that find their ways into armies at the end of long wars.

Perversely, a second cause of disappointment lay in the fact that so many of the returning British really *were* the same: those who had stayed till the bitter end and been interned by the

Japanese were considered to have a moral right to come back; but there was resentment against those who had dropped everything, abandoning their posts to save their skins, then returned after the war to claim their old jobs.

The continuing economic distress was, however, a more important cause of disappointment in the British administration. An easy-going, predominantly rural people like the Malays tended uncritically to blame the British for conditions that were, in fact, largely beyond their control. Most of the great rice-bowls of Asia were empty; paddy-fields in Burma and Vietnam had been abandoned or devastated. Siam alone was a seller and British Malaya turned to the Siamese. But in 1946 and 1947 the Siamese delivered only one-third of the rice they had contracted to sell Malaya. As Robinson records, a year after liberation the Malayan rice ration was less than a pound a head per week, compared with the pre-war consumption of nine pounds. A flourishing black market sent the general price level soaring to 400 per cent above the pre-war figure.

These conditions affected the Malays and the Indians more than the Chinese who, more resourceful and more urbanised, tended to collar existing supplies and profit from the black market. Yet paradoxically, the insurrection of 1948 was overwhelmingly a Chinese movement. But the paradox was more apparent than real. The Malayan Communist Party itself was overwhelmingly Chinese, and it was the MCP that controlled the Pan-Malayan Federation of Trade Unions. The reduced prestige of the British, the food shortage, the inflation, the slowness in rehabilitating the tin-mines: all these things played into the hands of the communists. The general strike called throughout Singapore and Malaya in February, 1946, was the beginning of a long series of communist-fomented labour disputes and disorders that went on until the start of the armed insurrection. The point is that this policy of militant industrial action would hardly have been possible, and would certainly have been unsuccessful, had it not been for the prevailing economic frustrations of the Malayan people.

Politically, the frustrations of the Malayan Chinese were a

more important factor in the rebellion than those of the Malays. Alternatively, the nationalistic frustrations of the Malays were important only to the extent that they enabled the Chinese communists to exploit an existing demand for independence. Apart from the local-born Chinese (the "Straits Chinese" or "Queen's Chinese"), the Chinese of Malaya sat like an undigested mass on the political body of Malaya. As in Vietnam, Siam or Indonesia, they remained Chinese, clinging to their language, customs and secret societies, and basically loyal not to their country of adoption but to China itself, and within China to their family or village of origin. But whereas in Vietnam, Indonesia and—to a lesser extent—Siam, they were a relatively small minority, in Malaya they were nearly as numerous as the Malays—and more numerous if Singapore was included in the calculation. The pursuit of fortune was their dominant, if not their exclusive, passion. Though economically privileged, they were politically underprivileged. In their great majority, they were not citizens of the country they lived in, debarred from certain offices and denied the right to own land.

That this state of affairs was potentially dangerous was recognised by the Colonial Office under the Labour Government that was swept into power in Britain in 1945. The Malayan Union project, offered to the Malay rulers in October of that year, would have conferred equal citizenship rights on the Chinese. It was, however, difficult to please everybody at the same time. Malay agitation, led by Dato Onn bin Jaafar, then Mentri Besar (Prime Minister) to the Sultan of Johore, forced the abrogation of the Malayan Union. The Chinese were thus left not merely without a political outlet but without even the prospect of a political outlet. The Malays, for their part, had agitated intermittently for independence since the Malay Nationalist Party had first raised the cry in the 'twenties. But they were not, even in the confusion of the post-war years, planning to achieve their ends by violence.

It would be misleading to attach too much importance to the political inferiority of the Malayan Chinese. It is certain that the great majority of them were much less interested in political advancement than in continuing economic opportunities; or, alternatively, that they were interested in political courses only to the extent that these might safeguard their economic interests. Once again, however, the existence of a palpable grievance was grist to the mill of the communists.

It was into this world that Chin Peng, the youthful and rising communist leader, emerged from the jungle after the Japanese collapse. He was 24. Born in Sitiawan, in south Perak state, he belonged to the Hakka community, sometimes called the "gypsies of China". The Hakkas were one of the two Chinese communities of Malaya among whom communism had made the greatest inroads (the other was the Hilams of Hainan island). His father owned a modest bicycle repair business. He attended first a Chinese then an English school, and at the second he appears to have come under the influence of the Malayan Communist Party. He joined the MCP when he was 18, in 1940. By the time the Japanese invaded Malaya, he was the leading communist in Perak. Taking to the jungle, he soon displayed a remarkable talent for organisation, creating food-lines and maintaining supply routes under the noses of the invading army. He gave every assistance to British troops, but made no secret, even in those early days, of his ambition to establish a communist republic in Malaya. Throughout the war, however, Chin Peng was only a local leader. The Secretary-General of the MCP was a mysterious individual called Loi Tak. According to Harry Miller, who gives an excellent account of Malayan communist activities in *Menace in Malaya*, Loi Tak was a Vietnamese who reached Singapore from Hong Kong in the 'thirties and was elected Secretary-General of the party in 1939. Chin Peng displaced him as party boss in 1947 after Loi Tak had fled with the party funds. He was then only 26. This was the same Chin Peng who had marched with the forces of the Commonwealth in the Victory Parade in London, and been awarded the OBE for his part in helping the British "Force 136" in the anti-Japanese resistance.

He, too, like Taruc in the Philippines, was defeated, though less decisively. In December, 1955, protected by a safe-conduct, he came out of the jungle for the first time for seven and a half years. At Baling, close to the Siamese border, he met Tunku Abdul Rahman and Mr. David Marshall, Chief Ministers of the Federation of Malaya and of Singapore, to discuss a negotiated end to the Emergency. His terms were: the right of his followers to return to civilian life and form their own political associations. The Tunku's terms were: formal surrender of the guerrillas to the properly constituted authorities, deportation of undesirables and a total ban on the Communist Party. A few days later, Chin Peng was back in the jungle, without hope of victory, but still defiant.

For all his courage, endurance, ruthlessness and capacity for organisation, Chin Peng was not a communist leader of the stature of Ho Chi Minh or Vo Nguyen Giap. He failed to appeal to the non-Chinese peoples of Malaya and gravely misjudged his chances of success. His tactics alienated the population, and when he changed them in response to orders from Peking, it was too late. He contributed nothing to the technique of guerrilla warfare, or to communist ideology.

4

Against British Rule

ANOTHER rebel leader who failed, though in vastly different circumstances, was Colonel George Grivas, the organiser and commander of the Eoka terrorists in Cyprus. More than with other rebel leaders, and for less intelligible reasons, the career of Colonel Grivas was a study in frustration. Born in 1898 at Trikomo, a village near Famagusta in Cyprus, he decided early in life that he would have a military career. He adopted Greek nationality after the first world war and worked his way through the Military Academy in Athens. His first experience of active service was on the defeated side in the ill-starred Greek invasion of Asia Minor in 1922—a bitter rebuff to those who, like Grivas, believed wholeheartedly in "greater Greece". At 30, as a staff officer, he was selected for special training at the École Supérieure de Guerre at Mailly where, it is said, he absorbed a measure of Marshal Pétain's anglophobia. When Italy invaded Greece in 1940 Grivas was lecturing at the Greek Training School in Salonika. Made chief of staff of the Second (Athens) Division, he held the post until the collapse of Greek resistance before the German invasion. Thereafter, his life entered its first conspiratorial phase.

Many years later, at the height of the Cypriot troubles, his followers or admirers attempted to give his name an aura of heroism. They created the legend of a Grivas high in the honoured list of leaders of the Greek resistance movement during the German occupation. The truth was less exalted. While communist and royalists bands were raiding German installations from the Greek mountains, Grivas was creating his first terrorist group in occupied Athens. He called it "X", and its members were mostly young cadets whom he had trained in Salonika, with a sprinkling of older unemployed army officers. "X" had twin objectives: externally, the wild irredentist dream of "greater Greece", stretching, on specially printed maps, over southern Albania, European Turkey and Cyprus; internally, the restoration of the Greek monarchy as an acceptable façade for a fascist-type régime of the extreme right. In a perverted way, the man must be credited with foresight. At a time when allied energies were concentrated on the overruling need of fighting the Nazis, Grivas was planning for a struggle which few had imagined: the coming struggle against communism. In retrospect, he seems, perhaps, to have been right for the wrong reasons and at the wrong time.

It was during this period of clandestine activity that Grivas first met Michael Mouskos, then deacon of the fashionable Ayia Irini church, and better known by his later style of His Beatitude Archbishop Makarios III. It may be deduced from their later relationship that Makarios then formed a high opinion of Grivas's single-minded pan-Hellenic ambition and of his capacity for organisation. Because "X" played no part in the resistance, it did not qualify for allied assistance. The allied mission to the Greek guerrillas, under Colonel C. M. ("Monty") Woodhouse, supplied arms to the major resistance groups, including the left-wing Elas, but not to "X"—a further source of anti-British grievance to the fanatical colonel from Cyprus. In *Apple of Discord*, his brilliant study of Greek politics in the transitional period immediately after the war, Colonel Woodhouse had this to say of "X":

> This body, later known as the direct-action instrument of the Royalist Right Wing under the leadership of Colonel Grivas, has claimed to have been a resistance movement during the occupation. If that claim were true, it would be classifiable as the only resistance organisation of the Right then active in Athens; but in fact its name was unknown until shortly before the Germans left; and even then the name signified nothing connected with resistance. Only in the years immediately after the war did it acquire significance: the sinister significance of a Klu Klux Klan.

These words were, of course, written some years before the terrorist outbreak in Cyprus, and Woodhouse cannot therefore be suspected of wishing to destroy Grivas's dubious reputation as a hero of the Cypriot "resistance".

For all his ruthless efficiency, Grivas built in "X" an organisation that was too small to be anything more than a sinister nuisance, and too limited in its scope to affect the course of history in anything but a marginal way. Grivas threw his thugs into battle against the communists in the first round of the Greek civil war, from December, 1944. But Elas, the communist-led guerrilla organisation, was far stronger than "X" and the other royalist groups put together. "X's" intervention did not halt the cold-blooded slaughter of hundreds of "fascists" and "collaborators" by the communists; it merely provided the KKE (Greek Communist Party) with a useful propaganda ploy to divert attention from its own excesses.

Between the first and second rounds of the civil war, British intervention had reduced the communist threat, the nomination of Archbishop Damaskinos as interim Head of State had brought a temporary peace, and a plebiscite had secured the return of King George II of the Hellenes to his throne. Grivas, who had played his part in the plebiscite by organising intimidation at the polls, celebrated the restoration as his hour of triumph. But in the cold light of the morning after, it turned out to be his hour of maximum frustration.

His was indeed a double frustration. The frustration of the soldier: the Greek general staff had overlooked him after the war when distributing medals for valour during the Italian and German invasions, and had failed to recall him to active service. The frustration of the political agitator: for all his monarchist efforts, both in action through "X" and in word through his newspaper *Ethnikos Kyrix* (*National Herald*), he was snubbed by the restored monarch and his courtiers. As Stephen Barber of the *News Chronicle* put it in an informative series of articles on Grivas in March, 1959, "Grivas, in the eyes of Greek sophisticates, was a vulgar fellow—a 'Cypriot donkey'." In his bitterness, Grivas had his own description of Athenian politicians, including the formidable General Papagos: "Faint-hearted traitors," he labelled them. And years later, in those remarkable diaries that fell into British hands in Cyprus, he wrote: "I am certain that when praises are awarded after the end of our struggle [for *enosis*] we shall be given crumbs while others will claim the victory. At least, this is what happens in Greece." Again, in his perverted way, he wrote prophetically.

Before the end of 1946, the second round of the Greek civil war broke out. That there was a second round at all was partly Grivas's doing. During the preceding months, he had turned his killers loose in Athens. Wearing masks, they would drive into working-class districts, pick their "communist" victims, pump bullets into them and speed off. When General Markos Vafiadis led his left-wing guerrillas into the second phase of the revolt, Grivas offered to lead "X" against them. Again he was snubbed. After a few more months of murders and brutalities, "X" began to break up. By 1949, when the civil war ended, Grivas, deserted by his followers, had reached a nadir of frustration. Like that later idol of youth, the late James Dean, he had become a rebel without a cause. It was then that Archbishop Makarios returned to Greece and renewed their old acquaintance. And from that point forward his story merges with that of the Archbishop.

Makarios was born on August 13th, 1913, at Ano Panayia in the Paphos district of Cyprus. Of peasant stock, he attended the elementary school in his native village. Destined for the Church, he entered the Kykko Monastery, then won a scholarship to the Pancyprian Gymnasium in Nicosia. It was the first of his many and precocious successes. With Makarios, indeed, the element of frustration is subtle and more difficult to isolate than with Grivas. The disgruntled "Cypriot donkey" had a marked talent only for banging his head against unyielding walls. Ever the espouser of lost causes, he seemed predestined to failure. Even his prodigious feat of holding an island of half a million people at bay and tying down 30,000 British troops with a few dozen gunmen, even that turned to ashes in the end. For was he not fighting for *enosis*? Yet in the end all the Cypriots gained—and only incidentally through his efforts—was a circumscribed independence which neither Grivas nor Makarios had asked for. But Makarios, though he shared that final frustration and in part authored it, seemed in contrast to be predestined for success. His difficult years were those in war-time Athens, where, as a student of law and theology, he was frequently near starvation. In 1946, after the liberation, he went to the United States for further study at Boston University. There, two years later, came his first big success: news reached him that he had been elected Bishop of Kitium. Breaking off his studies, he returned to Cyprus and was enthroned on June 13th, 1948. He was just under 35.

Like Grivas, but in the more humdrum sphere of episcopal finances, Makarios was a good organiser. He found his new bishopric in a chaos of unpaid bills and inadequate revenues. Keeping a tighter rein on expenditure than his easy-going predecessor, chivvying the richer churches for funds, organising special collections, the young Bishop soon converted the inherited deficit into a comfortable surplus.

Makarios had not, until that time, given outward signs of an
interest in politics. But when he was able to emerge from the early
problems of his bishopric, he fell under the spell of the man whom
he was to succeed as Archbishop, the aged Makarios II. Preaching
enosis, the Archbishop was arousing a fervour of popular feeling.
Makarios joined the movement, and it was after he had overtly
associated himself with it that he went to Greece in 1949 and
revived his acquaintance with Grivas, who indeed had been sent
to meet him by the Greek Government. He returned to the island
fired with enthusiasm for the idea of a plebiscite on *enosis*, and
won the Synod's approval for it. On January 15th, 1950, a Sun-
day, every person over 18 who was so moved entered a church
to sign his or her vote on an open petition calling for union with
Greece. It was no less conclusive than plebiscites usually are: of
the 224,747 entitled to vote, 215,108 or 95·7 per cent, were claimed
to have voted. Five months later, content, one supposes, with
the results of his eloquence, Makarios II died; and on October
18th, the Bishop of Kitium was elected, without opposition, to
succeed him as head of the Church in Cyprus. He was still
only 37, and many must have supposed that having reached
this pinnacle of fulfilled ambition, he would have rested on his
laurels.

By that time, however, Makarios was fired with the infinitely
frustrating aspiration of *enosis*. Moreover, by virtue of his new
office, Makarios had also become Ethnarch, or national leader, of
the Cypriots. This important point is sometimes puzzling to
citizens of countries where the Church devotes its major energies
to spiritual matters. But the tradition of clerical leadership in
Cypriot politics was deeply rooted long before Makarios III was
enthroned. As an autocephalous branch of the Greek Orthodox
communion, the Church of Cyprus has enjoyed the right to elect
its own head since the 5th century A.D. Under Byzantine rule, it
enjoyed immense power as the instrument of State religion.
Under Ottoman rule, the election of the Archbishop had to be
confirmed by a Berat of the Sultan. But once confirmed, his
temporal power was almost absolute. The tradition of clerical

authority was therefore venerable by the time Makarios III was elected; and so, too, was another feature of the Church of Cyprus which Christians of other denominations found puzzling during the Cypriot troubles of the 1950s: its association with violence. Sir George Hill, in his *History of Cyprus*, writing of the island under Ottoman rule, quoted from a letter written by the French consul in Cyprus to Talleyrand, the French Foreign Minister, in 1807:

> The Greeks would rather leave their country and live under the Turks than under their own Archbishop. The Dragoman, his instrument, and the grammateis and the collectors of the Kharaj have been terribly harsh these last years, using the bastinado and other tortures on those who could not pay; if they fled, their wives were tortured, even to the crushing of their breasts between two planks. If they failed to extract anything by such means, the collectors carried away even the doors of their houses. Thus the Archbishop and Bishops became wealthy.

This picture of the Church of Cyprus is, of course, one-sided. But there is no doubt that from the time of his election in 1950, Makarios devoted his best energies to the political campaign for *enosis*. The January plebiscite, spectacular though it had seemed, had proved no more than that the great majority of Greek Cypriots felt compelled to pay lip-service to the ideal of union with Greece. This was insufficient for Makarios. The relative indifference of the population seemed to threaten the political power of the Church. So did the only other organised political force of consequence on the island: the communists, who called themselves Akel ("Anorthotiko Komma Ergazomenou Laou" or "Reform Party of the Working People"). Akel was interested in *enosis* only to the extent that it might foreshadow the union of a communist Cyprus to a communist Greece. In 1949, the communists approached the Ethnarchy, suggesting joint representations to the United Nations. Snubbed by the Church, Akel obtained thousands of signatures to a petition urging a plebiscite on *enosis* under UN auspices. This was a concrete challenge to the political monopoly of the Church which it could not ignore; and it was this, perhaps more than anything else, which persuaded the Synod to adopt Makarios's scheme for plebiscite (while Makarios II was still alive).

To these threats or challenges—the indifference of the people and the increasing activity of the communists—could be added another: the strategic needs of the British in the Middle East. Ousted from Palestine, insecure in the Suez Canal Zone, the British were unlikely to weaken their hold on Cyprus, which indeed was increasingly being used for military purposes. One must suppose that all these factors played a part in Makarios's decision, after his election, greatly to intensify the campaign for *enosis*. He may well have thought that only by a more aggressive advocacy of the cause could he ensure the continued political ascendancy of the Ethnarchy. Whatever the reason, we find him returning to Greece time and again after his enthronement, attempting, at first without success, to enlist official support for the movement. These activities, culminating in Grivas's return to Cyprus at the Archbishop's invitation, are described in detail in a later chapter.

What are we to make of this militant cleric? The Greeks had no doubts: he was the supreme commander of the operations in Cyprus. On New Year's Day, 1956, some weeks before the deportation of the Ethnarch to the Seychelles, Archbishop Sophronios, in a proclamation on behalf of the Pan-Hellenic Committee for Enosis, referred to "the heroic struggle of the Cypriots, which is directed resolutely and wisely by Archbishop Makarios". Grivas, himself, in his captured-diaries, acknowledged the Archbishop's primacy; in a letter to him, dated May 23rd, 1955, Grivas described him as "the real leader of the national liberation struggle". And in the end, when talks between the British, Greeks and Turks had brought agreement about the future of the island, Grivas, in his last leaflet signed Dighenis, wrote these revealing words on March 9th, 1959: "Today after the Zurich agreement between Greece and Turkey has been accepted by Archbishop Makarios in London, I am obliged to order the end of the struggle." The Archbishop had brought "the leader" to Cyprus and had ordered him to fire; he had ordered him to cease firing, and Grivas had obeyed him again. The second of these fundamental orders must have been a good deal more difficult for Grivas to swallow than the first, and indeed he waited eight days after the Archbishop's return to Cyprus before proclaiming the end of the struggle. To fight was one thing: after the frustrations of the 1922 campaign, the war and the civil war, here at last was a chance to achieve at least one part of the old irredentist dream; Cyprus, at last, would be united with Greece. But to end the fight without having achieved *enosis*, that was a different and bitter thing. For Grivas, the end, like the beginning, brought frustration.

And for Makarios? Who can tell what went on in the private and subtle obscurities of the prelate's mind? Had he renounced *enosis* for good in October, 1958, when he told Mrs Barbara Castle, the British Labour MP, that he would settle for conditional independence? Or had he merely decided that a gradualist approach would bring greater dividends than direct action? Our lifetimes will tell.

It is always difficult, in a period of terrorism, to assess the true feelings of average citizens. Eoka was an organisation of a few dozen trained gunmen and saboteurs, with the backing of a few thousand exalted school-children. It must be assumed that any movement which feels obliged to kill three people of its own side for every two of the "enemy" is a minority one. A "death to traitors" campaign is necessary only when the "traitors" exist in large numbers. It is probable that the great majority of the population disapproved of Grivas's methods, even if they were in sympathy with his objectives. But terrorism blurs the outlines; it is useless to attempt to probe into people's minds when they are afraid to open their mouths to speak. It may be assumed, however, that the idea of *enosis* did exert a strong fascination over the minds of Greek Cypriots. That they felt, and feel, Greek is certain; mainland Greeks speak with envy of the classical purity of their language. If frustration is merely the denial of something you want, then the people of Cyprus were frustrated. I hope to show in Part II that they also had cause for frustration in the penny-pinching gradualness of Britain's approach to their political evolution. But it must also be said that in many of the things that bring frustration to colonial peoples they had relatively little cause for complaint. They had, for instance—and ultimately to the sorrow of the British—freedom of religion and education (though no facilities for higher education, which they naturally sought in Athens rather than London). Freedom of religion carried with it the political leadership of the Church; freedom of education meant Hellenic methods and standards; it also meant the glorification of the tattered heroes of the Greek War of Independence, in whose images the school-children saw the fighters of Eoka reborn. Economically, the people of Cyprus had been neglected rather than exploited by the British. A niggardly £500,000 a year was spent on official development schemes immediately after the second world war, and even in 1955 less than £1 million was spent; in 1956, when it was too late even to try to win over the Cypriots by financial generosity, the expenditure on official schemes rose sharply to £2,853,000. In general, however, Greek Cypriots affected to attach relatively little importance to material considerations, professing a preference for poverty under Athens to affluence under Whitehall. If these professions are accepted at face value, it does not seem as though economics played a determining part in the Eoka rebellion, although it would be fair to criticise successive British administrations for not even trying to disprove the Cypriot assumption that Britain was not really interested in the island. At all events, Eoka's rebellion coincided with an economic boom, in which the island's trade, capital development and employment were at peak levels. The British connection had brought the benefits of imperial preference, access to the London money market and, not least, freedom to emigrate to Britain and prosperous countries of the Commonwealth, such as Australia. Apart from a boycott of British goods, there was never an economic equivalent of *enosis*: even at the height of the disorders, emigration to Greece was a trickle, and thousands of Greek Cypriots were settling in the United Kingdom. The frustrations of Cyprus were those of unfulfilled dreams, rather than of restiveness under a paternalistic yoke.

* * *

It may seem invidious, and even insulting to Hellenic pride, to bracket Eoka and Mau Mau. And indeed there are not many similarities between them. Both, however, were terrorist organisations in revolt against British rule; and the countries in which they operated were both, anomalous though it has always seemed in the case of Cyprus, under the jurisdiction of the Colonial Office. Beyond that, the comparison need not be pressed, at least in this chapter.

In the Mau Mau rebellion, we meet a factor that does not exist in our other examples: the impact of an advanced civilisation on a primitive society. All colonial encounters are brutal, some more, some less, and whether or not physical violence is involved. But nowhere was the encounter more brutal than in Kenya where, on the one hand, the European arrival came late and, on the other hand, the local population was wretchedly backward. The British East Africa Association obtained its concession in 1887, and Kenya was transferred to the United Kingdom Government as recently as 1895. Even at that time, the peoples of east and central Africa were found to be "in an extraordinary condition of backwardness and ignorance", says Sir Philip Mitchell, a former governor of Kenya, in his book *The Agrarian Problem in Kenya*. Specifically,

> . . . they had no units of government of any size or stability . . . no wheeled transport . . . no roads nor towns; no tools except small hand hoes, axes, wooden digging sticks and the like; no manufactures . . . and no currency. . . . Perhaps most astonishing of all to the modern European mind, they had no calendar nor notation of time. . . . They were pagan spirit or ancestor propitiators, in the grip of magic and witchcraft, their minds cribbed and confined by superstition.

The glaring contrast in the levels of culture is an essential element in the situation that exploded into violence six or seven decades later. The psychological brutality of the colonial impact is explained by what Marxist writers would call "objective factors"; it was not, in any significant sense, a reflection of administrative shortcomings. It meant, however, that the frustrations of the colonised in Kenya were, in part, different in kind from those we have encountered in, say, Vietnam, Malaya or Cyprus. In effect, we are dealing in Kenya with two sets of frustrations: on the one hand, psychological and tribal; on the other, economic and political.

The psychological and tribal elements were concisely and admirably analysed by Dr. J. C. Carothers in *The Psychology of Mau Mau*, a report prepared for the government of Kenya and published in 1954 at the height of the emergency. Independent authorities have confirmed Dr. Carothers's findings, from which I borrow those elements that seem to have a bearing on frustrations of the Kikuyu tribe, of which Mau Mau was an emanation.

In general African terms, the outsider—the stranger to the group—is held to have no rights; if, in the opinion of members of the group, he has behaved badly, anything may legitimately be done to him. In other words, tribal sanctions apply within the tribe and its own protection, but not outside it. The stranger, then, is resented. This is not of course, peculiar to primitive Africans; nor, for that matter, is a trait noted by Dr. Carothers and other authorities: the absence of sanctions on moral behaviour towards strangers. The Nazis were equally uninhibited in their treatment of the Jews. But this puts the primitive African in poor company. In contrast, the great religions of mankind, though they may also distinguish against outsiders, limit discrimination to declaring heretics unqualified to enter paradise. But they all agree in making murder, even of strangers, an offence against the moral law.

And so, the resented stranger arrives. Were he weak, he would be exterminated. But alas, he is strong. The old gods are shown to be fallible; the stranger's gods, or God, must be worshipped. What is the source of the stranger's power? Is it religion? One suffer oneself to be converted. Is it education? One must study. At this point, however, frustration sets in. The Christian God is evidently a god for white men, for the black man, even after he has knelt in church, remains weak and poor. The white man's religion is a sham, for only the missionaries are prepared to treat the black man like a brother. The white man's education is a fraud and a deception, for even after studying in his schools and passing his examinations, the black man fails to get the good jobs or join "the establishment".

These observations are held to be applicable to Africans as a whole. In the particular case of the Kikuyu, Dr. Carothers argues that the tensions resulting from the impact of the European arrival were greater than in other tribes. The Kikuyu are forest people, at home in country which most Africans fear; in the forest the authority of the group is reduced and the individual's capacity to fend for himself is stimulated. "It seems to have been especially true of the Kikuyu," writes Carothers, "that much of life was spent in seeing what one could get away with." Although many Kikuyu are no longer forest dwellers, their forest tradition persists, and during the Mau Mau insurrection they returned to it naturally.

The Kikuyu's contact with Europeans and Asians has been closer and has lasted longer than that of other tribes. But contact has brought neither adaptation nor—for obvious reasons—assimilation. Instead, it has created, then deepened, frustration; and within the tribe itself it has created dangerous disparities. Envying, not unnaturally, the white man's power, the Kikuyu turned to learning with avid appetite. Proportionately more Kikuyu than members of other tribes reached the higher levels of education in Kenya. But in many cases education failed to open doors; and many Kikuyu, failing to make the educational grade, nevertheless considered menial work beneath their dignity and became discontented. On the other hand, many more Kikuyu, particularly the women, remained almost entirely without formal education; tensions within the tribe were therefore intensified. Moreover, the educated Kikuyu, however inadequate their attainments, acquired prestige and power—for good or evil—over other members of the tribe. Bearing in mind that these tensions and disparities of culture occurred in a society in which witchcraft was prevalent, their explosive character is easy to understand.

The special psychological frustrations of the Kikuyu lent a particular ferocity to the Mau Mau rebellion. They help to explain some of the more irrational aims of the movement. These aims were not all irrational, however. Some of them arose from understandable economic and political grievances—the second set of frustrations which I mentioned earlier. These aims, both rational and irrational, were: to recover land "stolen" from the Kikuyu; to destroy Christianity and restore ancient customs; to drive out foreigners and obtain self-government; to increase secular education; and, curiously, to abolish soil conservation.

The sense of grievance over the "stolen" lands went deep and is of fundamental importance. The "stealing" of the lands was probably not as deliberate as Mau Mau propaganda has made out. Dr. L. S. B. Leakey, the best-known authority on the Kikuyu and whose sympathy with their aspirations is patent, ascribes it largely to a monumental official misunderstanding of the Kikuyu system of land tenure, and to a series of natural disasters that hit the tribe at the turn of the century. He has explained the circumstances in great detail in his invaluable little books, *Mau Mau and the Kikuyu* and *Defeating Mau Mau*. To summarise them is to court the risk of oversimplification, but there is no choice. Between 1887, when the British East African Company obtained its concession, and 1902, when the first large-scale alienation of land took place, four major natural disasters ravaged the country: an epidemic of smallpox, an outbreak of rinderpest, a drought followed by a famine and an invasion of locusts. The death toll among the Kikuyu was enormous; estimates range from 20 to 50 per cent. Thousands of survivors moved *temporarily* from the stricken Kiambu district to more favoured areas. By 1902, when the first large wave of white settlers moved in, much of the land formerly under cultivation in Kiambu had reverted to bush. The settlers thus found a sparsely populated and apparently virgin region, large areas of which seemed to be ownerless. It happened also that this was some of the richest and most fertile land in Kenya, on highlands where altitude nullified the debilitating effects of an equatorial climate.

On the official side, it was assumed, on the analogy of experience farther south on the African continent, that these tempting lands could not have been privately owned, on the misconceived ground that the concept of land as property did not exist in Africa. In fact, however, all the (relatively small) area alienated by the British was private property, and thousands of Kikuyu families—on returning from their temporary refuge elsewhere—found themselves landless.

On the Kikuyu side, then, the deprivation of land was a genuine economic grievance—however innocent the British may have been in alienating it—and its restoration was a legitimate political aim. The destruction of Christianity and the restoration of ancient customs seem less rational aims to the European mind, though in fact they follow quite naturally from the tribal and psychological attitudes I have described. The resentment of Christianity arose from various causes. An important one was the brutal divergence between the preaching of the missionaries and the practices of the nominally Christian settlers; clearly, the black man failed to qualify for brotherhood. An even more important cause of resentment stemmed from the vigorous campaigning of the missionaries against old-established Kikuyu customs particularly female circumcision and polygamy. The first was considered by the Kikuyu as an essential element in the initiation ceremonies marking the advent of puberty in younger members of the tribe. In recent years, the operation has become increasingly severe, amounting in some cases almost to mutilation; from 1929, it was the subject of a sustained campaign of opposition by the missionaries, particularly the Presbyterians, who refused to admit circumcised Kikuyu girls to their schools.

Polygamy, likewise, was condemned as un-Christian. To the Kikuyu, however, this disapproval was unreasonable on two grounds: it was not explicitly condemned in the New Testament, and it fulfilled a legitimate social purpose in Kikuyu country. There was a chronic surplus of women and there were few outlets for unmarried women. Polygamy took care of both problems; and indeed, to the extent that it has been discontinued, there has been a corresponding increase in prostitution among the Kikuyu. This in turn has militated against the cohesion of the tribe.

Of the other Mau Mau aims, most are self-explanatory: the restoration of ancient customs is a corollary to the destruction of Christianity; the expulsion of foreigners is a demand that might be expected from a people convinced that all their misfortunes were caused by foreigners; the call for an increase in secular education is not surprising. The demand for the abolition of soil conservation, however, was at first sight astonishing in an agricultural people. Leakey explains it in terms of the Mau Mau leaders' desire to gain support among the women—the main cultivators of the tribe. The Kikuyu women were bitterly opposed to the government's soil conservation programme; to them, every hour devoted to the planting of wash stops and grass leys, or to the digging of contour trenches, was a wasted hour that might have been spent to better purpose in cultivating the soil. Moreover, these measures reduced the area available for cultivation; that they also improved the soil and increased its yield was an argument that fell on deaf ears.

Into this world of rapid and painful transition was born the presumed leader of the Mau Mau rebellion, Jomo Kenyatta. It might be thought that there was no doubt about the fact of his leadership, since he and four of his leading supporters were convicted of "managing Mau Mau". Not only were they found guilty and gaoled for long terms, but they also lost their appeals. On the other hand, an important part of the Crown's case rested on the evidence of one Rawson Mbogwa Macharia—who, in November, 1958, signed an affidavit withdrawing material portions of that evidence. The following April, Macharia was sentenced to twenty-one months' imprisonment for swearing a false affidavit; but the gnawing suspicion persisted that had the government of Kenya brought a charge of perjury against Macharia, he might have been sentenced on that charge instead of for swearing a false affidavit. Only a prosecution for perjury would have amounted to a rehearing of the Kenyatta trial, and the government of Kenya was criticised for having chosen the easy way out. Moreover, a number of writers, including Montagu Slater in *The Trial of Jomo Kenyatta*, have thrown doubts on the fairness of the trial.

At the beginning of Part I, I described Kenyatta as a "primitive politician". That this description is only half true is the essence of the Kikuyu tragedy. For Jomo Kenyatta is a highly educated man, capable, as his evidence at the trial amply demonstrated, of wit, sophistication and the telling repartee. It is hard, on reading his moderately worded statements, to believe that he was associated with the bestial practices of Mau Mau; hard, but not impossible in the light of his tribal inheritance. As Montagu Slater has pointed out, however, it should be remembered that in August, 1952, Kenyatta took a leading part in a large public meeting at which he denounced Mau Mau in a solemn Kikuyu curse, which was tape-recorded; that the worst Mau Mau atrocities occurred after his arrest and imprisonment; and that he was the leader of an open political movement—the Kenya African Union—whose rapid growth promised reasonably fast constitutional progress. Was terrorism necessary? Did it not take place against the wishes of Jomo Kenyatta and his associates?

These questions cannot yet be answered. At the time of writing, Jomo Kenyatta stands convicted and is serving his sentence. In any case, whether or not his conviction was justified on the evidence, there is no doubt that he was the leader of the extremist wing of the Kenya African Union which, consciously or not, fathered Mau Mau. His personal circumstances epitomised those of his tribe; his character and education mirrored the clash of cultures and the resulting tensions that burst into the open with the grisly oaths and murders of the Mau Mau association.

Kenyatta was about 50 when the emergency was proclaimed in Kenya in October, 1952. In other words, although he does not know the exact year of his birth, he must have been born about the time of the arrival of the first settlers and of the alienation of

Kikuyu land in 1902. One supposes that he must often have heard his elders discuss this subject when he was a boy. When he was about 10, however, he presented himself as an orphan at a Church of Scotland mission near Fort Hall. He gave his name as Kamau Wa Ngengi; he took the more patriotic-sounding name of Kenyatta many years later, in England.

He first went to England in 1929. The Hilton Young Commission had been investigating the land question in Kenya and the Kikuyu approached Kenyatta, asking him to put their problems before the authorities in London. Three of these problems were selected as of special importance or urgency: land, female circumcision (it was the year of the hostile Presbyterian campaign) and the need for independent schools. Only on the third did he make progress. The Kikuyu were given permission to open independent schools if they could build them and train the staff. By then, it was September, 1930, Kenyatta returned to Kenya with this concession, but came back to England the following year, staying away from Kenya until 1946. On his return to England he took up the issue of female circumcision with great vigour, protesting not only against the Church of Scotland's ban on circumcised girls in their schools, but also against the suggestion that the custom, in itself, was undesirable. During his evidence at the trial, he said:

> This custom which was and still is regarded as dear to the Kikuyu people, that is the circumcison of Kikuyu girls, was maintained by the missionaries as being cruel to the womenfolk, and we as Kikuyu maintained that it was a beautiful custom, and there was this disagreement.

He addressed meetings and wrote to the Colonial Secretary. He argued the case for female circumcision in person with the Moderator of the Church of Scotland and the Archbishop of Canterbury. The House of Commons appointed a committee to consider the question. The committee, in Kenyatta's words, "decided to recommend to the government the abolition of such a custom, and to educate the Kikuyu so that they would be in a position to decide which of their customs were good and which were bad".

The following year—1932—Kenyatta gave evidence in London before the Carter Commission on Kenya lands—yet another of the successive commissions which tackled, without solving, the basic problem of Kenya and of the Kikuyu. Since he was in Europe, Kenyatta took advantage of the opportunity to travel and educate himself. He travelled extensively, and twice went to Moscow, where he studied at the university from 1932 to 1934. Since it is doubtful that either Kenyatta or his people could have paid for these journeyings, and since they took him eventually to Moscow, it must be suspected that communist money paid for them. This is not improbable, as the Comintern was always on the lookout for promising colonial students; there is no evidence, however, that Kenyatta was ever a communist, and the British Communist Party has said that he was never on its list of members.

Back in England, he sank himself in anthropological studies at the University of London, under Professor Malinowski. The fruit of his labours was published in 1938 under the title of *Facing Mount Kenya*, which he wrote in an old, bathless but friendly house after meeting the colour bar in various places where he had tried to find lodgings. His distinguished professor considered him a highly intelligent pupil, wrote a foreword to the book and described it as "an invaluable document in the principles underlying culture-contact and change"—the basic conflict of his native land. There is no evidence that Kenyatta was anti-British at this time, despite his dampening experience of the colour bar among English landladies. It is said that he was known affectionately as "Jumbo" at his local pub. In between studies and casual jobs— for instance, as an agricultural labourer—he lectured for the Workers' Educational Association. And in 1942, he married Edna Grace Clarke, an Englishwoman, to whom, a year later, a son was born.

Two years before Kenyatta's marriage, the government of Kenya banned the Kikuyu Central Association, of which Kenyatta had been an official since 1925. He is said not to have known of this war-time ban until he returned to Kenya in 1946. He immediately asked the Governor, Sir Philip Mitchell, to revoke the ban. Sir Philip, without accepting this suggestion, advised him, in a spirit of friendliness, to reacclimatise himself after his long absence before re-entering politics. Kenyatta took the advice; for a year he devoted himself to his new job as principal of the independent Teachers' Training College. Then he founded, and accepted the presidency of, the Kenya African Union. Its success was dramatic. So was Kenyatta's. Like Dr. Banda of Nyasaland a decade later, he revealed himself as a mass orator of hypnotic accomplishment. Meetings of 40,000 to 50,000 Africans, many of whom had travelled from afar, were alternately entranced and excited by his oratory.

The programme of the KAU was nationalistic but with moral overtones. The land question was foremost and some of its leaders, including Kenyatta, clamoured for immediate self-government. Labour problems likewise concerned the KAU. But next to these great economic or political questions ran a parallel stream of demands or injunctions affecting the way of life of Kenyan Africans. In his speeches, Kenyatta laid emphasis on the need for hard work and the wickedness of sensual pleasures; thieves, prostitutes and parasites were the targets of his abuse. Often he explained that, ideally, the African should borrow what was good in the European, American or Asian ways of life, reject what was bad and retain all that was good in his own customs. English hats and English beer were bad and were explicitly condemned; the Kikuyu's circumcision of girls was good and the European must not be allowed to interfere with it.

Was Mau Mau the natural striking weapon of the KAU, "managed" by Kenyatta and his friends, as the Crown insisted at their trial? Or was it a hideous perversion of a legitimate political movement, conceived by insane criminals without the knowledge of Kenyatta, as, in effect, Montagu Slater and others have suggested? It is not my purpose to judge. All I have attempted to show is that given the frustrations of Kenyan Africans in general, and of the Kikuyu in particular, a rebellion of *some* kind was inevitable, sooner or later. And Kenyatta, whether or not he "managed" Mau Mau, was the natural leader of the ferment of rebellion that exploded in the Mau Mau insurrection.

* * *

I have already mentioned Dr. Banda of Nyasaland, and he deserves a few words to himself; for although, strictly speaking he was not the leader of an insurrection, he was certainly the leader of a movement that took a violent form in February and March, 1959, and that might well have developed into an insurrection if prompt police measures had not been taken. He therefore qualifies as a "rebel".

Like Kenyatta, Dr. Banda spent many years in self-imposed and educative exile; like Dr. Nkrumah of Ghana, he graduated in the United States. Unlike Kenyatta, however, he is a Christian, indeed a member of that very Church of Scotland which Kenyatta saw as one of his principal enemies. This religious divergence is hardly coincidental, for it merely reflects the curiously ambivalent rôle of the Church of Scotland in eastern Africa. In Kenya, the Africans regarded it as a white man's Church; and in Nyasaland the Europeans regarded it as a black man's Church. Both of these verdicts were—in the rough—correct. We have seen something of the rôle of the Presbyterians in Kenya; in Nyasaland, however, they set up an autonomous Church, the Church of Central Africa Presbyterian, which, by deliberate policy, was gradually Africanised. This Church certainly became the mouthpiece of Nyasas who opposed federation of their country with northern and southern Rhodesias for fear of permanent subjugation to the white settlers. The governments of both the Federation and Nyasaland itself blamed this opposition on the Church of Scotland and its central African offspring, and the Nyasaland Government drafted a secret white paper to prove its case. I have read this document, and I do not accept its findings, for it is hard to believe that the Church was in any way responsible for *creating* African opposition to federation, though it may well have helped to keep that opposition alive. The tensions of 1959 were largely the result of a series of official shortcomings which I describe in greater detail in Part II. The greatest of these errors was the deliberate failure to consult the Africans; one need look no farther for the cause of the frustrations of the Nyasas and of Dr. Banda.

He was born in 1906, and his first two names symbolise the meeting of primitive and technological cultures. It is said that a medicine-man cured his mother's barrenness by prescribing certain root herbs; in gratitude for his success, Banda's mother named him Kamuzu, which means "the little root". But he is usually known as Dr. *Hastings* Banda, for that was the name he chose for himself, in tribute to John Hastings, a missionary who had aroused his admiration. Restless, intelligent and ambitious from the first, he was soon dissatisfied with the limitations of the mission school which had taught him to read and write. Aged 12, he walked out of the family hut, without warning, clothes or money, and nearly a year later reached the white men's towns of South Africa. For four years he studied at night while interpreting between Nyasa labourers and their employers on the Rand goldfields. A lecture by Dr. Aggrey, an American Negro educationist, persuaded him to study in the United States, where he arrived in 1923, with £2 in his pocket. Americans, white and black, helped him to work his way through various colleges until, as the only black student at the University of Chicago, he graduated as Bachelor of Philosophy. Later, at Mecheray Medical College, in Nashville, Tennessee, he qualified as a doctor.

He left America in 1938, not for home but for Scotland, where he took his L.R.C.P. at Edinburgh in 1941. Eventually he settled down in the Kilburn district of London, to a large and successful practice, with 4,000 Europeans on his books. Dapper of clothing, gentle of manner, he presented the perfect but deceptive image of a GP at work. Deceptive, because the hard-working doctor was already a political leader and his modest surgery had become a meeting-place for politically minded African students. Some of them, like him, bear names that are now well-known—like Kwame Nkrumah and Jomo Kenyatta.

From his Kilburn home, Dr. Banda wrote innumerable letters

to the Nyasas, guiding and counselling, creating at long range the Nyasaland African Congress which his remittances helped to finance. Inevitably the Nyasa chiefs and party members who came to London in the early 'fifties to oppose federation acknowledged him as their leader. Uncompromising in opposition, he viewed the imposition of federation in 1953 as a betrayal of the Nyasas by their trustees and protectors. Bitter to the point of despair, he left England two years later, this time for a point nearer home— Ghana, where he wished to study the first of Britain's ex-colonies to have emerged to African statehood, in preparation for his homecoming after more than thirty years of exile. But before going home, he returned to London. The Federal Prime Minister, Sir Roy Welensky, had announced his intention of seeking independence for the Federation in 1960. This was the final challenge and spur to action. Dr. Banda took over the leadership of the Nyasaland African Congress, lobbied MPs, made speeches. Anti-communist from his American days, he saw a parallel between Hungary and central Africa. "That the European settlers want federation", he declared, "is no justification, any more than the fact that a section of the Hungarians wanted a Russian-imposed régime, for imposing an unwanted régime on the African people."

And so, shouting "To hell with federation", and, more Biblically, "I am like a Moses come home to my people", he returned to the land of his birth. Eight months later, after passionate speech-making had culminated in anti-European riots, he was arrested and sent to Southern Rhodesia. "I was wondering when you were going to come for me," he calmly told the police.

5

Post-colonial Rebels

IT could be argued that, basically, there are only two forms of government: parliamentary democracy and single-party rule. Scratch many a "parliamentary democracy" and you will find, thinly disguised, a single-party state. The former, however, without quotation marks, is a highly civilised and sophisticated process, evolved through the centuries and reflecting, in the last analysis, an attitude of tolerance. The latter is a crude and primitive makeshift, suitable for the politically unsophisticated. The essence of parliamentary democracy is the right to change governments peacefully at the polls; the opposition, being legal, may then take over. The single-party state is denied this advantage: opposition being illegal; it must reform itself, if at all, from within. The frustrations that explode into rebellion are therefore more likely to accumulate in the single-party state, which denies them an outlet, than in a parliamentary democracy, which affords them one. On the other hand, the apparatus of repression and intimidation is infinitely stronger in the totalitarian state, where power is a monopoly, than in the parliamentary democracy, where it is auctioned to the highest bidder every few years. Rebels are therefore more likely to be discouraged in single-party states than in those where opposition parties are legal. Conversely, where parliamentary rule is weak, inefficient or corrupt, rebels will be the more tempted to resort to force of arms.

These reflections, it will be seen, are as relevant to the next chapter, which deals with anti-communist rebellions, as to this one. Here and now, however, I am concerned with a phenomenon of the utmost importance to the emerging states of Africa and Asia: the post-colonial rebellion. The most striking examples of it come from Cuba, Indonesia and Burma.

The coupling of such apparently dissimilar examples as the first two is in itself a fascinating exercise. Both had been ruled by foreign powers. Both, as it happens, are island republics, though that is scarcely relevant; nor is the fact that both are large producers of sugar, though it may be more relevant to mention that both have large peasant populations and underdeveloped economies. More arresting—and challenging—than the similarities is the *contrast* between their forms of government at the time of the rebellions. For Indonesia was, in principle at least, a parliamentary democracy, whereas Cuba was, frankly and brutally, a dictatorship. It is useless, therefore, to seek to establish a correlation between forms of government and tendencies to rebellion in post-colonial régimes. It is far more rewarding to examine the facts of each case. And it will then be found that neither frustration nor misrule is a monopoly of any particular system of government.

Fidel Castro's successful rebellion is of special significance in Latin-America, where revolutions, as everybody knows, are two a penny. Its uniqueness does not consist in the fact that it resulted in the overthrow of a detested dictator, Fulgencio Batista. For in the previous few years, several other Latin-American *caudillos* had been overthrown: the relatively progressive but irresponsible Juan Perón in Argentina, Rojas Pinilla in Colombia, Pérez Jiménez in Venezuela, to name only three. Castro's originality was that he led a genuine popular movement, spearheaded by an army of fortune; in this he broke a standing rule of Latin-American revolutions: that governments are overthrown by the defection of regular armed forces. The revolutions of Argentina, Colombia and Venezuela, which conformed to the rule, are correspondingly of less interest to this study.

Cuba was ruled by the British for eleven months (1762–63), by the Spaniards for 135 years and twice by the Americans: from 1898 to 1901 and from 1906 to 1909. Its modern experience of freedom has therefore been brief and intermittent, for American intervention, in one form or another, continued until 1923, and American interest and influence have continued. With so recent an experience of colonial rule, the term "post-colonial" has more meaning in Cuba than in other former Spanish colonies of Latin-America. In Cuba as elsewhere, however, independence has been no guarantee of good government. To say that independent Cuba had known nothing but bad administration until Fidel Castro launched his rebellion is no more than the truth. General Gerardo Machado, who inaugurated the constitution of 1928, was overthrown by organised revolt in 1933. The Machado tyranny was replaced by the first Batista régime, which, even after the inauguration of a new constitution in 1940, was widely criticised as semi-military, although Batista had been freely elected that year.

Further free elections in 1944 brought in President Grau San Martín, who, under his successor, President Carlos Prío Socarrás, was accused of misappropriation of funds. President Prío, who had been elected in 1948, is generally considered to have been a greater respecter of civil liberties than of the public purse.

And so, Batista. . . .

General Batista returned to Cuba in 1949, after five years in exile. He formed a new party, the *Acción Unitaria Progresista* and announced that he would be a candidate at the new Presidential elections, due on June 1st, 1952. It was clear to him as to others that his chances of honest victory were small; and on March 10th, he staged a *coup d'état* and proclaimed himself President without benefit of popular support. The first of Cuba's rebel frustrations under Batista flows from the simple fact that he had come to power illegally; whatever the shortcomings of the three previous governments—of which Batista's first presidency was one—all three had been legally elected. Batista's seizure of power rudely interrupted Cuba's graduation course in parliamentary democracy.

Batista thus made his second start against a built-in current of resentment, particularly among the educated youth of the country. But there was more to the frustration of the intellectuals than a quarrel about legality. A further, and rapidly developing, source of frustration was the *nature* of the support enjoyed by Batista. Army officers pampered by their self-promoted President; brothel-keepers who made Havana a capital of vice with 10,000 licensed inmates; gambling racketeers, either local-born or imported from the United States; business-men allowed to share in Cuba's rising prosperity on payment of graft to Batista and his men; crooked politicians at the receiving end of monetary considerations—these were the people who supported the régime. It required no more than a modest dose of youthful idealism to be revolted by Batista's supporters, and a normal dose of youthful courage to revolt against them.

Graft and corruption were not, as we have seen, peculiar to Batista's régime. But under his two freely elected predecessors, these conditions had not proved incompatible with a reasonable degree of political and civil liberty. From the first, however, Batista ruled through fear of the police and army. Opposition to the régime thus rested on the triple grounds of illegality, corruption and depravity, and the tyrannical exercise of power.

It would be naïve and misleading, however, to suppose that Castro rebelled against Batista merely because he was running a police state. Indeed, the full rigours of official terrorism were imposed only *after* the rebellion had been launched and as a method of suppressing it; before that, the régime had been relatively mild. Fidel Castro, in fact, is the perfect example of the initial proposition in this book: that rebellions are made by rebels. He was a rebel by nature and in reality long before Batista's second period of power. In 1947, he was aboard a ship carrying 1,100 intending insurgents from the eastern Cuban coast, who aimed at invading the Dominican Republic and overthrowing its dictator, Rafael Leonidas Trujillo. Intercepted by gunboats, the ship turned tail and the attempt petered out.

In a sense, Castro had been nurtured in rebellion from his earliest years at Mayarí, fifty miles from Santiago de Cuba. He was born on April 13th, 1927—only four years after the last period of direct American rule had ended. Memories of Theodore Roosevelt's "big stick" were fresh and anti-*Yanqui* talk was normal in the Castro household. It would probably be fanciful to see in this an element in Fidel's later opposition to the Batista dictatorship which, for most of its course, enjoyed American support. More relevant is the fact that he grew up during the dictatorship of General Machado, "the butcher" or "the President of 1,000 murders" as he was variously known. (It is only fair to recall that it was largely owing to American influence that Machado was eventually overthrown.) In Castro's family and among its friends there was contempt for professional politicians and detestation for dictatorship. These sentiments had nothing to do with economic lack of privilege. Angel Castro, Fidel's father, though originally a penniless immigrant from Spain, owned a $500,000 sugar plantation by the time Fidel was born. Fidel was educated at Jesuit colleges, first in Santiago, then in Havana, already a visible and instructive centre of corruption. Later, at the University of Havana, he graduated in Arts and Laws. Deeply involved in student politics, he was twice arrested for activities that were certainly illegal by the lights of a dictatorship. Yet, paradoxically, it was presumably during this period of legal studies that Castro developed his obsessive opposition to the illegal exercise of power: to those who contest a dictator's right to govern, the "illegal" activity of opposition is, by definition, legal.

Few rebellions can have been so dominated by their leader as Fidel Castro's. Fanatical, impulsive, spellbinding, romantic, ascetic, idealistic, egotistical: these adjectives have all been used of him. And indeed he displayed the egotism that believed in his ultimate victory when others, including Batista, wrote him off as a fool and a failure; the fanatical concentration on a single goal that is the hallmark of the true rebel; the impulsiveness that led him, more than once, to strike too soon; the romanticism that made of him and of his ragged movement a living legend; the oratory that cast a spell over audiences, sometimes for five hours on end; the asceticism that imposed a puritanical code of behaviour on his followers of both sexes; and the idealism that aroused the youth of his country and gave a lasting impetus to his insurrectionary drive. All the adjectives, then, were deserved (as indeed were others that revealed themselves as soon as he came to power; but that is no concern of this narrative). Castro's movement was known simply as "el 26 de julio" from the date of his first and abortive attempt to overthrow Batista. In those days, he must indeed, with his thin face and gangling figure, have seemed a youthful Don Quixote, tilting at windmills. The year was 1953. Castro had been a candidate for Congress in the elections that never took place because Batista had seized power. From that moment Castro knew his own mind: he would overthrow Batista. He sold his law books and car, and recruited his brother Raúl and 150 friends. Between them they raised money—$20,000 according to one account—and bought arms and contraband uniforms. Don

Quixote had followers; he needed a windmill. The choice was symbolic: the Moncada barracks at Santiago de Cuba, symbol of Batista's illegal power in Oriente, province of Castro's birth. The leader's preparations had been pitifully inadequate and his choice of tactics was disastrous. At dawn on July 26th, Fidel Castro set off with as many of his followers as could fit into thirteen cars. They had scarcely reached the Moncada barracks when a jeep patrol challenged them. Castro drew a pistol and fired. The amateur rebels were soon surrounded; seventy-five of them were killed and most of the others captured. Castro himself was tried and sentenced to fifteen years in gaol.

There is no need, in this chapter, to follow Castro's career into its phase of success, which we pick up later. Instead, it is worth casting a second look at the frustrations of the Cuban people. I have suggested a connection between Cuba's under-developed economy and peasant population and the Castro rebellion, and indeed the connection is important. Though the *Fidelista* movement started with purely political aims, it waxed on peasant support and soon became agrarian and social in character.

As in Mexico before the great revolution of 1910, the peasants of Cuba were little more than serfs in the sense that they were bound to the land on which they lived and worked. But if they lived there all the year round, they worked only ten or twelve weeks of the year, during harvest-time. And half a million of them—in a total population of $6\frac{1}{2}$ millions—never worked at all. Even those who worked at harvest-time soon ran into debt, and because they bought their necessities on credit at stores owned by the companies that employed them, they were never able to seek better fortune elsewhere. To complete this picture of serfdom, one has to add a few more facts: about 80 per cent (in value) of the island's exports consist of sugar; only a fifth of the sugar-cane was grown on small plots owned by their farmers; three-quarters of the sugar was grown by tenant farmers whose plots were owned by the big companies; and the companies decided both the rent paid by the tenants and the price paid to them for the sugar they grew; more than two-thirds of the peasant dwellings had floors of beaten earth, nearly two-thirds had no lavatories and more than three-quarters no electricity; moreover, two-thirds of all Cuban families lived in one-room dwellings. Add to these figures a glaring contrast between the wretched peasant and the relatively prosperous urban worker; a high literacy rate, by Latin-American standards (more than 70 per cent); and the fact that many students are of peasant origin—and you have the ingredients of a rural revolutionary situation.

I have drawn most of these facts from various Chatham House publications, including the monthly review of the Royal Institute of International Affairs, *The World Today*, which, in its issue of May 5th, 1959, carried an article from which I quote:

> For the first few days after Castro landed on the Oriente coast in December 1956, his total following numbered only twelve. The majority of those who subsequently swelled his ranks were from Oriente, and most of them were students, often working in the towns. . . . His *maquis* forces were almost entirely peasants.

In these circumstances, it is not surprising that this movement of youthful intellectuals, mainly concerned at first with the legitimacy of power and corruption in the cities, should have turned into a peasant revolution obsessed with the need for land reform. Indeed, it could scarcely be otherwise: however hard Batista worked to label the movement communist (and although the *Fidelistas* certainly included communists), it derived none of its strength from the Marxist revolutionary class: the urban proletariat. On the contrary, Batista enjoyed the full support of the Secretary-General of the Cuban Confederation of Labour, Eusebio Mujal, whose unswerving loyalty was given in return for the dictator's backing in an earlier dispute with a rival labour leader. Castro evidently found it hard to realise and accept this fact. Twice—in August, 1957, and in April, 1958—he tried to call a strike. The second time, aiming high, he wanted a general strike. But both attempts, understandably, were failures. Thereafter, Castro relied on his willing peasants, who must have found it easy to believe that their poverty was due to the enrichment of

the pimps, drones and gangsters around Batista, or to the wickedness of the United States, on whose sugar import quota the
fluctuating prosperity of Cuba depended.

* * *

I have drawn a parallel between Cuba and Indonesia, and it is
time to show how imperfect it really is. The Indonesian rebellion
of colonels and economists was no peasant revolution, though one
does not have to accept at face value the statement of the rebel
government's "Representative for Europe and Ambassador-at-
large", Dr. Sutan Mohammed Rasjid, that "the struggle in Indonesia arose from political causes". Politics may have been pre-
dominant, but economic factors did play an important part in the
rebellion, as one would expect of a movement whose principal
political leaders were professional economists. Only these factors
were different in kind from the economic causes of insurrections
whose social antecedents were more humble. This was no Marxist
dream of an oppressed proletariat rising to shake off the chains of
its exploiters. Rather was it two other things, each distinct from
the other, and both distinct from the hypothetical proletarian
revolution. It was, on the one hand, a revolt of dissident regional
commanders who were dissatisfied with what they considered to
be the unfair distribution of revenues from the centre. And on
the other hand, it was a gesture of disgust, by some of Indonesia's
few monetary technicians, at the misuse of public funds by the
central government. It was not, as the British newspapers, perhaps in desperation, labelled it, a "right-wing rebellion" (its
guiding spirit, in economic terms, was Dr. Sumitro, an avowed
socialist, though perhaps of a rather Gaitskellian kind). The
desperation was understandable, for Indonesia's rebellions have
been legion, and this one was anti-communist; which seemed,
perhaps, to make it "right-wing".

It is arguable that most of the Indonesian Republic's troubles
go back to a single act of misguided nationalistic defiance. If
ever geography ought to have dictated a country's constitution,
that country is Indonesia. Three thousand islands on an arc of

2,500 miles; a people noted for its diversity of language, culture and even religion: how else but under a federal system could such a country be governed? The Dutch grasped this essential fact— and perhaps too well—and at the time of the transfer of sovereignty to the Republic, in December, 1949, the federal Indonesian state consisted of sixteen partner-states and autonomous territories. A smaller number would have sufficed, for administrative efficiency, but the principle was sound.

To the Indonesian nationalists, however, the federal structure of the State they had taken over was merely an instrument of Dutch imperialism, a perfect example of the old imperial principle of "divide and rule". Dorothy Woodman, whose book *The Republic of Indonesia* is a valuable presentation of the nationalist case and cause, quotes a typical argument. Hadji Agus Salim, who was at that time advising the Indonesian nationalists on foreign affairs, wrote:

> ... the creation of an increasing number of participating states and territories was purely artificial—a Dutch fabrication, aimed, originally, at avoiding the unconditional recognition of the sovereign Republic of Indonesia, and, subsequently, at the complete dismemberment of that Republic to enable the Kingdom of the Netherlands to restore their control over the former colonial empire in a less conspicuous form.

Given this prevailing trend of thought, it is not surprising that the idea of a unitary state rapidly came to be identified as the fulfilment of the nationalist dream. It was therefore not unexpected that the Indonesian leaders, as soon as sovereignty was transferred, began to destroy the Dutch-created Republic of the United States of Indonesia and build in its place the unitary state of the new Republic.

It was an ill-starred decision. Even in a continental country, a unitary state requires strong government; and even a strong government is often content with a federal structure, as are both the Soviet Union and the United States. From the outset, however, Indonesia was bedevilled by weak government and challenges to its authority. A federal structure might have saved the

Republic; paradoxically, a unitary state was bound to destroy its unity. Moreover, a unitary state meant, in effect, rule by Java, the central island. But Java, the most densely populated of the islands, with 53 millions of the total population of some 80 millions, was, almost by definition, the poor relation of the archipelago. Irrespective of the quality of the central administration, Java was bound to claim the largest share of the Republic's revenues, while contributing less to them, proportionately and absolutely, than some of the other units. Without further complicating elements, then, central rule was bound to arouse resentment in the other islands.

This situation has to be borne in mind if the rebellion is to become intelligible. I have tried to show that frustration was inherent both in the constitutional structure of the Indonesian Republic and in the distribution of its population. It remains to add that, with brief intervals, the Republic suffered from gross mismanagement at the centre almost from the day of its birth. This mismanagement is the core of the frustration that gnawed at the hearts of the rebels.

More communicative than most, the Indonesian rebels have consigned their grievances to paper, in a useful monograph entitled *The Birth of the New Indonesia*. There is no point in imagining their sentiments; to quote or paraphrase their own words will be more satisfactory. The rebels reproached the central government in general, and President Sukarno in particular, with having violated the existing constitution, tolerated or profited from corruption, and encouraged the growth of the Communist Party (PKI). They claimed that the clauses of the constitution providing for the autonomy of the outer regions had remained a dead letter; consequently, the economic needs of the regions had been neglected and the central planning bureau in Jakarta had concentrated on the needs of Java to the detriment of the other islands. To top it all, said the rebels, in approximate English which I leave unretouched:

> As a consequence of the maladministration of the country a crisis
> of authority has come into being. Key-positions in the government

as well as in vital private enterprises are seized and monopolized by members of the various political parties without regard to their capacities. It is quite clear that this tendency has degenerated into widespread corruption and briberies resulting in the disintegration of state-apparatus and the impoverishment of the vast majority of the Indonesian people.

It is clear that for the regional commanders the decisive issue was autonomy; for the distinguished politicians who joined, then led, them, it was maladministration. Both groups shared a determination to have the PKI outlawed; and both considered that the President had acted unconstitutionally in attempting to inaugurate a system of "guided democracy", in which he, of course, would be the guide. Indeed, the last two grievances overlapped: the core of President Sukarno's "concept" for a guided democracy was the creation of a National Council, which would advise the cabinet, whether or not its advice was sought; and since the National Council was to include the PKI, the communists were to be given a voice in the direction of the country's affairs, from which they had been excluded by tacit agreement among the other parties since their abortive insurrection at Madiun in 1948. In the early stages, the rebels did not ask for Sukarno's resignation. They merely called on him to resume the modest rôle allotted to him by the constitution; to that end, they advocated a resumption of the old partnership between Sukarno as President, and Mohammed Hatta as Vice-President, which had broken down by the time Dr. Hatta resigned in 1956. They also favoured the formation of a government headed by Hatta himself; it was not till it was clear beyond doubt that their demands were not going to be heeded that they decided to disown Sukarno and proclaim their separate government.

These grievances and demands were given expression in a document known as the "Palembang Charter" and issued over the signatures of the dissident army officers, including Colonels Hussein, Barlian and Sumual. These officers had met, to consider the situation and draft their "charter", at Palembang in south Sumatra, on September 7th and 8th, 1957. The Palembang

Charter was less a bill of rights than a political ultimatum—though without a time-limit. Under it, the rebels demanded: the return of Hatta to the top leadership in the affairs of state; the immediate replacement of the army high command (meaning the dismissal of the Chief of Staff, Lieutenant-General Abdul Haris Nasution, who had identified his career with loyalty to the President); decentralisation and regional autonomy; the establishment of a Senate (which would protect regional interests, neglected under the unicameral system); and the prohibition of communism "as a movement based on an internationally directed ideology which is contrary to the fundamental principles underlying the state-ideology for Indonesia".

The Palembang Charter was signed several months after the rebel colonels had been joined by the former Finance Minister, Dr. Sumitro Djojohadikusumo. In those months, Dr. Sumitro had built up the flourishing (but illegal) system of trade between the rebel areas of Sumatra and Celebes and the outside world, which was to provide the rebels with their revenues (while denying them to the central government). In Sumitro, and later in Dr. Sjafruddin, the Governor of the central bank, we find the frustrations of the able technician in the midst of chaos, corruption and inefficiency. There is no doubt that Sumitro and Sjafruddin himself had been the ablest of the Republic's Finance Ministers; both men may have had their share of luck (with the terms of trade), but this is true of successful generals as well as finance ministers. The fact is that Indonesia's reserves of gold and foreign currency rose steadily when they were in office and tended to drop as though by evil magic when they were out. The graph of the reserves rose, for instance, during the Natsir cabinet—the second after the transfer of sovereignty—when Sjafruddin was Finance Minister and Sumitro was Minister of Trade and Industry. It rose again, under the Wilopo cabinet (1952–53), when Sumitro was Finance Minister, and again after a sharp fall, under the Burhanuddin Harahap government, when Sumitro was back in office. True, the reserves continued to rise under the Sukiman-Suwirjo government, which succeeded Dr. Natsir's, but the rise, which was phenomenal, was due to the great boom of the Korean war, which sent the prices of Indonesia's greatest exports—rubber and tin—soaring to unprecedented levels. This was, in fact, a far from creditable period in the management of the Republic's finances. In an orgy of uninhibited spending, ministers placed orders abroad without bothering to inform the Ministry of Finance. The government fell just before the day of reckoning; Sumitro, back in office as Finance Minister in the Wilopo cabinet, discovered that orders placed abroad without registration either with the Ministry of Finance or the Foreign Currency Fund totalled $1,000 million. It was too late to prevent the crash, but afterwards, by a prudent import-control policy, the new Finance Minister set the graph climbing once again. In the meantime, Dr. Sjafruddin had been appointed Governor of the Bank Indonesia where, once more, he practised his belief in sound finance.

This apparent digression is essential if one is to understand the kind of frustration that drove these able—indeed, respectable—men, both fathers of large families, into the discomfort and uncertainty of rebellion. In both cases, it was the frustration of the sound technician prevented from doing his job. For Sumitro, it was the frustration of seeing his good work undone in each of the Ali Sastroamidjojo cabinets (1953–55 and 1956–57); for Sjafruddin, particularly in the last two years before he joined the rebels, it was the frustration of the paid official at the mercy of irresponsible policies and without a say in deciding them. For both, perhaps above all, there was the frustration of seeing the intriguing politicians of Jakarta steadily making a mess of a rich and beautiful country, while the PKI, as steadily, grew in numbers and influence, all under the eye of a demagogic President.

Something of this frustration comes through in a passage in the rebel booklet I have mentioned and in which one fancies to have detected the hand of Dr. Sumitro:

> And when one looked somewhat deeper into Jakarta politics, it was obvious that a reasonably good government was only left in power as long as it was deemed necessary to tolerate it in order to clear the financial mess that had been left by its predecessors. But as

soon as the monetary reserves were at a reasonable level and inflation had been curbed, the good cabinet was brought down by the
machinations of a limited number of "nationalist" and communist
leaders and their fellow-travellers. It was against the interests of this
group that a good cabinet should be allowed to embark upon its
work of economic and social progress; once it had seen to it that
some money was again available to the State Treasury, the forces of
corruption and depravity were put into power again.

I am not at all sure that an objective observer would agree with
every word of this analysis, but I have no doubt that its author
believed every word of it. He, and others like him, including the
two ex-Prime Ministers Natsir and Harahap, felt frustrated in the
entangling undergrowth of Jakarta's political jungle. That, in the
last analysis, is why they joined the dissident colonels in Sumatra.

For all that, the rebellion was a body without a head. True, the
rebel government proclaimed on February 15th had a Prime
Minister, but until then the body had been stumbling forward
without a brain to direct its footsteps and co-ordinate its movements. Economic co-ordination had been provided by Sumitro,
but despite his energy and ability, he neither aspired to political
leadership nor would have been acceptable if he had. Intellectually
brilliant, he was considered inadequate in terms of mass appeal
and authority; moreover, he was reproached with having played
too small a part in the struggle for independence. The military
rebels, though co-operating with each other, were laws unto
themselves; the man they eventually picked as their Commander-
in-Chief, Colonel Kawilarang, was in Washington as Military
Attaché when the rebellion broke out, although he had been involved in the early stages of dissidence against President Sukarno
(that indeed was why he had been transferred to Washington).
The lack of leadership was, of course, a major cause of the initial
failures of the rebellion. In adding to our portrait gallery of
rebels, therefore, I am faced with the choice between including all
the leaders or selecting one knowing that he could not be, in all
senses, regarded as the leader. To sketch them all would be
tedious for the reader; I therefore select the man who did become

the rebel Prime Minister, and who stayed on in the Sumatran jungle to carry on the struggle after the Indonesian army had walked over the rebel defences in April, 1958.

Dr. Sjafruddin Prawiranegara is not fashioned in the image of a rebel. I remember him as a bland-faced man with spectacles. He is, however, a man of great physical courage who played a fairly important part in the fight against the Dutch. For a brief period, indeed, it was a spectacular rôle. When the Dutch launched their second police action against the Indonesian Republic in December 1948, bombing Djogjakarta and arresting the Republican leaders, Dr. Sjafruddin proclaimed an emergency government with himself as Prime Minister. At the time of the action, he was Minister of Economics; he had flown to Sumatra a week earlier and it was there that he read his proclamation. A man sensitive to humour, as he is, must have enjoyed the irony of proclaiming himself Prime Minister once again, but this time in defiance of the recognised authorities of the Republic—again from Sumatra, but nearly ten years later.

He was born at Anjerkidul, in west Java, and belongs to the Sundanese minority—a factor that may help to account for a basically rebellious character. In his chosen field of economics, however, he has always been a pillar of orthodoxy. After graduating from Jakarta's Law College, he specialised in taxation. Sharp of wit and intolerant of obtuseness, he had no time for the financially reckless politicians who directed Indonesia's fortunes after independence. Appointed head of the Bank Indonesia, he did not trouble to hide his views. In 1953, he warned the politicians that Indonesia was living beyond its means and could not afford to prolong the irresponsible euphoria of the first years of independence. One element of that euphoria was the seven-hour day; Sjafruddin called a return to the eight-hour day. Another element was the discouragement of foreign capital; he preached the need of it if the dreams of rapid development were ever to materialise. Profligate spending had become general; he recommended economies and the consolidation of the gold reserves. Those prescriptions made the doctor unpopular with the demagogues of the capital. But his expertise was generally regarded as unassailable.

Yet in the end he, too, found the insecurity of insurrection preferable to the frustrating security of a high post in Jakarta. His speech at Padang on February 15th, 1958, proclaiming a rival government of the Republic, explained why he made this bitter choice. In it, he accused the Sukarno régime of tolerating corruption and unleashing official terror against political opponents. The words he used are worth quoting:

> When Mr. Djody Gondukusomo was Minister of Justice in the Ali Arifin (Sastroamidjojo) cabinet, he received hundreds of thousands, maybe even millions of rupiahs, from several Chinese, as bribery to get entry permits into Indonesia. One case was proven in court, for which he was sentenced to several months of imprisonment. But his appeal for mercy was granted by President Sukarno in contradiction with the advice of the Supreme Court. This convicted ex-minister is now sitting as member of parliament, allegedly as representative of the people and to defend the interests of the people.
>
> But let us compare it with another case. A sub-inspector of police in Tjiandjur, with many children and a small salary, has been convicted for committing a graft of several thousands of rupiahs. He was sentenced to one year imprisonment. He appealed for mercy to President Sukarno, but his appeal, in contrast with Mr. Djody Gondukusomo's appeal, was rejected outright.

Sjafruddin went on to talk of "thousands of young hoodlums" who, he said, had been hired by the President to "unleash terror and intimidation against everyone who dares to oppose the President's political concept".

With this speech, the die was cast. With this speech also the old nationalist dream of the unitary state finally came tumbling down. Whatever the outcome, this country of 3,000 islands could never again be ruled from the centre.

*   *   *

There are striking parallels between the post-war histories of Burma and Indonesia. Both countries became independent after the second world war. Each had its dominant race: the Burmese were to Burma what the Javanese were to Indonesia. Both suffered communist insurrections in 1948, though the Indonesians gave their communists much shorter shrift. Both had to contend with fanatical Moslem rebellions: the Darul Islam in Indonesia, and in Burma the Mujahids in the extreme north of Arakan. Above all, both were plagued by separatist movements. To the superficial onlooker this seemed stranger in Burma, which is a land mass, than in Indonesia, which is an archipelago. But in ethnic terms, the Union of Burma, too, is an archipelago, for the dominant Burmese are surrounded by distinct peoples, such as the Shans, Mons, Karens and Karennis, Kachins, Pa-O and others. Each of these peoples has nationalist inclinations and each of them, to a greater or lesser degree, took up arms against the government shortly after independence. As a result, insecurity was a major national problem for many years after independence had been gained.

In common with other tempting parallels, however, this one should not be pushed too far. In Indonesia, the case for a federal constitution was always strong, both for geographic and for economic reasons: a number of federated states, each perfectly viable, could easily be carved out of the Republic of Indonesia. But in Burma, the ethnic minority regions were in most cases, deficit areas, incapable, on their own, of constituting viable states. It is not surprising, therefore, that the makers of the constitution of the Union of Burma should have decided on a structure that looked federal but, in practice, was not. As Dr. Hugh Tinker put it in his thoroughgoing study, *The Union of Burma*:

> The relationship of state governments with the Union government appears to be that of dutiful adolescents to a severe parent. As long as the children behave in a way which the father approves, they are permitted a reasonable degree of freedom. But immediately they assert an independence which is contrary to the parental wishes, they are reminded sharply of their dependence. Although the constitution permits (Ch. X) under formidable safeguards a right of secession from the Union, it is doubtful if this right would be per-

mitted to be exercised. With regard to the Karens, there is no doubt: the legislation under which the Karen State came into being (Constitution Amendment Act, 1951) included a section 181(10), which definitely denied any right of secession to the new state.

More succinctly, the Burmese constitutional adviser, Chan Htoon, quoted by Dr. Tinker, observed: "Our constitution, though in theory federal, is in practice unitary."

It would be a mistake to blame Burma's separatist insurrections on the ambiguities of a constitution which, on the whole, the experts have admired rather than condemned. But it can hardly be a coincidence that on the one hand the strongest insurrectionary challenge to the Union government came from the Karens, while on the other hand the amendment granting them a state was not passed until 1951—four years after the adoption of the constitution; and indeed the Karen state—known as Kawthulay or "Flowery Land"—was not officially proclaimed until July 1st, 1955. In any event, the Karen rebellion, was a major challenge to the Union government: at its height, in 1949–50, the Burmese Prime Minister, U Nu, estimated that the rebel force, known as the Karen National Defence Organisation (KNDO) numbered 10,000 fighting men. Because of its scope and its character as a post-colonial rebellion, the Karen insurrection deserves some attention.

Two temptations must be resisted: the desire to oversimplify a fairly complicated situation, and a tendency to saddle one side with all the blame. Unlike many peoples who fight for their independence, the Karens do not appear, at any time, to have been independent, though the related Karennis ("red Karens") were and entered into treaty relationship with the British. The Karens, as an ethnic group, may number two or three millions; their spokesmen have had a natural tendency to inflate the figure, which the government of Burma put at 1,367,673 in 1949. Most of them are Buddhists and some are animists, but the most dynamic—and bellicose—among them are the 220,000 Christians; and among the Christians those who most deserve these adjectives are Baptists. Indeed the Baptist missionaries are credited—or blamed

—for at least a share of the Karens' refusal to recognise the rule of Rangoon in their areas. Unlike the Burmese, who are thought to be of Tibetan origin, the Karens are of Chinese origin and speak a tonal language of Sinitic extraction. In common with most of the dissident Burman national groups, they are hill people.

In the second world war, the Karens gave good and loyal service to the British, and in Major Hugh Seagrim of the Burma Rifles they had, in effect, their own Lawrence of Arabia. After the British had retreated before the advancing Japanese, Seagrim organised a Karen resistance group in the mountains of the Salween district. In this endeavour, he was greatly helped by the traditional antagonism between the Karens and the Burmese. The combination of this antagonism and the Karens' loyalty to Britain labelled the Karens, in Burmese eyes, as "collaborators" and enemies. In 1942, the Burma Independence Army—that forcing ground of political leaders—seems to have decided to teach the Karens a lesson. On March 21st, 150 men of the BIA arrived at Papun, in Karen country, and accused the Karens of being pro-British when they demurred at a request for arms. On April 4th, the local chief of the BIA, Boh Nya Na, was ambushed and killed with some of his followers. Next morning, the BIA lined up seventeen Karen elders and mowed them down with automatic rifles. In another incident, the BIA massacred more than 150 Karens, including a cabinet minister, his British wife and their children.

Against this background, it is scarcely surprising that the Karens felt disinclined, five years later, to entrust their destinies to the Burmese. At that time, however, the cry was not for independence but for continued British rule—a lonely discord in the general chorus of anti-colonialism that followed the war. When it became obvious that the British were handing over Burma, a determined minority of Karens decided to fight for independence, egged on, it is said, by some Britons who were ashamed that their country had abandoned the Karens.

The Burmese leaders, including Aung San, were aware of the wisdom of consulting the minority peoples if independent Burma was to be established on a stable basis. But little attempt was made to bridge the gap of suspicion that separated the Burmese from the Karens. In July, 1946, in the dying days of British rule, the Karens sent a four-man delegation to London to plead—unsuccessfully—for home rule. In December, Aung San left for London to negotiate independence with the Attlee government, but without including any representatives of the minorities in his delegation; the Attlee-Aung San agreement followed, but although it promised independence within a year, it made no mention of the aspirations of the minorities.

At that time, the Karen Central Organisation was one of the bodies constituting the main Burman independence party, the Anti-Fascist People's Freedom League (AFPFL) and the Karen leader Saw Ba U Gyi, was a member of the cabinet. Another Karen, San Po Thin, called on Ba U Gyi to resign as a token of dissatisfaction with the Attlee-Aung San agreement. He did, and San Po Thin immediately took his place as a wholehearted collaborator of the Burmese. Only a small minority of the Karens supported San Po Thin, however; the great majority joined a new body which Ba U Gyi founded: the Karen National Union. And the new KNU demanded a separate Karen administration.

Ignoring them, Aung San called a conference of hill peoples at Panglong in southern Shan state, on February 12th. The four Karen observers at the conference were not consulted, though the other hill peoples agreed to co-operate with the government. In March and April a Frontier Areas Committee, headed by a Labour MP, Lieutenant-Colonel David Rees-Williams (now Lord Ogmore), conducted a rapid inquiry among the hill peoples. The committee heard confusing demands from the Karens: those of the Salween district, for instance, demanded a separate administration, as far as possible under direct British control, while those of the Shwegyin area asked to be joined to the Salween, but could not make up their minds whether they wanted the Salween district to be separate or part of Burma. In the end, their views were simply ignored.

Apart from San Po Thin's followers, the Karens boycotted the elections to the Constituent Assembly in April, 1947. The more disgruntled among them set about creating their National Defence Organisation (KNDO), though the best-known Karen leaders, including Ba U Gyi, favoured a peaceful settlement. There was still time to preserve the peace, and indeed the government—under U Nu, who had replaced the murdered Aung San—appointed a Regional Autonomy Commission with that end in view. The commission, on which the Karens were well represented, was charged with inquiring into the question of autonomy for the Karens, Mons and Arakanese. On the Karen side, Ba U Gyi pledged the loyalty of the KNU to the government. But he no longer controlled the extremists of the KNDO, who, under their commander, Mahn Ba Zan, were planning their insurrection.

In this powder-keg a mere spark was needed for an explosion, and the Burmese provided a naked flame. The Karen Union Military Police had been withdrawn from certain areas and disarmed. On Christmas Eve, 1948, Burmese members of the Auxiliary Union Military entered churches in eight villages in one of those areas, and murdered more than eighty Karen Christian worshippers. The Karen national insurrection then burst in full force.

Those, in bare outline, are the events that led up to the Karen rebellion. They are described—with academic impartiality—by Hugh Tinker in *The Union of Burma*; and with partisan sympathy by the late Ian Morrison in *Grandfather Longlegs*, his biography of Major Seagrim. Morrison quotes a document from an unnamed Karen leader which deserves mention in any study of Karen frustrations and aspirations. The document stated categorically that "the hill Karens wish to remain under the direct control of a British governor" for reasons which I briefly summarise:

1. The Karens are mostly illiterate and do not understand Burmese. They owe their liberation to the British.
2. The Karens do not wish to be exposed to Burmese hooliganism and violence. They prefer orderly administration.
3. The Burmese leaders have no plans for the development of the Karen hills areas.

4. Given a separate area, the Karens could excel other districts in various respects.

5. The Karens can never forget Burmese atrocities in 1942.

6. The Karens are bewildered that the British have let them down.

Touching as was the Karen desire to remain under British rule, it was quite unrealistic. So was the demand for independence that came from an extremist minority, if only because the Karens were so scattered that it was difficult to find a reasonably viable area in which they would have been in a majority.

When all this has been said, however, a large share of the responsibility for the protracted Karen insurrection must be laid on the Burmese nationalist leaders, particularly Aung San. Preoccupied only with getting independence in the shortest possible time, the young Burmese leaders brushed the Karens aside, and in so doing invited rebellious violence.

In international terms, the Karen rebellion was far less important than Indonesia's revolt of colonels and economists. But the lesson it contains for the governments of newly independent countries is equally relevant. For them as for the maturer democracies of the West, it is always wise to seek the consent of the governed. Only governments that dispose of overwhelming force at the centre may ignore this principle with impunity. And even those could avoid an unnecessary wastage of military assets by talking before striking.

6

Against Communist Rule

As the 'fifties showed, rebellions are not a monopoly of the capitalist world. The demonstrations of this fact of life in Hungary and elsewhere may have privately disconcerted many communist agitators, but in public their line was ready. Marxist theory identifies revolution by the people with communist revolution. It follows that any revolt, on however large a scale, against a communist government must have been organised and led by "reactionaries" or "enemies of the people". The orthodox doubtless find intellectual comfort in this argument, but the serious student of affairs cannot help noticing that it rests on a false assumption: that the Communist Party represents the people.

Realising the falseness of this assumption, the serious student is not surprised to find that all the major anti-communist rebellions have been great popular movements, and that—with the partial exception of Tibet—they have been spontaneous outbreaks, without incitement, organisation or leadership. I have four examples in mind: the workers' uprising in east Berlin in June, 1953; the Tibetan rebellion against Chinese communist rule, culminating in the Dalai Lama's escape to India in March, 1959; the revolt of the Vietnamese peasants in November, 1956; and of course the great Hungarian uprising which, by an arresting coincidence, took place a few days before the events in communist Vietnam.

Three of my four examples are of anti-colonial uprisings: in Tibet against China; in Hungary and east Germany against Russia. Even in north Vietnam, it could be argued that the peasants were revolting against a system of administration alien to their traditions, although they almost certainly thought of their action in the simpler terms of turning around to kick the officials who had been oppressing them. Another point should be noted: in all four of my examples, a large number of workers or peasants, or both, rose spontaneously against administrations that claimed, above all, to speak in the interests of workers and peasants. Thus these rebellions are doubly instructive, for they were both anti-imperialist and popular. Yet by communist definitions, imperialism and communism are mutually exclusive terms, and it is impossible for the people to revolt against itself, i.e. against the Communist Party. It is, in fact, difficult on the evidence, to avoid two conclusions: that communist imperialism is a good deal harsher than "capitalist" imperialism has been in the twentieth century; and that workers and peasants, no less than intellectuals and surviving "bourgeois" elements, resent communist methods of administration.

These conclusions are useful correctives to communist fallacies. They may even boost the morale of elderly and retreating imperialists, like the British, French or Dutch, who may reflect complacently that, by and large, their worst days of colonial oppression are over, whereas for the communists they are just beginning. But alike in terms of power and from the rebel standpoint, there is little comfort in this reflection. For one more observation must be added to those I have already made: the four anti-communist rebellions I have cited were all crushed with ruthless disregard for human life and suffering. There is indeed a case for the proposition that the popular rebellions of the 'forties and 'fifties started with good chances of success where the ruling authorities were non-communist, and with none where communists controlled the government. This is scarcely surprising, on historical grounds alone and leaving ideology out of the question. Communist imperialism was about thirty-five years old when the Hungarians revolted in 1956, dating it from 1921, when the young Soviet régime, under Lenin, finished reconquering the areas of Asia that had revolted against Russian domination after the collapse of Tsarism. In the 'forties, when the British, French and Dutch faced their great post-war trials, each had ruled over alien peoples for several centuries. The late Sir David Kelly was right when he observed in *The Ruling Few* that nations lose their empires when they lose the will to rule them. The communist imperialists have not yet lost the will to rule people who would reject them instantly if given the freedom to choose their rulers. (In fairness to communists, the French retained the will to rule much longer than the British.)

This argument supposes the existence of a "communist imperialism". Some people, not necessarily communists, would deny it, on logical or historical grounds, arguing that imperialism is one nation's dominion over another. But there is no doubt that communist theory has introduced a new element into the concept of imperialism. Communists assert that the advent of "socialism" in every country of the world is historically predetermined; but paradoxically, they reserve the right to give history a push in the right direction. In Europe alone, this interpretation of history has led to the enslavement of nine nations. But the communists go farther than earlier imperialists in that there is a corollary to their theory of historical determinism: once communism is established in a country it would be a "betrayal of the cause of the world proletariat" to allow it to be overthrown. Hence the Soviet intervention in Hungary, which merely claimed the right to free elections and neutrality. In one sense, then, communism is an instrument of older imperialisms—Russia's or China's—but in another sense it has an independent existence. The term "communist imperialism" therefore seems to me fully justified.

Unless and until communism modifies its character (when, in any case, it would cease to be communism as we know it), it would be vain to suppose that communist authorities will take the slightest notice of a chapter on the frustrations of people under communist rule. For the only logical lesson of these frustrations, and of the permanent tendency towards rebellion which they cause, is that the communists should make room for others. That, however, is the one thing they cannot do while remaining communists. I write these words, therefore, because I feel this study would be incomplete without them, not in the forlorn hope of influencing the course of events.

I may perhaps, however, permit myself to deal with the three lesser rebellions in relatively summary fashion. Of the two Asian ones, only the Tibetan one made big headlines in the Western press and then only in its later stages. Indeed it was a more sustained and, internationally, a more important insurrection than the north Vietnamese one. Yet in one respect the Vietnamese uprising is the more interesting of the two; for it was a clear case of a rebellion against communist rule, imposed not by foreigners but by nationals of the rebels' own country.

Few people in western Europe outside France have had the time or the desire to interest themselves in the affairs of Indo-China. But in 1954 the newspaper-reading public could scarcely help itself: the siege of Dien Bien Phu, the defeat of the French Union Army by the Vietminh, the Geneva conference, M.

Mendès-France's race against time to bring peace within a month or resign—these events dominated the news in the first seven months of the year. Many people with no particular interest in Indo-China are therefore aware that under the Geneva agreements Vietnam was partitioned, as Germany and Korea had been. It is also common knowledge that in the first few months after partition, nearly a million refugees, mostly Catholics, fled to the nationalist south after the communists had taken over the Red River delta in north Vietnam from the defeated French. It is perhaps hardly astonishing that the arrival of the communists in the predominantly Catholic areas of Phat Diem and Bui Chu should have caused a panic. It is all the more interesting, then, to note that the peasant revolt of November, 1956, had nothing to do with the French defeat or with sudden panic. In fact, it took place in an area where the communists had been in continuous and undisputed control since the Japanese defeat in 1945. The main centre of disturbance was Quynh Luu, a Gulliverish-sounding village in the province of Nghe An in northern Annam. It is an area with a long revolutionary tradition; indeed, as I mentioned in Chapter 1, that famous revolutionary, Ho Chi Minh, was born in Nghe An. Only in 1956 the peasants were in revolt against *him*.

I am concerned with rebel frustrations, and it is less difficult to reconstruct the background than might be supposed. Hanoi radio and the communist press of north Vietnam threw a good deal of light on it; a junk-load of refugees from Nghe An reached the south to tell their tale; and, as it happens, I myself reached Saigon less than three weeks after the events, and went on to Hanoi where I made my own inquiries. The backbone of the great body of discontent was the land reform programme initiated by Ho Chi Minh's government at the end of 1953. The Agrarian Reform Law was passed by the National Assembly of the Vietnam Democratic Republic Law on December 4th, 1953; that is, in the closing stages of the Indo-China war. It called for the confiscation of lands belonging to "treacherous, reactionary, cruel and twisted" landlords; but landlords who had taken part in the resistance against the French were specifically exempt from confiscation. In their case, the law provided for forced sale of land, against special treasury bonds repayable in ten years at $1\frac{1}{2}$ per cent interest.

In the event, the distinction between "patriotic" and "reactionary" landlords was soon blurred. The Lao Dong (communist) Party sent teams of "cadres" to every village north of the dividing line along the 17th parallel. These teams had orders to find landlords. In fact, by that time few Vietnamese landlords were left, for most of them had long since fled to the relative safety of the south; in any case, north Vietnam was mainly an area of smallholders. No matter: the cadres had orders to find landlords and they did. The technique was to find the poorest peasants and promise them land if they would denounce the "cruel landlords" in the midst. The temptation to pay off old scores, or merely to satisfy one's hunger for land, proved irresistible. So "landlords" —mostly peasants marginally richer than the poorest—were always found. As soon as they had been denounced, they were hauled before an *ad hoc* "people's tribunal", where witnesses were produced to accuse them of various crimes and brutalities. To be accused was to be convicted, and there was no right of appeal. Most of the "landlords" convicted by these methods were done to death on the spot, often after prolonged torture; thousands of others were gaoled or sent to labour camps. The holocaust went on for more than two and a half years, then was abruptly called to a halt in August, 1956. On the 17th, President Ho Chi Minh announced, in a "letter to the peasants", that the party and government had agreed on a programme of reforms. People wrongly classified as "landowners" or "rich peasants" were to be reclassified; landowners who had supported the revolution were to be given special consideration; and "errors" in the land reform policy were to be rectified.

During the summer and autumn, the government sent further teams into the villages, this time to inquire into peasant grievances and into the judgments of the people's courts. Several hundred imprisoned "landowners" were freed, and the cadres responsible for abuses were arrested. There was, however, no provision for the resuscitation of the dead.

On November 2nd, Hanoi radio announced that three leading officials, including the Secretary-General of the party, Truong Chinh, had been relieved of their posts. Ho himself became Secretary-General.

It will be seen that the Nghe An disturbances took place *after* the announcement of impending reforms and of the "rectification" programme. In fact, the frustrations of the peasants were even worse than before, if only because it was plain to them that the sufferings of the past three years, the terror, the denunciations, the brutalising atmosphere of the people's courts, had not improved their lot. They were still subjected to high taxation and compulsory sales of produce; officially, the collection of taxes was admitted to be a "hard, complicated and revolutionary task". Worse still, most of the peasants—with certain specified exceptions—were subject to compulsory labour, being obliged to work for thirty days in the year on public construction projects at very low wages. Moreover, they were not allowed to travel, even within their own province, without special permission. It was the combination of these circumstances that proved explosive.

The trouble started on November 9th. The International Commission for Supervision and Control of the Geneva Truce had sent a team to Nghe An province. The inhabitants of Quynh Luu heard that the team was passing through the village, and, disregarding threats from the communist cadres, succeeded in handing over a bagful of petitions. The content of these petitions, as quoted by President Ngo Dinh Diem of south Vietnam in an appeal to the United Nations, throws further light on the frustrations that preceded the outbreak. The peasants requested that members of their families arrested or deported during the land reform be freed; that properties unjustly seized be returned; that the right to be informed of the internal and external situation be recognised; and that the population should be allowed to change its "zone of residence"—that is, move to south Vietnam.

On November 10th, the authorities sent a group of cadres to a neighbouring village, Cam Chuong, where the people had gathered to hear whether the Control Commission was going to take action. The villagers refused to listen. In the afternoon there were a few scuffles between them and local communist troops. After nightfall, an army mission was sent to reason with the demonstrators who were becoming increasingly restive. On the 12th yet another mission was sent to the villages. This one was composed of high-level party members and Nghe An provincial officials; it was taken prisoner, *en bloc*, by the local militia, which had sided with the villagers. On the 13th, clashes took place between the villagers—many of whom had seized arms—and the troops. In the evening, massive reinforcements were sent to the area, and after fierce fighting restored order.

It is difficult to gain a clear idea of the scale of the uprising. According to Hanoi radio, 4,000 villagers took part in it; but eyewitnesses—including, of course, participants—put the number at 13,000 to 15,000. This seems more probable, since it took some 6,000 crack troops to crush the revolt. About half a dozen villages were affected, and Hanoi radio admitted that "numerous" soldiers had been killed or wounded. Five "reactionaries" were tried in Hanoi on April 24th and 25th, 1957, for having engineered the uprising. One of the defendants was acquitted and the others were sentenced, not to death as might have been expected, but to hard labour for terms of four to fifteen years.

I have told the story of the Nghe An affair in some detail, because it is a little-known but instructive and self-contained example of rebellion against communist rule. The Tibetan rebellion has had far more publicity and was far more prolonged; I shall therefore not attempt a detailed account of it. Instead, I shall summarise the main facts and attempt to isolate the reasons for Tibetan resentment under Chinese communist suzerainty.

The Chinese communists invaded Tibet in October, 1950, and in May, 1951, imposed an agreement on the Dalai Lama, Tibet's spiritual and temporal ruler. This agreement gave China the right to station troops in Tibet and to control Tibet's external relations; in return, Peking undertook to respect Tibet's autonomy. In particular, there was to be no change in Tibet's special form of Buddhist religious structure, or in the authority of the

Dalai Lama. In May, 1956, a rebellion broke out among the Golok tribesmen in the north-eastern frontier region; and almost simultaneously a much larger insurrection started among the traditionally martial Khamba tribesmen. The Khambas inhabit an area that straddles the official frontier between Tibet and China proper; on the Chinese side they overlap into Sikang—which, in a world of universal self-determination, would be part of Tibet. The Tibetans, indeed, claim it, but in the last days of the Manchu dynasty, the Chinese general "Butcher" Chao Er-feng, pushed the border far to the south-west towards Lhasa. The Chinese Nationalists maintained a claim to all the Tibetan territory east of Chao's farthest advance, and the Tibetans, lacking map-makers and diplomats, were unable to enforce a counter-claim. In their turn, the Chinese communists took over the Nationalist and Manchu claims; they went further, however, by incorporating Sikang into Szechwan province. This enabled them to claim that the Khamba rebellion was the work of a feudal minority inside China and to deny it any connection with Tibetan nationalism. Soon, however, this claim became untenable, as the rebellion spread into indisputably Tibetan territory. By the end of 1958, the Khambas had drawn near Lhasa.

The final explosion came early in March, 1959. A rumour that the Chinese communists intended to kidnap the Dalai Lama swept through Lhasa on March 10th. That day the *Kashag* or cabinet met, revoked the 1951 agreement and proclaimed Tibet's independence. Anti-Chinese demonstrations flared into riots. The "rebels"—who included nearly all the members of the Kashag—prepared to smuggle the Dalai Lama out of the city, and called on the Khambas to help. Carrying their ancient rifles and on horseback, the Khambas rode into Lhasa—and into Chinese artillery fire. For two full days the resistance controlled Lhasa, and it took the Chinese six more days to regain control. To do so, they had used the methods introduced by the Russians in Hungary two and a half years earlier: indiscriminate bombardments of buildings and massacres of Tibetan civilians and soldiers alike. For two days, according to Tibetan eyewitnesses, the Chinese burned the bodies of their victims on funeral pyres. The Tibetan dead ran into thousands, but the Dalai Lama had escaped to India.

That is the bare framework of facts: a minor rebellion (the Goloks), a major one (the Khambas) culminating in a desperate popular uprising. But why? What had happened between 1951 and 1956 to make the Tibetans revolt?

If one looks at the Tibetan revolt in historical perspective, one sees immediately that it is nothing new for Tibetans to rebel against Chinese; in 1750 they massacred the Chinese in Lhasa, and in 1911 they drove the Manchu army out altogether. There are thus strong elements of Tibetan nationalism and anti-Chinese sentiment which played their part in the insurrection of 1956. Indeed, the Khambas had fought the Chinese for months after the invasion of 1950, before they had had a chance to learn what communism meant. But the point that interests us in this chapter is that, over and above the element of nationalism, there was an anti-communist element which, in the end, was at least as important a cause of the revolt.

According to most accounts, the trouble between the Chinese and the Khambas began in October, 1954, when the Chinese ordered the Khambas to hand in their arms and ammunition. The Khambas ignored the order and consistently resisted its enforcement. A year later, the Chinese attempted to tax the Lamaseries; then came "land reform", on the·familiar pattern, with trials of landlords "denounced" by their serfs.

The Dalai Lama himself, at his important press conference at Mussoorie on June 28th, 1959, gave a specific account of Tibetan grievances against the Chinese communists. If this account is accepted, even in part, these grievances make the word "frustrations" seem inadequate. He accused the Chinese of "an attempted domination of the Tibetan religion and culture, and absorption of the Tibetan race". In substantiation, he charged the communists with having killed 65,000 Tibetans since 1956; of settling five million colonisers in north and north-east Tibet alone (a number far greater than Tibet's previous population) and planning to settle four million more in central Tibet; of destroying more than 1,000 monasteries and imprisoning many Lamas; and of launching a deliberate policy of exterminating Buddhism.

Peking's real intentions became clear from April, 1956, when the Chinese communists set up a "preparatory committee for the autonomous region of Tibet". The committee was charged with introducing "democratic reforms"; this, the Tibetans soon discovered, was Marxist jargon for "communism". Certain Tibetans were, of course, prepared to co-operate in this policy. One of them, Sherab Galtso, the deputy-governor of Chinghai, sounded the first note of alarm in June, 1956, in a speech before the National People's Congress—the Chinese communist parliament—in Peking. Referring in cryptic terms to "an unpleasant incident" in "certain Tibetan areas of Szechwan", he listed the causes of disturbance as: improper measures of land reform, the commercial tax on monasteries, the registration of farmland and stock and the collection of weapons from the Tibetans.

The Chinese had created a Tibetan political party as an instrument for extending their political control over Tibet. It was called the *Mimang Tsongdu* (People's Village Council). By the autumn of 1956, it was clear that the weapon had recoiled against its makers; the Mimang Tsongdu had taken over the political direction of the anti-Chinese resistance. With the Khambas in revolt, passive resistance had spread over the rest of the country. By the beginning of 1957, the Chinese realised that the Tibetan people as a whole was against them; and in May they formally renounced the attempt to impose communism on their unwilling colony. Or rather, they postponed it. This remarkable admission of temporary defeat was made in a lengthy statement by Chang Kuo-ha, the Chinese communist Resident in Lhasa. Reporting on the work of the preparatory committee, Chang complained of "inadequate detailed study of the general objective conditions", of "insufficient consultations" and "failure to develop the initiative and organisation of Tibetan cadres". He announced that "democratic reforms" would not be carried out during the period of China's second five-year (that is, not before 1962), and that whether they would be carried out during the third plan would depend on conditions at that time. Many Chinese cadres who had been stationed in Tibet were to be transferred to "other areas of the fatherland", where they would take part in "socialist construction". This admission of failure was accompanied by a frank admission of its cause: "Certain conditions are necessary to carry out peaceful reforms in the Tibetan area, such as the demand of the masses of the people for reforms, the support of personages of the upper strata, and so on." The jargon, though frank, was euphemistic: in plain English, the Tibetans did not want communism.

We need not look farther than Chang's report or Sherab Galtso's speech for the frustrations of the Tibetans, from peasants to priests and nobles. They valued their privacy, and it was invaded; they were content with their ancient theocratic system, and the communists interfered with it; they saw no reason for land reform, and the communists began to impose it. The postponement of "reforms" in 1957 had come too late; the Tibetans no longer wanted an autonomy which the Chinese had violated: they had set their eyes on full independence.

*　*　*

At the time of writing, too little is known of the political direction of the Tibetan rebellion to draw any useful conclusions from it. We know that some political guidance was provided by the Mimang Tsongdu, and that a rôle of some importance was played by a former Tibetan Prime Minister, Mr. Lu Khang Ha, who went into exile in 1956. But it seems unlikely that the wild Khambas paid much attention either to the Mimang Tsongdu or to Mr. Lu Khang Ka. From all accounts, the Khamba leaders—whether Andrutshang, the "Robin Hood" of the rebellion, or Andu Mamgyal Dorje, commander of the "Army for the Defence of Religion", as the Khambas styled their volunteer force—were independent-minded in more senses than one.

What can be said is that the final explosion of popular resentment in Lhasa was more typical of anti-communist rebellions than the uprising of a tribe like the Khambas, with their reputation for liking a fight. Certainly there is a striking similarity between the revolts of Nghe An and Lhasa on the one hand and, one the other, the rioting of German workers in east Berlin in June, 1953, and the national uprising of the Hungarian people in October, 1956. All four events were acts of despair by ordinary people who could stand no more and were willing to risk their lives in unequal contest against impossible odds. All four were leaderless and spontaneous.

In all four cases, again, similar effects were produced by similar causes—a fact which is explained by the uniformity of communist practices and which further justifies the term "communist imperialism". By 1953, the full rigours of Stalinist communism had been imposed on eastern Europe. In the factories, the system of workers' norms—that is, quotas of work—was in force; every so often, norms were raised, automatically reducing the wages of the majority of workers—a process of "pauperisation" which proved Marxist prophecies to be applicable to communism rather than capitalism. On the land, forced deliveries to the state had been decreed. But Stalin died on March 5th. And at the beginning of June, some relaxation of Stalinist severities seemed to be on the way. On May 28th, the Russians separated the command of the Soviet forces from other occupation functions, and on June 5th the new office of High Commissioner was filled by Mr. Vladimir Semeonov, former political adviser to the Soviet commander in east Germany. Mr. Semeonov was considered a moderate, and six days after his appointment the German communist authorities revoked an order depriving non-productive people of ration-cards and decreed that agricultural holdings confiscated for failure to fulfil production quotas be returned to their former owners. A few days later, however, this apparently liberal policy was rudely halted by a decree raising workers' norms. On June 16th, the workers of east Berlin assembled to protest against the new norms. They carried slogans demanding freedom and the return of prisoners of war in Russia. Ministers appealing for order were shouted down. Next day, the demonstrations gathered strength and turned to violence. Russian flags were torn down and government buildings set on fire. Alarmed, the Soviet military authorities sent tanks to fire on the demonstrators who, by this time, had been joined by a number of east German police. Similar clashes took place in Magdeburg, Leipzig, Gorlitz, Halle and Jena.

It is impossible to summarise the Hungarian uprising as I have summarised the three other anti-communist revolts. Nor is it, in my opinion, so necessary that I should. For a few days, Hungary was wide open to Western journalists, some of whom wrote excellent books on the uprising; thousands of eyewitnesses escaped to tell the story; and, not least, the report of the United Nations special committee on Hungary, published in June, 1957, stands as a permanent record of communist barbarism. What concerns us here is the condition of the Hungarian people under communist rule.

Most students of communist Europe agree that the oppressive features of Stalinist administration were even more marked in Hungary than elsewhere. The power of the AVH—the secret police—was arbitrary and all-pervasive, and its methods were of the utmost brutality. The absence of all personal freedoms was total, and the economic exploitation of workers and peasants as unrelenting as anywhere. Moreover, the internal exploitation of Hungarians was paralleled by external exploitation of Hungary by Russia. As with the other satellites, the Russians imposed unequal trade agreements on Hungary, buying its produce at arbitrary prices well below world levels and exporting Russian products at artificially high prices. One of Hungary's principal forced exports to Russia was uranium ore which, if sold on the world market, could have brought the Hungarians valuable foreign exchange.

The architect of Hungarian Stalinism was Matyas Rakosi, secretary of the Hungarian Workers' (communist) Party. He was almost universally detested in Hungary. Even the Hungarian White Book, *The Counter-Revolutionary Forces in the October Events in Hungary*, issued by the collaborationist Kadar government, described Rakosi's policy as "criminal" and the cause of "deep indignation and a broad popular movement". The Twentieth Congress of the Communist Party of the USSR, held in Moscow in February, 1956, encouraged the satellites to believe that liberalisation was on the way. In Hungary, in particular, it encouraged the hope that Rakosi would soon be removed. In fact, he was not dismissed until July, and even under his successor, Erno Gerö, de-Stalinisation was slow. As the summer wore on, the Hungarians came to feel they had been cheated of their expectations. On October 19th, the news that Mr. Gomulka, the new Polish party boss, had successfully defied the Russian leaders and secured a new deal for his country aroused great enthusiasm in Hungary. On the 23rd, mass demonstrations of students, factory workers, soldiers in uniform and others took place in Budapest. It was on that day that the AVH fired on the demonstrators before the radio building, sparking the national uprising.

The demands of the demonstrators provide the clearest possible picture of the frustrations and grievances of the Hungarians. These demands were expressed in various petitions, some of which are reproduced in the UN report. The most comprehensive of the petitions was the one drawn up in the form of a resolution passed by a plenary meeting of students of the Building Industry Technological University on October 22nd. It contained sixteen points, of which I summarise the most important:

1. The immediate withdrawal of all Soviet troops.

2. The election of new leaders in the Hungarian Workers' Party, by secret ballot.

3. The formation of a new government under Imre Nagy (who did, of course, become Prime Minister for a few days, and was eventually executed).

4. "Matyas Rakosi, who is primarily responsible for all the crimes of the recent past and for the ruin of this country, should be brought home and brought before a People's Court of Judgment."

5. General elections, with universal suffrage, secret ballot and the participation of several parties. The right to strike.

6. Complete equality in Hungarian-Soviet relations.

7. The re-examination of Hungary's planned economy with an eye to Hungarian conditions and the vital interests of the Hungarian people.

8. "We demand frank and sincere information concerning the country's uranium deposits, their exploitation and the Russian concession. We demand that Hungary should have the right to sell the uranium ore freely at world market prices in exchange for hard currency.

9. Revision of norms in industry and minimum living wages.

10. Revision of the agricultural delivery system; equal treatment for peasants farming individually.

11. Release and rehabilitation of innocent political prisoners; repatriation of prisoners of war and civilians deported to the Soviet Union.

12. Freedom of the press and radio.

13. Removal of the statue of Stalin—"the symbol of Stalinist tyranny and political oppression". (Students toppled the massive statue that very evening at 9.30.)

14. Restoration of the old Hungarian coat-of-arms; new national uniforms for the Hungarian Army.

This document, which reads pathetically in retrospect, epitomises the sufferings of the Hungarians—students, peasants and workers, the people in whose name communist parties claim to govern. Equally, it reflects the peculiar character of communist imperialism: its suppression of national feelings and symbols; its imposition of economic hardships to be redeemed at some date in a receding future; its suppression of civil liberties; and its exploitation of a people in the interests of a larger power's foreign and economic policy.

In Hungary, as in Vietnam, Berlin and Tibet, the people revolted in a period of slight relaxation and disappointed hopes. It is scarcely surprising that disappointed hope should prove a stronger stimulus to rebellion than no hope at all. It is important to note, however, that there have been, as far as we know, no anti-communist rebellions of importance during periods of total repression. This suggests that repression, like Maxim Litvinov's peace, is indivisible. To relax is fatal: as an imperialist, Stalin could give points to Khrushchev.

is much nearer a solution than either India or China. But in Algeria's case, the paradox of a problem—pauperisation—aggravated by scientific success is matched by a further paradox: only the French, whom Algerian Moslems blame for their misfortunes, are likely to alleviate them.

Alleviation, however, is a further problem of the present and future which does not concern this book. If one is looking for the causes of the Algerian rebellion, one must include *clochardisation*. But this stage of my inquiry concerns those causes which are due to avoidable official errors; it would be unfair to the French administrators of Algeria to place the pauperisation of part of its Moslem population in that category, just as it would be unfair to saddle Batista with the blame for Cuba's one-crop economy.

It is, of course, far from easy to be fair both to the rebels and to authority. Rebels tend to blame all their misfortunes on authority, and clearly, if they do so with sufficient enthusiasm, they provide themselves with a justification both for rebelling and for the sometimes unpleasant methods they adopt. Similarly, officials tend to blame rebellions entirely on rebel perverseness or on factors beyond control. For instance, I have heard Frenchmen dismiss the entire Algerian rebel leadership as a bunch of criminals. Another familiar French argument is worth closer attention. It is that all, or nearly all, post-war insurrections can be traced back to the war-time resistance movements, particularly in France. I have no doubt that the example of movements in which the saboteur and *franc-tireur* were heroes has been contagious. And I am aware of the further argument that if it was morally right for a French *maquisard* to shoot a German in the back, it must be right for a Greek Cypriot to shoot a British soldier in the back. But there are flaws in these arguments and limits to their validity. In the first place, the war-time resistance movements were not the only model: Eoka derived inspiration from the exploits of the bandit-heroes of the Greek War of Independence rather than from the *maquisards*, and Fidel Castro looked to the Spanish civil war for successful methods. In the second place, the familiar comparison between the French *maquisard* and the Eoka fighter is misleading. Surely the relevant question is: was it right for the French resistance men to shoot collaborators, and for Eoka men to "execute" traitors? It is not within the scope of this book to answer this question; I set it only to show that there are more ways than one of drawing a parallel.

Having said this, I do not deny that there is a connection between certain post-war insurrections and the war-time resistance movements. But the connection is hardly that of cause and effect. The real connection is that the resistance movements provided a model for methods of guerrilla warfare and terrorism; that they provided some of our rebels with experience of guerrilla conditions and with arms for future use; and that, even when they did not have direct experience of the resistance, it helped to condition their conduct of operations. No one may suppose, for instance, that the Malayan and Filipino rebellions of 1948 would have taken the form they did if their leaders had not taken part in resistance movements against the Japanese. On the other hand, the models—as I have said—were varied: thus the Vietminh in Indo-China derived its fighting inspiration and methods almost entirely from Mao Tse-tung's theories of revolutionary war, as he had exposed them, notably, in *Problems of War and Strategy*.

No, just as it would be unfair to blame the authorities for conditions beyond their control, so it would be letting them off far too lightly to attribute insurrections against their rule to the supposed criminality of rebel leaders or to their capacity for imitation. That the causes of our rebellions have included avoidable official errors is, I hope, apparent from the first part of this book. To repeat all those I listed or mentioned in passing in that part would be tedious. This part is concerned with isolating the kind of official errors or shortcomings that tend to cause rebellions.

There are, in fact, two kinds. One covers sins of omission: the disregarding of early warnings, the failure to take political action in time. The other covers sins of commission: actions that aggravate rather than improve a situation, policies that defer the day of reckoning, while merely ensuring that the price to be paid will be higher than it need have been.

In particular terms, examples are not lacking. Western intelligence services were aware of Ho Chi Minh's activities for many years before 1946. In 1931, he was using Hong Kong as a base to stir up trouble in the French concession in Shanghai. The British police gaoled him for two years. The French had long been aware of his activities, and indeed tried unsuccessfully to extradite him from Hong Kong. Nor were the French unaware of the general phenomenon of Vietnamese nationalism, as distinct from the particular problem of Vietnamese communist agitation represented by Ho Chi Minh. A Vietnamese nationalist party started an uprising in 1930 after several unsuccessful attempts to assassinate French officials. Repression was swift: several leaders were arrested and executed. Preventive policies were non-existent rather than slow. In consequence, Vietnamese nationalism was ripe for communist exploitation in the 1940s.

Similarly, the French police were aware of the activities of Belkacem Krim and other Algerian militants long before the insurrection of 1954. And French administrators were aware of Algerian nationalism in its milder political manifestations. The warning had come early. The first Algerian nationalist organisation of consequence, "L'Etoile Nord-Africaine", was founded in France in 1925. It made way two years later for the Parti du Peuple Algérien, which was driven into clandestinity in 1939. In 1947, two years after the war, Algerian nationalists founded the Mouvement pour le Triomphe des Libertés Démocratiques (MTLD). The militant FLN (National Liberation Front) resulted from a split in the MTLD in 1954. This year of insurrection came nineteen years after the formation of the first nationalist group in 1925. In that time, French endeavours had brought great material benefits to Algeria, but few political advantages to Algeria's Moslems. Indeed, neither politically nor economically were Algerian Moslems "integrated" into the French population as a whole; yet they were denied a nationality of their own. These facts are known, or at any rate knowable, though the French Fifth Republic has been showing itself nearly as allergic to the truth as the Fourth. For those interested in the full story, I can do no better than recommend a search for *La Révolution Algérienne*, by the Swiss writer Charles-Henri Favrod—remembering, however, that it is basically a collection of facts and documents that incriminate the French. It is hardly a matter for wonder that Algerian nationalism, denied peaceful political outlets, ripened for exploitation by apostles of violence.

I have no wish to pick on the French. But the convulsions that marked the breakdown of the French colonial empire after the war were inherent in the Constitution of the Fourth Republic. The Constitution enshrined a unitary concept of empire: the French Union, each member of which, in the last analysis, entrusted its destinies to Paris. Moreover, the Constitution ensured weak government and a strong, but irresponsible, parliament. It therefore did not allow for peaceful evolution in overseas territories and guaranteed that no government would be strong enough to carry through evolutionary policies. In contrast the British Commonwealth was based on the concept of peaceful evolution towards self-government and independence. There being no such thing as a constitution of the British Commonwealth, there were no legal obstacles to the evolution of dependent territories. True, the concept of peaceful evolution was open to different interpretations. Winston Churchill had made it clear that he did not feel called upon to preside over the dissolution of the British Empire. But in the important years, from the standpoint of this argument, Clement Attlee was in power. By giving independence within the Commonwealth to India, Pakistan and Ceylon, and outside the Commonwealth to Burma, the Labour Government in 1947 did not avoid bloodshed; but the blood was not shed by British soldiers, and the odium, inconvenience and expense of several colonial wars were avoided.

British policy was less happy in Malaya and disastrously short-sighted in Cyprus. In both places, there had been ample warning. The Malayan Communist Party was founded in the 1920s; by 1937 it was playing a leading part in the wave of strikes that rolled over Malaya. Rapid progress towards self-government was not, at that time, envisaged. This indeed is true of other colonies besides Malaya. The looming threat of war in Europe engaged most of the attention and energies of the colonial powers. The conferment of self-government, and eventually independence, was doubtless a goal, in the eyes of the British, but a distant one, to be reached in the good time of the colonial power.

During the war, the defeats and humiliations inflicted by the Japanese on the colonial powers throughout South-East Asia made many British politicians and administrators realise that the time-table for independence would have to be advanced. In India, a long history of resistance, both violent and passive, gave urgency to this awareness; in Malaya, despite the warning of 1937, the deceptively placid atmosphere made the need seem less pressing. Yet two factors ought to have made the Colonial Office realise that troubles lay ahead. One was military defeat. The Japanese Army never invaded India; in Malaya, it inflicted on the British Army its greatest humiliation of the entire war. Thereafter, things could never be the same.

The second factor was a more specific warning of impending danger. The British had had a unique opportunity to know their future enemy by direct contact. For two years, a British liaison group, known as Force 136, had worked with the communist-led guerrillas fighting against the Japanese. The character of one of the guerrilla leaders, Chin Peng, his fanatical courage and determination, were well-known by the time the Japanese surrendered in 1945. Yet three years later, he was back in the jungle leading his old comrades in an insurrection that proved costly to the British as well as to the Malayan people and government.

It is not, however, certain that the Malayan insurrection could have been prevented by political action (though hindsight suggests that preventive arrests and deportations might have been effective). Nor perhaps should excessive blame for lack of foresight be put on the Colonial Office. The nature of the international communist conspiracy was probably insufficiently known at that time. Even the most rapid and enlightened constitutional advances might not have prevented the insurrection, for it had been planned outside Malaya and timed to coincide with similar outbreaks in Burma, Indonesia and the Philippines. Since these three countries had already won or been granted independence it seems probable that the Malayan Communist Party would have struck when it did even if the British had left Malaya by 1948. The communist aim in all four countries was to set up "people's republics". Where a colonial administration existed, as in Malaya, it was to be driven out; where an independent government was in power, as in the other three countries, it was to be removed.

In Malaya, however, conditions were more favourable for the insurgents than they need have been. Constitutionally, a false start had been made with the abortive plan for a Malayan Union introduced in 1945. Malay resentment had been fanned by the proposal to grant equal citizenship to the Chinese. By the time the Malayan Union project had been withdrawn in favour of the more realistic Federation of Malaya, two important years had been wasted.

In Cyprus, the mistakes were worse and the excuses far feebler. There, warning was really ample. The *enosis* movement began in the middle of the nineteenth century, and was already strong when the British took over Cyprus from Turkey in 1878. Awareness of the emotional links between Greeks and Cypriots is of long standing. Without this awareness, Sir Edward Grey, then Foreign Secretary, would presumably not have offered Cyprus to Greece in 1915. (The price was that Greece should join the allied powers. If Greece had been willing to pay it, the troubles of forty years later would not have occurred.) Turkey recognised the British annexation of Cyprus in 1920. Peace reigned on the island for the next eleven years, but only because the Greek Cypriots, during that time, clung to the hope that their aspirations could be fulfilled by peaceful means. These were the years of "memorials" to the British Government; constitutionally, they were wasted years. Violence erupted, as it was bound to sooner or later, in October, 1931. Before the rioters had been suppressed, Government House had been burnt down.

It would be wrong to think of the violent warning of 1931 as an isolated event, of no relevance to the disturbances of the 1950s. The process of warning was indeed continuous. Thus in 1937, a Committee for Cyprus Autonomy was formed in London. In 1939, the Committee presented the Colonial Office with constitutional demands. (Establishing a precedent that found later imitators, the then Colonial Secretary, Mr. Malcolm MacDonald, replied that the great majority of the Cypriot people was not discontented with the present administration; progress towards representative government would be gradual.) The warnings continued during the war, with the formation of a left-wing party (Akel) calling for popularly elected bodies, and a right-wing party (the National Party) calling for *enosis*. The long list of further warnings and neglected opportunities could be extended through the years, indeed until July 28th, 1954, when the Minister of State for the Colonies, Mr. Henry Hopkinson, in a memorable debate in the House of Commons, made it clear that Cyprus belonged, in his government's view, to the category of territories which, "owing to their particular circumstances, can *never* expect to be fully independent". The italics are mine. But Mr. Hopkinson spoke at the twelfth hour; the small word "never" made terrorism inevitable.

If the undue delaying of concessions engenders political frustration and creates the conditions of rebellion, the refusal to carry concessions to their logical conclusion invites insurrection. Those, it seems to me, are among the lessons of the unhappy story of Cyprus. No one could have been franker than Mr. Hopkinson in July, 1954. Indeed, reasons of domestic politics may be found for his frankness; his "never" was a reassurance to the right-wing Conservative MPs who had been shocked by the British withdrawal from the Suez Canal base, and a warning to the Opposition that it was wasting time and breath. In thinking of domestic politics first and of international implications second if at all, Mr. Hopkinson was doing no more than conform to a general rule of political behaviour. But he may since have had cause to regret his words. Denied hope, a people, or a group claiming to represent it, will be driven to desperate courses.

I have written of the undue delaying of concessions. This does not imply a philosophy of appeasement. A concession made to gain tranquillity will almost certainly not gain it for long. If concessions are to bring lasting returns, they must not be made in isolation; they must be seen to be part of a programme and to lead to a definite and desirable goal. I am aware that I have begged the question: "Desirable to whom?" This is the crux. The potential rebel desires the earth: independence. The colonial power, if enlightened, will not deny this desire, though seeking to achieve it in conditions that will preserve at least some of its commercial or cultural privileges. Britain did reasonably well in India. So did the United States in the Philippines.

Other colonial powers have been less enlightened. By insisting on retaining the substance of power, as France did in Indo-China and the Netherlands did in the Dutch East Indies, they ensure the total loss of their overseas territories. True, the British also lost their major colonial possessions in Asia, but they paid and suffered less in the process—and kept more after conceding independence.

The example of Vietnam is particularly striking. I shall leave until another chapter a discussion of whether the Indo-China war could have been prevented and, if so, whether the price would have been worth paying. But another hypothetical question is of equal interest: could the French have won the war? In the sense of keeping Vietnam, Laos and Cambodia for France, I do not believe victory was possible. In the sense of defeating the Vietminh insurgents, I am persuaded that they could have won. In that event, Vietnam would not have been divided, as it was under the Geneva agreements of 1954 which ended the war; and France would have retained permanent links of friendship with a united and independent Vietnam, and perhaps a favoured commercial position in that country.

This, I suggest, was a goal that the French, as well as the Vietnamese, would have found desirable. It was never achieved, in the first place because the French wrongly thought that the only alternatives before them in Vietnam were victory for the

French or victory for the Vietnamese communists; whereas another alternative existed: victory for the Vietnamese nationalists. In reality, this was a war that France, as an old-fashioned colonial power, could not hope to win; but France could have ensured the victory of Vietnamese nationalism over the communist perversion of nationalism known as the Vietminh. This indeed was, or ought to have been, the idea behind "the Bao Dai experiment".

It was not, *per se*, a bad idea. I shall not concern myself, at this stage, with the character of Bao Dai. What does concern me is the idea itself and how the French went about executing it. Superficially, the idea was to find an alternative to Ho Chi Minh and the Vietnamese communists, a Vietnamese nationalist leader with sufficient prestige to rally around him those nationalists whose faith in Ho Chi Minh had been shattered. This, it was thought, would enable the French to settle the future of Vietnam without reference to the Vietminh. The circumstances should be remembered. The Vietminh had proclaimed the independence of Vietnam on September 2nd, 1945. Protracted negotiations to define the relationship between the new Democratic Republic of Vietnam and the French Union had broken down in the summer of 1946. The keywords in these and later Franco-Vietnamese negotiations were always "independence" and "unity". Independence was open to differing interpretations; unity meant the union under one central government of the three provinces of Vietnam: Tonking, Annam and Cochin-China. The French had refused to grant Ho either a degree of independence which his followers would have accepted, or the union of the three provinces, preferring to encourage, for their own ends, Cochin-Chinese autonomy. A series of bloody incidents during the autumn culminated in a general uprising against the French on the night of December 19th. The Indo-China war had begun.

Bao Dai had abdicated as emperor of Annam a week before the Republic was proclaimed. He then joined Ho as "supreme political adviser". But his attempt to work with the Vietminh was short-lived. By the time the insurrection began, he had been a refugee in Hong Kong for some months. The French first toyed with the idea of appealing to him in the spring of 1947. But at that stage they had not begun to think of him as an alternative to Ho Chi Minh; their first idea was to weaken Ho's position by negotiating with Bao Dai as well as with him. The growth, during 1947, of a nationalist current of opinion favouring the return of Bao Dai persuaded the French that they stood to gain by approaching him. But the decision to do so was made by the French cabinet only on December 23rd, 1947—one year after the outbreak of war.

The spirit in which this decision was made is important. The French considered Bao Dai a man of weak character who would yield on the issues which Ho had contested. They thought of him as an instrument for the re-establishment of French paramountcy throughout Vietnam. On the other hand, the Vietnamese nationalists who clamoured for Bao Dai's return thought of him as a leader who would rally to himself the support of the intellectuals and peasants who had committed themselves to the Vietminh. They hoped he would extract more from the French than Ho and his team of negotiators. There was thus a fundamental contradiction between the motives of the French and those of the nationalists for desiring the ex-emperor's return. In these circumstances, the "Bao Dai experiment" was doomed to failure from the start: it was vain to hope that Bao Dai could rally popular support if he was to be denied the means of satisfying popular aspirations.

The French, who ought to have known better, were shocked to find that Bao Dai was no less insistent than Ho on securing independence and unity. Since the French were still not disposed to yield, Bao Dai's attitude made for protracted negotiations. In fact, it was not until March, 1949, that Bao Dai agreed to return to Vietnam as Chief of State. He had secured "unity"—subject to a "free consultation of the populations concerned"—but hardly independence. The agreements of March 8th, to which he was party, did indeed recognise Vietnam's independence, but hedged it around with so many restrictive clauses that the term was meaningless. Even so, more than twenty-six months had elapsed since the outbreak of war. "Too little" complemented "too late".

It was vain, under these conditions, to suppose that Bao Dai would play the part expected of him, or to expect the Vietnamese nationalist army to fight with a spirit comparable to that of the Vietminh insurgents. It was not that the soldiers who enlisted under Bao Dai's banner were any less brave or resourceful by nature than the Vietminh guerrillas, for they were all Vietnamese; it was that they were an army without a cause. The French disaster of Dien Bien Phu was inherent in the 1949 agreements; even without the massive short-range military help of communist China, the Vietminh would have had its victory.

That was the reality. Yet hypothetically, the French expeditionary corps could have won its war, not of course for France, but for Vietnam. A promise of real independence undiminished by reservations in favour of France, and implemented in good faith within the limits imposed by the state of emergency, would have given Bao Dai the power he needed and his army a cause to fight and die for. But the French acted in bad faith. They never intended to give the substance of power to Bao Dai, nor real independence to his country. They sought to keep all, and in the end they lost all.

The British in Malaya demonstrated what the French might have done in Vietnam. They also demonstrated that under the conditions of Malaya or Vietnam, the protecting power could win a military victory but not, in absolute terms, a political one. True, a political victory was also won in Malaya. Only it was a victory for the Malayan people against communism; Britain's share in the victory was moral rather than material: the Federation of Malaya did not remain a British colony, but it did decide to join the Commonwealth. This, I suggest, was the most the French could have hoped for in Vietnam: victory in military and moral terms and an independent Vietnam within a modified French Union.

I believe this to be essentially true, even though the comparison between Vietnam and Malaya ought not to be laboured. A parallel exists, but a limited one. Both countries are in South-East Asia. Both suffered communist-led insurrections in the name of anti-colonialism. But there the parallel ends. In scale the two situations were not comparable: in Vietnam the insurrection turned into a major war, in which two large armies were locked in combat; in Malaya, the insurrection never got beyond the guerrilla phase, and on the British side it was a large-scale police action with troops, rather than a military campaign. But there is enough truth in the parallel to make the comparison of methods valuable. In Vietnam, the French fought an old-fashioned military campaign, brilliant under the late Marshal de Lattre de Tassigny, defensive and defeatist under General Salan, foolhardy under General Navarre. In terms of results, however, the conduct of the war was almost irrelevant, for political action had created the conditions of defeat, not victory.

In comparison, the British displayed in Malaya a combination of military and political wisdom which has no place in a chapter devoted to official shortcomings. There was, however, little of political wisdom in Cyprus or Kenya. In Cyprus, from 1954 to 1957, there was almost certainly, on the British side, a positive will *not* to reach a settlement. Pure repression, unaccompanied by political action, was shown, once again, to be inadequate. In Kenya, against a tribal and primitive insurrection, police measures proved apparently successful. But success has clearly been shown to have been temporary. The political causes of the Mau Mau rebellion, especially the inequitable distribution of land, were not removed. And progress towards representative government was despairingly slow. In consequence, the Mau Mau was reviving, under another name, by 1958.

The early 'fifties are indeed scarcely a credit to Britain in its dealings with nationalism in east and central Africa. In 1953, while the Mau Mau insurrection was in full swing, the Conservative Government of the day created another potential insurrectionary situation by federating the two Rhodesias and Nyasaland without consulting the African majority of the population. Yet to the extent that the Africans had had a chance to express their views they had shown themselves hostile to the whole idea. And even if no African had ever spoken his mind on the subject, it ought to have been evident that Africans would oppose a scheme which seemed bound to condemn them eventually to share the fate of their brethren under the *apartheid* policy of the Union of South Africa. True, the new federal constitution enshrined the concept of "partnership" (between white and black); but the Africans had few grounds for trusting their European rulers, despite the willingness of the Southern Rhodesian Prime Minister, Sir Godfrey Huggins (now Lord Malvern) to leave native affairs in the north largely in the hands of the British Government, and to give his blessing to "partnership".

Despite the dangers of federation—which burst into violence in the widespread riots of March, 1959—nobody could accuse the British Government of lightly endorsing the project. But from the first, British legislators were more concerned to prevent the Balkanisation of central Africa than to rule with the consent of the governed. This was perfectly understandable in the 'twenties, when the problem first arose and when the possibility that the African colonies might one day become independent seemed too remote for legislative action. But thirty years later, there was less justification for observing the same order of priorities.

Of those thirty years, more than twenty were dissipated in official procrastination or hesitation. The Hilton-Young commission in 1929 examined the possibility of linking Northern Rhodesia and Nyasaland with British East Africa, but failed to produce an agreed report. The Bledisloe Commission in 1938 inquired into ways of bringing about a closer association between the Rhodesias and Nyasaland. It reported in favour of amalgamation of the three territories as an ideal solution, but ruled it out at that time because of African suspicion of Southern Rhodesian native policy. This was the early warning which governments so often get but ignore.

The second world war intervened, and the reports were taken out of their pigeon-holes in the changed world of the 'forties. One of the factors of change was the rapid evolution of the dependent territories of Africa towards the independence which the more advanced peoples of Asia had achieved or were achieving. It was admittedly a factor difficult to measure or assess. If events are any guide, it was brushed aside in the deliberations that led to federation in 1953. When the relatively enlightened South African Government of Field-Marshal Smuts fell in 1948, interested British politicians made much of the argument that Southern Rhodesia was now in danger of being drawn into the Union, of whose native policies—under the Nationalists—there was general disapproval in Britain. This herring was probably redder than most, since it was difficult to believe either that the Rhodesian politicians would wish to be swamped by their southern neighbours or that the Afrikaner Nationalists would welcome a large influx of British settlers. The argument was used, however, to justify the amalgamation or federation of Southern Rhodesia with neighbouring territories; and indeed it sounded more respectable than the scarcely mentioned truth: the determination to prevent the emergence of Nyasaland as a black African state. On economic grounds, the union of the two Rhodesias made sense: the balanced economy of Southern Rhodesia and the copper-rich but unbalanced economy of Northern Rhodesia would naturally complement each other. The poor relation, Nyasaland, would also benefit from the association, which would provide an outlet for emigrant Nyasa labour. Moreover, from the point of view of the Colonial Office, Nyasaland was an unwelcome charge on the British taxpayer; while it was not intended, at first, to abandon the responsibility for administering Nyasaland to the proposed federal government, federation was seen as a logical way of relieving the financial burden. The feelings of the Nyasas were no doubt taken into account, but were brushed aside, on the assumption that the evident economic benefits of federation would ultimately lead to political acquiescence or even support. This was, of course, a strong argument, for it was difficult to see a promising future for an independent Nyasaland without federal links. But it was clearly an error of the first magnitude to proceed with federation without first converting the Nyasas to the arguments in its favour. After all, there were three million Africans in Nyasaland and only 8,000 Europeans. There was worse to come, however.

The negotiations that led to federation were initiated by the Labour Government of Mr. Attlee (as he then was), and the federal constitution was outlined in a White Paper produced by officials of the local governments and of Whitehall in 1950–51. The fact that the Labour Party, after its defeat in the 1951 general elections, voted against the Bill, should not therefore be claimed too seriously as a sign of superior socialist wisdom. Federation, in its initial form, was a British error rather than a party one.

Federation began smoothly and indeed comfortingly for hostile Africans. With the opening of Dr. Walter Adams's University College in Salisbury, racial partnership seemed to take a giant step forward. The Africans of Nyasaland received back half a million acres of alienated land. The emergence of Mr. Garfield Todd as Prime Minister of Southern Rhodesia seemed to open up a new vista of liberalism. On the economic side, booming copper prices and the Kariba dam project seemed to promise a rising standard for all under federation.

The feeling of optimism was short-lived; a series of events in 1956 and 1957 dispersed it. But although many more observers could now see the dangers ahead, events were allowed to move forward under their own momentum. The key occurrences were these: the accession of Sir Roy Welensky to the federal Prime Ministership in the autumn of 1956, the introduction of the Federal Franchise Bill and of a Bill to amend the Constitution of the Federal Legislature, both in the British Parliament in the autumn of 1957, the overthrow of Mr. Todd in the Southern Rhodesian elections of the spring of 1958, and the return of Dr. Hastings Banda to Nyasaland the following summer. The Africans found it hard to see in the massive personality of Sir Roy Welensky anything but a living symbol of settler domination. The two Bills they considered frankly discriminatory, and as such the African Affairs Board, which had been set up to safeguard African interests, denounced them. This was the first time the Board had had occasion to fulfil its function. But it was overruled by the British Government, which used its majority to pass the two Bills through Parliament. When Sir Roy started to call for dominion status for the Central African Federation by 1960, he was not only going beyond the existing agreement between the Federal and British Governments, but simply asking for trouble. The agreement, which had been reached in 1957, merely called for a conference in 1960, with the limited objects of confirming the goal of a federal state with full Commonwealth status and laying down a time-table. Even these relatively modest aims were too much for the Africans, to whom they seemed to make independence inevitable, however gradual the time-table. And independence, whether within or outside the Commonwealth, meant the removal of Colonial Office protection and permanent domination by the Rhodesian settlers. Sir Roy's advocacy of dominion status by 1960 was bound to aggravate African fears and suspicions. Crying "To hell with federation", Dr. Banda returned from his long exile.

As we have seen in Part I, Dr. Banda had been organising opposition to federation from abroad. When he returned he called for the secession of Nyasaland from the Federation and for internal self-government. And he threatened passive resistance if these demands were not met. When he and several hundreds of his followers were arrested in March 1959, it was alleged, in the Federation and in the British Parliament, that he had been plotting a massacre of the Europeans. The Governor of Nyasaland, Sir Robert Armitage, attempted to substantiate this allegation in a letter to Mr. Lennox-Boyd, the British Colonial Secretary, on March 18th, and published as a White Paper five days later. Both the allegation and the attempt to substantiate met with a good deal of scepticism in Britain, though the charge was not, *a priori*, improbable in the circumstances I have outlined. I have no wish, however, either to prove or to disprove the assertion that violence was planned. The only points I have to make are these: if Sir Robert Armitage really believed that Dr. Banda and his followers were about to slit the throats of the settlers, then the Protectorate authorities were, of course, right to order the arrests, and the British Government was right to support them; on the other hand, the authorities really cannot shift all the blame for the alleged situation on to the shoulders of Dr. Banda, however inflammatory his speeches may have been: the political dangers of federation ought to have been clear in 1953, and even clearer in 1957. If Dr. Banda had not led the Nyasas to the verge of rebellion, somebody else would have. Official shortcomings were never more in evidence.[1]

It must be owned, however, that the British have been more successful than the French, and even more so than the Dutch, in adapting themselves to the changing trends of post-war history. The Dutch, like the French, were determined to regain their colonial empire after the war (the British were equally determined to reinstate themselves in Malaya, but had already adjusted themselves to the necessity for constitutional evolution). The Indonesian nationalists had proclaimed a Republic of Indonesia, by agreement with the Japanese, on August 17th, 1945, two days after the Japanese surrender. Although the Dutch gave *de facto* recognition to the Republic, they soon attempted to undermine and isolate it. Finally, unburdened by yearnings to come to terms with Indonesian nationalism, they launched two punitive expeditions against the new state. In strictly military terms, the two Dutch "police actions", as they are known, were successful. In political terms, they were disastrous. Indeed, they appear to have been launched without regard for the possible political consequences; certainly the Dutch did not regard them as a prelude to constructive political progress in agreement with the nationalists.

In simpler terms, the police actions were an attempt to by-pass Indonesian nationalism. Although the Dutch captured the principal Indonesian leaders during the second action, they had not destroyed the republican army, which carried on the fight from the hills and jungles. Nor had they reckoned with the pressure of world opinion. The force of mere opinion might, indeed, have been ignored. But the pressure of the United States, both within and outside the United Nations, could not. In the end, the Dutch

[1] The Devlin Report, published some months after these lines were written, supports these views.

released the captured leaders and invited them to a round-table conference at The Hague in September, 1949. The main outcome of this conference was Dutch recognition of Indonesian sovereignty over the territories of the former Netherlands East Indies (though not over Dutch New Guinea). Repression had failed.

It was an irony to find the Indonesian republican leaders cast in Dutchmen's rôles less than a decade later. In the intervening years, their authority had been challenged by rebels of many hues. These challenges were indeed so numerous that at no time could the Republic claim to control every square mile of its scattered territories. But the challenge of February, 1958, was different, both in scale and in character, from previous challenges. As we have seen in Part I, it was made not by cranks or fanatics but by sensible men, including some of Indonesia's few able technicians and administrators. These men were not communists, nor were they agents of the Dutch. They did not seek to truncate the territory of the Republic. Their challenge was to the authority of the Republic everywhere; their claim was to the entire territory of the Republic, on the ground that the central government had failed the people and forfeited its right to rule in their name.

One reason why this rebellion of colonels and economists is important is that it demonstrated the fallacy of a proposition dear to fighters for independence in dependent territories: that most of the people's ills are caused by colonial oppression and that, in consequence, the removal of the oppressors will usher in the millennium. I am not sure that the more sophisticated leaders of Asian independence movements have ever privately believed this proposition to be true; but they have often, in varied ways, publicly proclaimed it.

The 1958 rebellion also showed that a post-colonial government, if challenged by a group of rebels within the nation, will tend to behave in much the same way as a colonial government. It will fail to make concessions in time or to reform itself; when the challenge becomes acute, it will resort to repression. Its political initiatives will be inadequate and belated. In consequence, it will fail to match military successes with political gains. Thus the rebellion is of vital and enduring interest. Its lessons ought to be studied in every newly independent country in Africa and Asia, and in every dependent territory about to assume the distressing burdens and illusory joys of sovereignty.

There is no need to go over the ground already covered in Part I, but certain aspects of the rebellion are particularly relevant to Part II. We have seen that the rebellion really began long before the proclamation of a revolutionary government in February, 1958, with the creation of autonomous military councils and the organisation of illegal trade from the outlying islands. The central government's reactions to this curious challenge to its authority were either inept or irrelevant. The military command areas in Sumatra were re-divided—a measure which, as even General Nasution, the army Chief of Staff, remarked, "solved the military problem in Sumatra, but not the political one". More far-reaching, but scarcely more relevant, was President Sukarno's "concept" of a guided democracy. The President proposed to form a national government of all the political parties, and to create a National Council representing all groups and strata in the community. The National Council would be empowered to offer advice to the cabinet, whether or not the cabinet had asked for it. Many Indonesian politicians were quick to see that the main effect of the President's "concept" would be to give the highly organised Communist Party (PKI) a share in the machinery of government, from which it had until then been excluded by tacit agreement among the other parties.

President Sukarno had announced his "concept" in February, 1957, two months after the first rebel military council had been set up in Sumatra. It was not until the following September that he called a National Conference in Jakarta to discuss the problem of regionalism. Some of the rebel colonels attended, but not all. The conference produced pious statements, including a declaration committing the President and the former Vice-President, Dr. Hatta, to "resume their co-operation in the interests of the state". But Dr. Hatta, who had resigned nine months earlier, had his own views on what constituted "co-operation". The old partnership was never resumed. Even if it had been, however, it would not have made much difference. On their return to Sumatra, the colonels called a conference of their own at Padang and decided to continue the struggle against the central administration.

Things had gone far, but probably still not *too* far. A leader, less permeated by a sense of his personal importance, more willing to tackle specific problems with specific remedies, might have saved the situation; President Sukarno chose to make it worse. Like other inadequate leaders, afraid or incapable of taking the right action, he resorted to diversion. A United Nations debate on Dutch New Guinea had produced a vote unfavourable to Indonesia. A month later, in December, 1957, President Sukarno ordered the seizure of all Dutch estates and enterprises in Indonesia and the expulsion of all Dutch citizens. Not all Indonesians approved of this drastic course. One of those who protested was the future Prime Minister of the rebel government, Dr. Sjafruddin, who described it as "high-handed" and "a flagrant violation of our constitution". Thus the anti-Dutch action, far from rallying all Indonesians around Dr. Sukarno, as he may have hoped, merely deepened the division. Within a few weeks of it, Dr. Sjafruddin had proclaimed his "Revolutionary Government of the Republic of Indonesia".

The sequence of events in Indonesia, from 1956 to 1958, was thus instructively similar to those that preceded the anti-colonial insurrections I have already mentioned. Certainly, the authentic theme of "too little, too late" recurs with familiar insistence. But what, in fact, would have been "enough"? Probably nothing short of President Sukarno's resignation, which pride and attachment to power ruled out.

The totalitarian governments that run into trouble of this kind face a similar dilemma: whether to cling to power and misguided principles while the situation gets worse, knowing that eventually they may have to make room for others, or else to get out anyway. Fulgencio Batista had no answer to Fidel Castro's challenge beyond repression, which ended in flight. Similarly, no com-

PART III
PRELUDE TO VIOLENCE

I
The Pattern of Insurrection

WE have shared the frustrations of the rebels and peered over the shoulders of men who failed to mitigate them in time or at all. The hour of insurrection is at hand: frustration is about to explode into violence. What form is that violence likely to assume? How do the rebels prepare for action?

The pattern of insurrection is, in fact, strangely consistent. Whatever the country or the circumstances, insurrection *tends* to follow a sequence of three phases: terrorism, guerrilla warfare and full-scale war. That is the tendency, but the pattern is not always completed: not all rebellions reach the second phase, and fewer still the third. But in most cases, it is safe to assume that the rebels intended to round off the sequence, even if they have been stopped, or paused of their own accord, at the first or second stage. Terrorism is the natural weapon of men with small resources, fighting against superior strength. It dramatises their cause and—at least in the early days—enforces the loyalty of waverers. Cubans and foreigners who might have been unaware of Fidel Castro's uprising in its earliest stage could not ignore exploding bombs in the cinemas and gambling-dens of Havana. The communist insurgents of Vietnam, Malaya or the Philippines shared this with Mau Mau, Eoka or the FLN—that terror was their first arm.

In some instances, it remains the only arm. To many readers of newspapers, there is indeed an instant association between rebellion and terrorism. An unfortunate association, in some respects, for the two words have different moral connotations: rebellion may or may not be "good", but terrorism cannot be anything but "bad". In fact, as Part IV tries to show, terrorism is an inefficient, and often self-defeating, instrument of rebellion. Not all terrorists may realise this at the outset, and many of the men who perform the deeds—as distinct from those who order them—may actually enjoy the performance. There will always be candidates for licensed sadism, whether permission comes from above or from the underground. But the pattern of the rebellions that have been allowed to run their course suggests that when the opportunity comes, the rebels will drop terrorism in favour of guerrilla activities, or at least relegate it to second place.

Guerrilla warfare, however, necessitates a minimum of arms, suitable terrain and well-knit organisation. Outright war, the third and ultimate stage of rebellion, needs even more: a steady and incessant flow of heavy as well as light arms, the whole-hearted support of the majority of the population, perhaps help from abroad. Lacking these advantages and even the more modest requisites of guerrilla war, insurgents will be limited, or driven back, to terrorism, even though their self-interest dictates broader offensive tactics. Conversely, a major aim of established authority is to deny the rebels the advantages they seek. The three phases of rebellion are thus a barometer of relative strengths. On the one hand, this barometer measures the success of the rebels in adding to their fighting capacity. On the other hand, it measures the success of the authorities in denying them the opportunity for stronger action.

This general pattern may be the rule, but it is not an invariable one. The anti-Sukarno rebellion in Indonesia neatly reversed it in the first year. I have found it hard to avoid the word "respectable" when describing its leaders, the banker Sjafruddin, the academic economist Sumitro, among them. These were men to whom the notion of terrorism must have been repugnant, no less than it would have been to Mr. Cobbold of the Bank of England and Mr. Gaitskell of the Labour Party if by chance they had taken refuge in Edinburgh and challenged the seat of power in Westminster. The mental association of Benbella and guns or bombs is not intellectually shocking; substitute Sjafruddin for the Algerian rebel and the association becomes incongruous. Perhaps this helps to explain why the anti-Sukarno rebellion failed to conform to any of the usual rules. It began where rebellions ought to end, and then only if they are successful: with the proclamation of a government. This was rapidly followed by phase three, when the central government launched its offensive against the rebels in Sumatra and Celebes in April and May, 1958. The defeat of the rebels in phase three drove them into phase two—guerrilla actions from the mountains and jungles against the central government's forces in the towns. Shortly afterwards came phase one in a fairly mild form: the firing of plantations or rubber storehouses, often after the owners had been warned.

It is clear that the phases of rebellion, though they normally run in the sequence I have described, are not mutually exclusive: they may, and often do, co-exist and overlap. In Malaya, from 1948, and in Palestine from 1944, terrorism expanded into a kind of guerrilla war and co-existed with it (though after a while the Malayan communists, too weak for real war, were driven back to terrorism). In the Egyptian Canal Zone, in Cyprus and in Kenya the rebels never graduated to phase two, though not for the same reasons. Winston Churchill had described the Canal Zone incidents of 1951 as "a kind of guerrilla war", but that was stretching the language: the incidents amounted to no more than terrorism, and indeed nothing more was needed for the British quit the base. Neither in Cyprus nor in Kenya were the rebels ever strong enough to leave phase one for phase two. In Vietnam, Algeria and Cuba, on the other hand, rebellion ran its full course, from terrorism, through guerrilla war, to outright war. It is worth noting that in the Algerian rebellion, terrorism died down during 1957, when the Army of National Liberation was at its strongest and set battles were being fought; but it revived, particularly in metropolitan France, after the French military successes of 1958.

2

Cairo and the FLN

WHEN it comes to planning for action, similarities between various rebellions are fortuitous. It is no surprise that all intending insurgents collect arms and discipline their followers. But beyond that there is no uniformity: the individuality of circumstances ensures variety.

Few of the rebellions we are dissecting were entirely home-grown. In most of them, external influences played a part, often a major one. In all the communist insurrections, such influences are inherent. In the Algerian uprising, the Arab world as a whole has always played a major part: money and material aid from Egypt and the Arab Middle East, territory and moral support from the sister-nations of the Maghreb. Eoka would never have started without Greek help (for that matter, there could hardly be an *enosis* movement without Greece).

The external influences ought not, however, to be exaggerated. Nobody who has read the earlier chapters of this book will doubt that, in my opinion, the real causes of rebellions are always domestic; or conversely, that the external causes that matter concern the relations between local populations and distant colonial authorities. It would be foolish or self-deceptive to blame the Cyprus disorders entirely on the Greeks or the Algerian rebellion on the Egyptians. Yet that argument was the core of the official French line on Algeria and, to a lesser degree, of the British line on Cyprus. Even the communist-led.insurrections in South-east Asia were not exclusively caused by communist machinations: the soil must be fertile if the seed is to take.

With these reservations in mind, it is still true that at a given moment external help and advice can be of great importance to the rebels. It certainly played a considerable rôle in the Algerian rebellion, though not the dominant part ascribed to it by Jacques Soustelle and other French writers, or better still by the official

French dossier on Algeria, prepared in Algiers for the benefit of the French delegation to the United Nations. The 1956 supplement to this curious document dismisses the causes of the rebellion in this sentence: "The Algerian rebellion is incontestably a movement inspired and actively supported by foreign countries which interfere impudently in the internal affairs of France."

It is scarcely in doubt, however, that in the late 'forties a number of young Algerians (and Moroccans and Tunisians) were trained at the military school in Baghdad. Nor that in 1951, most of them took up residence in Cairo. That old North African rebel of the 'twenties, Abd el-Krim, who had escaped to Cairo from French captivity, had, it seems, originated this military initiative. By 1951, a nucleus of trained North African rebels existed in Cairo. These young officers received little or no help from the last governments of the dying Farouk régime. But their chance came two years later, when General Nagib's young officers overthrew the monarchy. The Egyptian Army thereupon provided further advanced training to some sixty North African officers.

A late arrival in the forcing ground of Cairo was the future leader of the rebellion, Mohammed Benbella. He arrived in 1952 shortly before the Egyptian revolution, after escaping from prison in Algeria. His term in gaol had marked the failure of an earlier attempt at armed rebellion. In 1949 Benbella had been appointed chief of the OS (Special Organisation), a terrorist organisation founded two years earlier by Messali Hadj's Algerian People's Party. Benbella's mission was to accumulate arms, explosives and money. Some of the money he secured by leading a daring raid on the central post office at Oran, which brought the OS three million francs. But in 1950 the French police struck. Benbella and his closest followers were arrested, the war material was seized and the OS dismantled.

During this time, the ageing Messali had been losing ground to the extremists in the People's Party, including one of the future ministers in the Algerian rebels' "provisional government", Dr. Lamine Debaghine. In broad terms, the extremists stood for military action and Messali's followers for political action. In 1954 the latent split burst into the open. The extremists of the People's Party broke away to form the CRUA (Revolutionary Committee for Unity and Action). Of the moderates, some rallied around Messali and others favoured collective leadership. The CRUA became the hard core of the FLN or National Liberation Front. Thereupon Messali created the rival MNA or National Algerian Movement.

By the time the Revolutionary Committee was formed, Benbella had become an important personage in Cairo. Two Egyptian officers had been assigned to help him create an insurrectionary general staff. According to Soustelle, in *Aimée et Souffrante Algérie*, this general staff was to have operative control over French North Africa as a whole, presumably in furtherance of Colonel Nasser's pan-Arab ambitions. The concern of Benbella and his confederates of the Special Organisation had always been, however, with the independence of *Algeria*, regardless of what the future might hold for the other countries of the Maghreb. In any event, the French Government under M. Mendès-France moved rapidly towards the granting of independence to Tunisia, after bringing peace to Indo-China in July, 1954. Whatever the truth of suggestions that an insurrection in North Africa as a whole was planned in Cairo, there was clearly going to be little necessity for an armed rebellion outside Algeria itself. Nor indeed was there one elsewhere, although terrorist outbreaks forced the pace of independence in Morocco.

Soustelle's theory of an Egyptian plot predominantly responsible for the Algerian rebellion is, in other respects also, difficult to sustain. Serge Bromberger, whose right-wing approach would prejudice him in its favour, records in *Les Rebelles Algériens* that the special North African commandos trained in Baghdad and Cairo played no part in the rebellion. Soustelle mentions, as though to prove his point, that one of them was captured carrying arms in Kabylia shortly after Soustelle's own arrival in Algeria as Governor-General. But according to Bromberger, the captured man was the only one.

I have no interest in denying the part that Egypt did play in the rebellion. Indeed, the capture of the ship *Athos* by the French off the coast of Oranie on October 16th, 1956, dramatised the issue. And the *Athos* was certainly not the only ship sent from Egypt to the Maghreb with a cargo of arms for the Algerian rebels. For that matter, the FLN received massive gifts of money from other Arab countries, particularly Iraq and Saudi Arabia. But it would be misleading to think of the Algerian rebellion as primarily inspired by Egypt; whatever aid and comfort may have come from the Egyptians, this was certainly a genuinely Algerian movement.

The capture of Benbella and other Algerian leaders, in flight from Rabat to Tunis, on October 22nd, 1956, was a political blunder on the part of the Frenchmen who ordered the diversion of their aircraft to Algeria, and of the government that approved it. But it had one merit, which journalists or historians could appreciate as well as the French Deuxième Bureau: the documents seized on the prisoners and the interrogations that followed threw light on the naturally obscure events that preceded the outbreak of November 1st, 1954.

Four men, it seems, planned the rebellion: Benbella and Boudiaf (both captured on the flight to Tunis), Belkacem Krim and Ben Boulaid. And they did their planning at least as much in Switzerland as in Egypt. Between March and September, 1954, two or more of these four men met in secret several times in Switzerland. It was there that the Revolutionary Committee (CRUA) was conceived. It was there, at the first meeting in March, that the conspirators decided to order the former members of the OS to return to Algeria from France, where many of them had gone after being amnestied. But it was in Algiers itself that Boudiaf, back from Switzerland, summoned the twenty-two members of the Revolutionary Committee to tell them that violent action had been decided upon, and that the Algerians could count on Egyptian help. This, the day of organisation, was July 10th. The twenty-two brought out a map of Algeria and divided it into six wilayas, or combat zones. A commander was appointed for each, except the sixth zone, comprising the wild southern territories where the CRUA had no organisation. It was again in Algeria that a series of decisive meetings was held in October, 1954. At the first of these, Boudiaf called together the zonal commanders to plan the details of the organisation of the new rebel army which, on that day, was baptised the Army of National Liberation. D-day was agreed on; it was to be November 1st at zero hour.

From August onward, rebel groups had been organised on the basis of three cells of three men each, plus their chief, making ten in all. Rifle practice and training in the throwing of hand grenades (using round stones) took place at night. In October, the clandestine cells were welded into the rudiments of an army. On October 20th, all the groups were summoned to the village of Ouled Amor ben Faled in the first zone (the Aurès region of eastern Algeria). There they took an oath of allegiance on the Koran. Two days later the group leaders were summoned to the house of Ben Boulaid, commander of the first zone, at Lambese. They were told the date of the insurrection but ordered to keep it secret from their men until further notice. On that day, the leaders printed many copies of a tract drafted in Cairo and announcing the creation of the FLN and its military arm, the ALN. After the evening meal, the leaders dispersed, to meet again on October 30th, a few hours before D-day.

Of these activities, the French authorities were, at the time, almost totally ignorant. A specimen of the home-made bombs that exploded on D-day in Algiers, Oran and Tlemcen was on the desk of the Director of Security in the first of these cities at the time of the explosions, writes Bromberger. His information was that the action would start on November 2nd, and he had planned to swoop on the workshop where the bomb had been made, on November 1st. A few days earlier, Algiers had had wind that something was afoot in the Arris district of the Aurès region. The Administrator of Arris was summoned to the capital, where he said: "No, I can't see any signs of trouble. All is quiet at the moment." In the more general terms used by Soustelle—"the administration floated like a rudderless raft on the surface of a deep sea which it did not know how to sound". Beyond that, the secret had been well kept.

3

Athens and Eoka

IN Cyprus, too, the secret was well kept, although it was clear from many warning signs that trouble of *some* kind was brewing. I have traced the depressing course of events in the first parts of this book. What concerns me here is the period that immediately preceded the terrorist outbreak of April, 1955: the organisation of the terrorists and the external influences at work on them.

Greece played a part in the Cyprus disorders analogous to that of Egypt in Algeria. It supported Eoka politically and diplomatically. Its representatives made speeches, in effect on Eoka's behalf, in the United Nations. The state-controlled Athens Radio rivalled Cairo Radio in its incitements to violence. To complete the parallel, the organisation of Eoka was largely planned in Greece, where the smuggling of arms to Cyprus has been undertaken. The *Athos* case, which so shocked French public opinion has its parallel in the *Ayios Georghios* case. This Greek schooner, registered at Hydra, was seized on a beach at Khlorakas in Paphos district on January 25th, 1955, while its crew were unloading more than thirty cases of explosives. The crew consisted of five Greek nationals. In the cases were 10,000 sticks of dynamite made in Greece; further cases contained small arms and ammunition, also made in Greece. Aboard the schooner was a professional saboteur of Greek nationality, Anarghyros Karademas, an ex-commando in the Greek Army and a former officer in the Greek Air Force.

The leader of Eoka himself, Colonel Grivas, though a Cypriot by birth, had made his career in Greece, as we have seen in Part I. His diary, captured by the British security forces in the summer of 1956, established the fact that Eoka maintained a supply organisation in Greece and that the smuggling of arms took place with the connivance of Greek officials. The seizure of further consignments of Greek-made arms showed that the *Ayios Georghios* case was not an isolated one.

These incidents were the natural outcome of Archbishop Makarios's sustained and successful efforts to enlist the active support of the Greek Government and public for the cause of *enosis*. From the time of his election in 1950, Makarios directed his efforts into parallel channels: agitation and organisation in Cyprus, propaganda and persuasion in Greece. At first, he found the government of the late Field-Marshal Papagos unresponsive to the point of indifference. Papagos was probably not, in fact, indifferent to *enosis*, but he was less interested in it than in maintaining good relations with Britain as a traditional friend of Greece and a provider in time of need. Makarios, on the other hand, had not wasted his war-time years in Greece. He was a familiar of the techniques of intrigue that were the sustenance of Athenian political society, so brilliantly described by C. M. Woodhouse in *Apple of Discord*. One of these techniques is the organisation of support *outside* the government: in the opposition and the press, and among public figures. By this method, an unrelenting pressure can be built up, to which in the long run the government can hardly fail to respond. So it was in Athens. By frequent visits, Makarios forged his political alliances. He persuaded the aged Spyridon, Archbishop of Athens, to become president of a Panhellenic Committee for the Union of Cyprus. The committee was reported to have raised £120,000 after appealing for funds in August, 1953. With his friends, Makarios enlisted widespread support in the press and launched the propaganda organ *Voice of Cyprus (Phonitis Kyprou)*.

Papagos gave in, according to plan, in the autumn of 1955, when his government adopted the cause of *enosis* as its own. True, by that time Greece was receiving aid from the United States and was therfore no longer dependent on Britain. The conversion was made official, after consultations with Makarios, with the announcement on March 1st, 1954, that Greece would raise the Cyprus issue at the United Nations. Thereafter, Greek sponsorship of *enosis* at the UN was a regular event.

It is consistent with the Greek decision to sponsor *enosis* (thinly disguised as "self-determination for the people of Cyprus") that the services of the state-controlled radio should be made available to Makarios. Despite Greek protestations to the contrary, the support of Athens Radio was clearly not a spontaneous manifestation of sympathy, but a deliberate plan, discussed and agreed between the Greek authorities and the Ethnarch. This conclusion is implicit in the radio's sustained incitement to specified acts of violence, duplicating similar threats in leaflet form by Eoka. But further, it is the only conclusion that can be drawn from various instances of collusion. For instance, on August 27th, 1954, Athens Radio relayed a speech made by Makarios five days earlier at a mass "prayer meeting" at the Phaniromeni Cathedral in Nicosia, summoned by the Archbishop to pray for the success of the Greek Government's initiative before the United Nations; the point is that the relay was of a recording of the speech which, according to the announcer, had been made secretly on the spot. The recording must clearly have been arranged with the Archbishop. More conclusive still were the broadcasts of June 21st and June 23rd, 1955, giving the texts of Eoka leaflets which were distributed only later in Cyprus itself.

During the second half of 1954, there was little actual violence on the island, apart from three acts of sabotage against the Electricity Authority's installations in August; but the warning signs of an impending outbreak were numerous and unmistakable. The Archbishop's own menaces were mostly veiled and indirect, although he did say, in an address to the National Assembly in Nicosia on July 23rd: "It is only through the exercise of violence that the British can be made to understand." The Bishop of Kyrenia was less reticent and, on occasion, called on his flock to emulate the deeds of foreign terrorists; on August 15th, for instance, he said: "Kenya will get its freedom because Mau Mau kills people. The English soldiers are leaving Egypt because the Arabs are every day killing them. The great peaceful (*sic*) battle is beginning." Demonstrations and the daubing of slogans on walls were further danger signals; so was the appearance, in July, August and September, of an anonymous pamphlet entitled *Enosis*, containing threats to "traitors" who were identified by name. But there was no specific evidence of a deliberate conspiracy, beyond persistent rumours. One of these circulated in August; its burden was that a terrorist organisation, on the model of the royalist "Khi-ites" in Greece, had been formed in Cyprus. In October, the police received reports that Greek saboteurs were being infiltrated into the island and that Greek consignments of arms had been shipped. There was, however, no confirmation of these reports.

With the *Ayios Georghios* case in January, 1955, the substance behind the rumours and reports began to emerge. During the inquiry that followed the seizure of the ship, the prosecution produced a document disclosing the existence in Cyprus of a "National Front for the Liberation of Cyprus" (Emak). The purpose of this organisation was said to be "to struggle secretly and by revolution" to overthrow the government of Cyprus and secure the union of Cyprus with Greece. The main terrorist organisation, known as the "National Organisation of Cypriot Combatants" (Ethniki Organosis Kyprion Agoniston), or Eoka did not come into the open until April 1st, 1955. On that day, concerted acts of sabotage occurred in Nicosia, Larnaca, Limassol and elsewhere. For the first time, pamphlets signed by the leader "Dighenis" (Grivas) appeared under the imprint of Eoka. The rebellion had begun.

The secret history of the months of preparation has been reconstructed from two sets of documents seized by the British security forces in 1956: the minutes of the Ethnarchy Council meetings and the Grivas diaries. As I noted in Part I, the association between Archbishop Makarios and Colonel Grivas was already of long standing by the time the terrorist campaign began. It is scarcely in doubt that though Grivas called himself "the leader", Makarios was—until his exile—the initiator of policy and Grivas his chosen instrument. Thus in 1951, Makarios invited Grivas to Cyprus to advise him on the organisation of a nationalist youth body which later formed the nucleus of Eoka. This body was Peon (Pankyprios Ethniki Organosis Neon, or "Pancyprian National Youth Organisation"). Two other organisations played a part in the preparations for the rebellion, and should be mentioned. They are: Ohen, the Orthodox Christian Union of Youth (Orthodoxos Khristianiki Enosis Neon) and Pek, the Pan-Agrarian Union of Cyprus (Panagrotiki Enosis Kyprou). The first of these was a religious club, directly controlled by Makarios, whose nominee, the priest Papastavros, was its president. Papastravros provided recruits for Eoka in the months of preparation. The second organisation, Pek, was, nominally, purely secular: a network of village farmers' clubs under a central committee. But the Archbishop gained control of it in 1953 through the appointment of his protégé Andreas Azinas, as Secretary-General. A previous Secretary-General, Socrates Loizides, had been forced to return to Greece in 1949 after his illegal activities had been uncovered. Loizides, a Greek national, was a former Greek army officer trained in sabotage. He was one of the men captured when the *Ayios Georghios* was seized.

The period of active preparation in Cyprus began in August, 1954. In that month, Makarios called a secret meeting of "enosists", including Zaphirios Valvis, a Greek national who had been Grivas's principal lieutenant and political adviser in the days of "X". This meeting decided to organise for violence. Valvis was assigned to the organisation of arms shipments from Greece. Grivas himself arrived in Cyprus on November 9th, apparently at the invitation of Makarios. At that time, the Archbishop was in the United States. But his messengers, particularly Azinas of Pek, immediately made contact with Grivas. It was Azinas, again, who asked Grivas for a report on the preparations, to be sent to Athens by diplomatic courier for the information of Makarios on his arrival from the United States. This was on December 23rd, 1954, a month before the seizure of the *Ayios Georghios*. Azinas's predecessor, Loizides, had returned to Cyprus with Grivas. It was he, with the help of the priest Papastavros, of Ohen, who organised the recruiting of men and youths for Eoka, from the

conspiracy" have been used as bogy-terms for so long that they have become almost emotive. As a corollary, they have lost much of their impact. It is as well, therefore, to give precision to one's meaning. The communist parties of Asia were all established by the Russian-controlled Comintern in the 'twenties and 'thirties. The abolition of the Comintern in 1943 misled many people into believing that the Soviet leaders had abandoned their plans for fomenting world revolution. They had, in fact, abandoned only an obsolescent instrument for the furtherance of this aim. Less than five years later a new instrument, better adapted to the changed circumstances of the post-war world, was created. This was the Cominform, Moscow's new channel for campaign orders to communist parties everywhere. The Cominform's work was supplemented by communist-controlled "front" organisations— movements of youths, students, women, trade-unionists and others, designed as communist "transmission belts" to the masses. These fronts originated from the International Youth Rally of 1941, and the first of them was the World Federation of Democratic Youth, established three months after the end of the second world war. In February of the same year (1945), Stalin had announced that the Soviet Government still adhered to the doctrine of world revolution.

The soil of South-East Asia was indeed fertile for revolution immediately after the war. It was not, however, uniformly fertile for *communist* revolution. A strong, competing tide of nationalism was in full flow. The Japanese occupation of the Pacific area had encouraged local nationalists, both positively and negatively: positively through the puppet administrations set up by the Japanese, particularly in Burma and Indonesia; negatively by irreparably damaging the white man's prestige. Moreover, the suddenness of the Japanese collapse in August, 1945, caused a hiatus between Japan's surrender and the arrival of allied forces in Indo-China, Malaya and Indonesia. This hiatus was exploited to the full by local communists and nationalists. In Burma, the British forces had re-established themselves before the collapse of Japan, and indeed collaborated with the Japanese-trained Burmese

Army, under General Aung San, in the final stages of the campaign. In the Philippines, the American Army had returned and defeated the Japanese before the final collapse of Japan.

In all these countries, the communists set themselves the task of capturing the leadership of the nationalist movements for their own ends. They were not completely successful anywhere, though they came near to success in Vietnam, where the veteran communist Ho Chi Minh emerged in 1945 as the unquestioned leader of the nationalists and as President of the provisional government of the Democratic Republic of Vietnam. (Ho furthered his success, incidentally, by dissolving the Communist Party of Indo-China—which he had founded—in 1945. This gesture was made with the same intent, and carried much the same significance, as the dissolution of the Comintern in 1943. It persuaded the minority of waverers among the nationalists that Ho was prepared to subordinate communist theories to national leadership. But the Communist Party was resurrected under another name in 1951, as the Lao Dong Dang or Workers' Party.) In Burma, the Philippines and Indonesia, the nationalist pretensions of the communists were, in varying degrees, irrelevant. The Labour Government in Britain was ready to hand over sovereignty to the Burmans. The Americans were pressing ahead with their promise of independence for the Philippines which was, in fact, proclaimed by President Truman as early as July 4th, 1946. The Dutch were far less disposed to surrender their sovereignty over the East Indies, but Dr. Sukarno had proclaimed the Indonesian Republic in August, 1945, without the benefit of communist assistance. In Malaya, where the British were in no hurry to hand over their authority, the Communist Party, whose membership was overwhelmingly Chinese, had little claim to speak in the name of the Malay majority of the population.

In one important respect, however, the communists were well placed to launch insurrections. They were armed, experienced in warfare and organised into fighting units. In Vietnam, Malaya and the Philippines, they had led or formed the hard core of resistance to the Japanese. In Burma, they had been associated with it, through membership of the Anti-Fascist People's Freedom League. In Indonesia, they enjoyed no such advantage, as there had been relatively little militant resistance; there was, however, an anti-Japanese underground, led by the Socialist Sutan Sjahrir and by Sjarifuddin, who revealed that he was a communist only in 1948. The Philippine communist leader, Luis Taruc, likewise came into the open as a communist only that year, after leading the Hukbalahaps (People's Anti-Japanese Resistance Army), first against the Japanese, then against the independent Philippine Government.

Despite the similarities I have mentioned, the internal situations of Malaya, Burma, Indonesia and the Philippines were naturally not alike in all respects in 1948, the year of insurrection. (In Vietnam the war was fifteen to eighteen months old when the communist rebellions broke out elsewhere in South-East Asia.) In Malaya, there had been 300 major strikes in 1947, but there were few outward signs that insurrection was about to break out. In March, 1947, the Secretary-General of the Malayan Communist Party, the mysterious Loi Tak, had disappeared with the party funds. His place had been taken by the youthful Chin Peng, OBE. Although it was not generally known, the party had decided in 1946 to overthrow the government and establish a people's republic, and the wave of strikes in 1947 was intended as a prelude to direct action. This decision, however, appears to have been taken in isolation; it was not until after the establishment of the Cominform in the autumn of 1947 that the Malayan party, in common with other Asian communist parties, began to receive policy instructions from Moscow through the Cominform journal, *For a Lasting Peace, for a People's Democracy*.

In Burma, the situation was complex. The AFPFL (Anti-Fascist People's Freedom League) had gathered various political groups under one banner, but their unity did not long survive the war. In February, 1946, one of the communist leaders, Thakin Soe, broke away from the Burmese Communist Party and set up a rival Communist Party, of Trotskyist tendencies, known as the Red Flags. The main Communist Party, under Than Tun, conducted anti-government and anti-Buddhist propaganda and fomented labour troubles. For these activities, it was expelled in October, 1946. Banditry, terrorism and murder were rife in many part of Burma. A year after its expulsion, the party pledged itself to help the government stamp them out, apparently as a means of resuming collaboration with the AFPFL on the eve of independence. This pledge was, however, short-lived. Shortly after it had been given, the Cominform was formed, and when its directives began to reach Burma, early in 1948, the party turned a spectacular somersault. Thus it had welcomed the Attlee-Nu agreement of October, 1947, providing for the implementation of the Burmese Assembly's vote in favour of independence, and had declared its support for the interim government of Burma; but on January 4th, 1948, when independence was proclaimed, the Communist Party denounced it as a false independence which imposed an economic and military stranglehold on Burma.

In the Philippines, the Hukbalahaps or Huks—who were by no means all communists—had welcomed the Americans back as liberators from the Japanese. But the Americans tended to lump them all together as communist bandits, and in fact the Huks soon did come completely under communist control. I have already pointed out that with the rapid granting of independence, the Philippine Communist Party was hardly in a position to exploit nationalist aspirations. On the other hand, the flagrant and widespread agrarian abuses were grist to the mill of the communists. If there had been no communist party in the Philippines, there would still have been peasant unrest and probably peasant rebellions. But the communists were well placed to turn the peasants' grievances to their own advantage. Thus peasant insurrections raged intermittently under communist direction almost from the moment of the Japanese surrender. By 1948, the Huks were still in control of certain rural districts in eastern and central Luzon. Taruc, the communist leader, and several other Huks, had been elected to the legislature, but they did not take their seats. Early in 1948, there were increasing clashes between the Huks and the constabulary. Then in April, President Roxas died and was succeeded by Elpidio Quirino, whose first act was to grant an amnesty to the Huks, on condition that they surrendered their arms. But by that time, the new Moscow directives had reached Taruc. Although he had personally negotiated the amnesty terms in Manila, he withdrew again to the hills and reopened hostilities on a larger scale. It was only then that he revealed he was a communist.

In Indonesia, in contrast to the other countries of South-East Asia, the communists emerged from the war as a small group without much prestige or influence. Apart from Sjarifuddin, their leaders had spent the war years abroad. Yet between 1945 and 1948, they made astonishing progress. They worked both above and below ground, infiltrating into many of the national organisations that sprang up after the Japanese defeat and intriguing for political power. Thus they gained control of the trade-union body Sobsi (Sentral Organisasi Buruh Seluru Indonesia, or Central Organisation of All-Indonesian Labour), of the Indonesian Socialist Youth Organisation (Pesindo, or Pemuda Sosialis Indonesia) and, above all, of the National Union of Indonesian Students, which was affiliated to a world communist front, the International Union of Students.

As an example of intrigue, the communist leader Tan Malaka forged the signatures of President Sukarno and Vice-President Hatta on a document transferring all power to him in the event of their deaths. He then spread reports that they had been killed by the British, and tried to talk the socialist leader Sjahrir into joint action to take over power and expropriate all foreign properties without compensation. He was gaoled by the Republican authorities in March, 1946.

Also gaoled at that time was Mohammed Jusuf, who, after the war, had set up a communist party under the pre-war name of Partai Kommunis Indonesia (PKI). He and his followers had been conducting a terrorist campaign against the Republican authorities. It turned out later, however, that neither Tan Malaka nor Jusuf was a true—that is, a Moscow-line—communist. Tan Malaka, released after two years, formed a "national" communist party, the Partai Murba or Proletarian Party, and fought on the government side against the communists. And Jusuf's PKI was not the genuine article. The real PKI was re-established in May, 1946, by one of its pre-war leaders, Sardjono. That spring, Sardjono had returned to Indonesia from Australia, where he had spent the war years. Other returning communist exiles joined him, notably Alimin, who had been abroad for twenty years, first in Moscow, then with the Chinese communists in the caves of Yenan. Under Alimin's vigorous leadership the PKI regained prestige and a large membership.

When 1948, the year of rebellion, opened, Sjarifuddin, still nominally a socialist, was Indonesia's Prime Minister. As in the other South-East Asian countries, events were moving on a pre-ordained course. The parallel with Burma is particularly striking. In Burma, the communists had welcomed the independence agreement with Britain, then turned against it on orders from Moscow. In Indonesia, the communists first welcomed, then denounced, a truce agreement with the Dutch. This agreement was named after the US Navy transport *Renville*, in which it was signed on January 7th, 1948. The Renville agreement halted the fighting that had started with the first Dutch "police action", launched the previous July with the object of recapturing from the Indonesian Republic those territories that were of the greatest economic value. A fortnight after the signing, Sjahrir took his followers out of the Socialist Party and formed the Indonesian Socialist Party, leaving the crypto-communist Sjarifuddin with the rump of the socialists. After a further fortnight, Sjarifuddin merged his own followers with army and labour groups in a communist-controlled People's Democratic Front (Front Democratic Rakjat or FDR). This is where the parallel with Burma becomes precise. In February, the newly formed FDR was supporting the Renville agreement; in March it denounced it. Simultaneously, it called for the nationalisation of all foreign properties without compensation. It was not by coincidence that this reversal was made after the return to Indonesia of the delegates who had attended the Calcutta Youth Conference in February.

In Indonesia's case, however, Moscow's responsibility for the insurrection of 1948 has been established with greater precision than in neighbouring countries. The insurrection broke out with a communist call to arms issued on September 18th, 1948. The man who issued it was Musso, yet another communist leader who had returned after many years in exile, spent, in his case, mostly in Moscow. Musso, however, had returned to Indonesia only on August 12th. Travelling under the name of Suparto and with a false passport, he represented himself as the secretary of a young man called Suripno. This Suripno, another communist, was returning to Indonesia from Prague, where, on behalf of the Indonesian Government, he had signed an agreement with the Soviet consul. Musso had brought with him the Soviet order to launch an insurrection against the young Indonesian Republic.

From Moscow, the circumstances must have looked favourable. The unpopular Renville agreement had brought down the Sjarifuddin cabinet. The respected Vice-President, Dr. Hatta, had formed a government, but unrest was rife and anti-Dutch sentiment seemed to indicate that the Republican leaders would be tied up elsewhere if the communists decided to strike. Only one thing was lacking: the PKI, despite its progress, was not prepared for violent action.

As soon as Musso arrived, he took over the leadership of the PKI and began his preparations. The communists set up their rebel headquarters at Madiun, a trade-union centre, where they already had a following. They started a "Red Army School" and trained between three and four thousand armed men. Musso and his companions appear to have realised that this force was insufficient and that further months of preparation were needed if the rebellion was to be a success. Their hand, however, was forced when some of their followers prematurely started anti-government disturbances and the loyalist army began to march on Madiun. It was then that Musso issued his call to arms.

The communists were given little time to find out what hit them. By the end of September the Republic's troops had captured Madiun. On October 25th, President Sukarno announced, in an Order of the Day, that the rebellion had been crushed. All the PKI leaders except Musso were captured; and in December they were all shot. Those who lost their lives in that way included Sjarifuddin; Musso himself was killed in action.

Malaya has already engaged much of our attention and comes back into the picture several times before this study closes. A few words ought, however, to be spared for the rebel preparations. As I have mentioned, an armed insurrection had been decided on, in principle, as early as 1946. But in Malaya, as elsewhere, principle was translated into practice through the policy decisions of the Calcutta Youth Conference. A delegation from the Malayan Communist Party (MCP) had gone to Calcutta, where its members were told to be more militant and passed a resolution calling on the peasants and workers to seize power "by any means". The plan of action seems to have been discussed in detail between the MCP leaders and the Australian communist L. L. Sharkey, who spent two weeks in Singapore on his way home from Calcutta. This incident was disclosed by the former Australian communist Cecil Sharpley, in his book *The Great Decision: The Autobiography of an ex-Communist Leader.*

The plan was conceived on a large scale and on the Chinese communist model. It envisaged three phases: the establishment of "liberated areas" serving as recruitment bases; the enlargement of the "liberated areas"; and their merging to produce a "liberated" country. As we shall see in later chapters, the MCP guerrillas scarcely achieved the first phase, let alone the others. In the spring of 1948, however, the party saw no reason for pessimism. It set about resurrecting the war-time Malayan People's Anti-Japanese Army, under the more appropriate title of Malayan People's Anti-British Army. Then, at the end of 1949, the rebel force was renamed "Malayan Races' Liberation Army"—an ingenious attempt to bask in the reflected glory of the victorious Chinese People's Liberation Army while concealing the fact that the Malayan force was almost entirely Chinese.

5

Conspirators in Contrast

THE Vietminh insurrection of 1946 does not belong to the group of rebellions we have just examined. As I have mentioned in earlier chapters, the Vietminh movement, in its initial stages, was far more than a mere communist movement. The men who prepared and launched the insurrection were, however, communists. But it cannot be said that they took their orders from Moscow, which had not yet created the Cominform, or from Peking, which was not yet a communist city. The foreign influences at work in the early years of the Vietminh were not, indeed, communist ones at all. In retrospect, they were unexpected: the Chinese Nationalists, who sheltered the Vietminh when it was formed in Kwangsi in 1941; the Americans of the Office of Strategic Services (OSS), who supplied it with arms; and a number of Japanese army officers, who offered their services to the Vietminh after the Japanese capitulation.

As we saw in Part I, the real organiser of the insurrection was Giap, not Ho Chi Minh. From the autumn of 1945, this gifted man devoted the greater part of his energies to the creation of an army. More realistic than Ho, he doubted the possibility of reaching a lasting agreement with the French. More militant, he did not shrink from violence. When Ho went to France in June, 1946, for the Fontainebleau conference on Vietnam's place in the French Union, Giap stayed behind to prepare for war. At that time, his army still numbered no more than 31,000 men—about a ninth of the powerful force that defeated the French Union Army in 1954. Aware of his weakness, Giap set up bastions or centres of resistance (*chien khu*) in the mountains of Tonking. These centres were to serve as bases for guerrilla forces to be sent to the plains by night.

Giap decided that the *chien khu* would be defended, in the last resort, by the regular army. Beyond that, however, his guiding principle was decentralisation. Self-defence groups and para-military formations were set up in every district. Party control was ensured by the creation of Resistance Committees in every province, charged with co-ordinating the actions of local People's Committees and of the army. Intensive courses in Marxism-Leninism were organised within the army. Above each high-ranking officer, Giap placed a political commissar, charged with political control and instruction and given the authority to purge resisters or deviationists in "liberated" areas.

Giap's overriding problem was a shortage of arms, which limited the expansion of his army. This he remedied with his usual energy and resourcefulness. In control of the Chinese frontier region, he sent his agents beyond the border, to buy weapons indiscriminately from nationalist or communist irregulars, and even from the communist regular army. Junks were loaded with weapons and ammunition, in Hong Kong, Kwang-tung or Hainan island, then unloaded in the twists and turns of the Bay of Along, to find their way to the *chien khu* in the mountains.

For money, Giap used requisitioned gold, silver and jewels. When these ran out, he offered stolen banknotes of the Banque de l'Indochine to the arms traffickers of Hong Kong; at home, the French currency had been replaced by Ho Chi Minh piastres. And when the French notes declined in value, as they were bound to, he exported everything he could find in the factories deserted by the French—opium, vegetable oils and even rice, although famine was spreading in Tonking. By the time the Fontainebleau nego-tiations had broken down in September, Giap's preparations were well advanced. By December he was ready to strike.

The preparations I have described constituted the secret phase of the Vietminh insurrection. How much the French knew of these preparations is hard to say; but at any rate the preparations were secret in intent. In other respects, developments took place in the full light of day. The Democratic Republic of Vietnam was already a state, recognised *de facto* by the French. Its army was official and visible; it had a government of live ministers. No more complete contrast could be imagined than that between the prelude to violence in Tonking and the dark happenings that preceded the Mau Mau rebellion in Kenya. Even the origin of the name "Mau Mau" and its meaning are unknown. All that is certain is that the founders of this secret terrorist society were former members of the Kikuyu Central Association, banned in 1941 for its subversive activities. Towards the end of 1948, a number of them started agitating in Nairobi. Under a "save the land" slogan, they spread the rumour that the British were planning further "thefts of land" from the Kikuyu. The occasion, they said, was to be the raising of Nairobi to city status. They called for a boycott of the celebrations, at which the Duke of Gloucester was to represent the King. Shortly before the Duke arrived, these men mustered hundreds of Kikuyu at Kiambaa in the Kiambu district. It was the first mass taking of the Mau Mau oath.

Thereafter, the leaders of the Mau Mau, from Jomo Kenyatta down, concentrated their energies on increasing the membership of their society. This simply meant that the oath had to be administered to ever-widening circles of the tribe. Simultaneously, arms were being stolen, mostly by domestic servants and in small quantities at a time. By the time the emergency was declared in October, 1952, Mau Mau stocks must have been fairly substantial.

The preparations were thorough and cunning. The Kenya African Union, unlike the Kikuyu Central Association, was a legal body. The Mau Mau leaders were members of the KAU and used its meetings as a cover for their own activities. A pyramid of power was built, resting on a base of cells, rising through district committees to the apex of the Central Council. Each committee had its "askaris" or police, charged with duties that varied from the provision of sentries to the murder of tribesmen who refused to take the oath. Each office holder in the committees or the Central Council had a deputy. The value of this self-perpetuating device was strikingly demonstrated when 130 Mau Mau leaders were arrested on the proclamation of the emergency; the deputies carried on in their stead.

6

Rebels in the Open

CONSPIRATORIAL methods played curiously little part in our last pair of rebellions: that of the Indonesian colonels and economists, and the *Fidelista* movement in Cuba. In these, our post-colonial rebellions, the preparations were strangely open. In Indonesia, indeed, they were, for all practical purposes, publicly proclaimed. There had, in fact, been a conspiratorial phase, but much earlier, in the last weeks of 1956; when the open revolt came, in February, 1958, the preparations were almost as open as the final break. In this, as in most other respects, this *sui generis* rebellion established its own rules. In effect, two or even three separate rebellions merged into one: a conspiracy of dissatisfied colonels, a movement of regional defiance and a revolt of political malcontents.

As we saw in Part I, there had been dissatisfaction in the Indonesian Army for several years. In October, 1952, guns had been turned on the presidential palace in a bloodless, mysterious and abortive revolt known as "the affair of the colonels". In 1955, Colonel Zulkifli Lubis, later acting Chief of Staff, had forced the resignation of the inefficient Sastroamidjojo cabinet. Now, in mid-1956, Dr. Ali Sastroamidjojo, an elder member of President Sukarno's own National Party (PNI), was again in power. The first sign of trouble came in the early hours of August 13th, when armed soldiers roused the Foreign Minister, Dr. Ruslan Abdulgani, from his bed. Their leader, Major Djuhro, carried an order for the minister's arrest, signed by Lieutenant-Colonel Kawilarang, Commander of the West Java military district. The order accused Dr. Abdulgani of corruption. Mrs. Abdulgani telephoned the Prime Minister, who telephoned the Army Chief of Staff, Major-General Nasution. And Nasution ordered the minister's release. A few hours later, Abdulgani was on his way to London to represent his country at the first Suez Canal conference.

He was later cleared of the charge of corruption by an independent inquiry commission.

It was soon plain that Kawilarang was not alone. Lubis, the rebel of 1955, announced that he supported Kawilarang's order for the Foreign Minister's arrest, and he condemned his Chief of Staff for intervening. Nasution does not appear to have replied in public. What he said in private is not known. But it is clear that Lubis and Kawilarang began to gather around them like-minded officers, much as Brigadier Kassem must have in Iraq before the *coup d'état* of July 14th, 1958. But the Indonesian officers were less versed in the art of secrecy. On October 5th, General Nasution announced that there was a danger of a military coup against the government. Four days later, the official army spokesman, Colonel Pirngadie, announced the arrest of a number of officers who, he said, had plotted to overthrow the government and set up a military junta. One of them was Major Djuhro, the bearer of the order to arrest Abdulgani. Another month went by; Lubis, the conspirator, was at his post as usual. On November 9th, he was ordered to appear before General Nasution and answer a charge of disobeying military orders. It was only then that he went into hiding. On the 21st, after another leisurely interval, army headquarters stated that Lubis had organised a plot to overthrow the government and "change the ideology of the state". He was charged with desertion. Little effort, however, seems to have been made to find him. It was freely said in Jakarta that he was still there, and that he was armed with a secret weapon: the dossiers of colleagues and politicians which he would cause to be published if arrested. According to the Nationalist paper *Merdeka*, the plot that had misfired was aimed at the removal of President Sukarno as well as his Prime Minister. The arrest of Abdulgani was to have been the first move. When the minister escaped arrest, the coup had been postponed till October 5th, then to November 20th. Then, after all, it had not taken place, presumably because some of the officers who were to have taken part had been arrested.

There was a similar inadequacy about the preparations for the "formal" rebellion of February, 1958. We saw in Part I that a National Conference, called in Jakarta the previous September, had failed to solve the conflict between the outer islands and the central administration in Java. This conference was preceded and followed by rebel meetings in Sumatra. The first of these took place at Palembang (South Sumatra) on September 7th and 8th, 1957. All the dissident colonels were there: Lubis, Simbolon, Hussein, Sumual and Barlian (Kawilarang had been "exiled" to Washington as military attaché). Together they drafted the document known as the Palembang Charter—a public act of defiance which has been described in earlier chapters—and set up a National Anti-Communist Front.

The National Conference dissolved on September 15th in a cloud of nebulous rhetoric and declarations. Hussein and Sumual had gone to Jakarta for it, but not Simbolon or Lubis. On the 21st and 22nd, some of the dissident colonels met again, with Sumitro, the ex-Finance Minister, at Padang in central Sumatra. They decided that the National Conference had accomplished nothing, and pledged themselves to "struggle" against the central administration. The Padang meeting was private but hardly conspiratorial: indeed, the participants sought publicity for it. They appear to have given little thought to the possibility that their defiance might culminate in civil war, although this was not excluded. A rebel account of the meeting, written at the time, merely said: "In the final analysis, it is of course not impossible that the central government will engage in physical pressure in the military sense." With so slight a concession to reality, it is perhaps not surprising that the rebels made virtually no defensive —or offensive—preparations.

Nor, it appears, were any preparations made for a possible *coup d'état* in Java, the real centre of power. All that was done was to alert other potential dissidents, such as Kawilarang in Washington and Colonel Warouw, the military attaché in Peking. After the Padang meeting, Hussein and Barlian went to Macassar, in south Celebes, to inform Sumual of their decisions. When the showdown came, the following April, all the original rebels stood united except Barlian, the local commander in south Sumatra, who had declared himself "neutral". This defection greatly facilitated the central government's operations.

Another important failure was that of leadership. It was not that the rebels lacked leaders, but that they had too many. None of the colonels was the undisputed Number One. In the important phase of preparations, the ship was rudderless. When the rebel government was proclaimed on February 15th, 1958, Colonel Kawilarang was at last appointed Commander-in-Chief. But at that time he was still in Washington, and his acceptance was by no means certain. Much time and energy had been expended in trying to persuade the respected former Vice-President, Dr. Hatta, to take the leadership of the rebellion. Contact had been made with him during his visit to Peking after the National Conference, and again in Tokyo on his way back to Jakarta. Each time he had refused to commit himself to unconstitutional courses. When Dr. Sjafruddin of the Bank Indonesia joined the rebel colonels at the end of 1957, he became their Premier-elect, partly *faute de mieux,* partly because he had the aura of prestige of one who had already been a Prime Minister.

Even when the decision to proclaim a revolutionary government was taken—at the beginning of February—the rebels dithered and delayed their ultimatum until the tenth. The ultimatum called for the dissolution of the then cabinet of Dr. Djuanda and the appointment of Dr. Hatta and the Sultan of Jokjakarta, a former Defence Minister, as *formateurs* of a new cabinet. It was bound to be rejected. Yet almost nothing had been done to prepare for the inevitable consequences of the proclamation of a revolutionary government five days later. The die, however, had been cast.

*   *   *

In its early stages, Fidel Castro's rebellion in Cuba was even more amateurish than the Indonesian rebellion. But the Cuban rebels had many assets, both positive and negative. On the positive side, they had an undisputed leader from the very beginning, the spontaneous sympathy of an oppressed peasantry and a marked talent for publicity of which the most striking demonstration was the kidnapping of the world motor-racing champion, Juán Fangio, with no other object than to draw the world's attention to the rebel cause. (In this, they succeeded.) On the negative side, they benefited from the unpopularity of the dictator, General Fulgencio Batista, and from the reluctance of the armed forces to give battle on his behalf. They also benefited from the dictator's reluctance to take his young opponent seriously. Gaoled for fifteen years after the failure of his rag-taggle attack on the barracks at Santiago de Cuba in 1953, Fidel Castro was released under a general amnesty in 1955. It was then that the period of plotting began.

In exile, first in the United States, then in Mexico, Fidel Castro consorted with other disgruntled rebels. Some were rich men, others poor; most spent their time in the sterile intrigues of political exiles. But Castro was looking for fighters, not intriguers. He found them in Mexico. He was looking for arms and money, and these too he found, across the border in McAllen, Texas. There in the Casa de Palmas Hotel, Castro conferred one day in the summer of 1956 with ex-President Carlos Prío Socarrás. Prío had been ousted from the Presidency by Batista; he was rich with the spoils of office—scarcely a man after Castro's heart, save for a shared hatred of the dictator, but with the means to finance an insurrection. He promised Castro arms and money.

Castro's next need was for training in guerrilla warfare, the art of the insurgent. This, too, he found, in Mexico City. His tutor, Colonel Alberto Bayo, had learned his trade in the hard school of battle against General Franco in the Spanish Civil War. Castro had assembled eighty potential rebel fighters. For several months, the Spanish colonel drilled them in the mechanics of guerrilla fighting, from marksmanship to map-reading and the manufacture of utility bombs.

This time, Castro had prepared his attempt. But he had neglected the essential precaution of absolute secrecy before the moment of action. With his eighty followers, he set off from Tuxpam on the Gulf of Mexico on November 26th, 1956. Their craft was the 62-foot yacht *Gramma,* a gift from ex-President Prío. But Batista was ready for them. When the rebels landed on the southern shore of Oriente province six days later, they ran into the murderous fire of the 1st Regiment. Only twelve survived. But they included Fidel Castro, his brother Raúl and a young Argentino with a talent for guerrilla fighting, Ernesto "Che" Guevara. Concealed in the marshes, they tramped twenty days to the natural stronghold of the Sierra Maestra mountains. If Castro had neglected the need for secrecy, Batista in turn had neglected the need for a follow-through. Castro and his stragglers were allowed to get away. Overconfident a second time, Batista lost Cuba.

7
Lessons for Both Sides

THE maze of facts we have traversed leads, I suggest, to certain reasonably firm conclusions. The first and most obvious is a lesson for intending rebels: absolute secrecy in the phase of preparation is an essential condition of success. Failure to observe this elementary rule cost the anti-Sukarno rebels serious initial setbacks. A similar failure almost cost Fidel Castro his life as well as the success of his rebellion.

My second conclusion is of interest to those in authority rather than those outside the law. External influences and intervention may be of great importance (China's intervention was decisive in Vietnam), but they cannot, by themselves, *initiate* a successful rebellion. This, surely, is proved by all the relevant examples. Greek help to Eoka and Egyptian help to the FLN certainly made the self-assumed task of the Cypriot and Algerian rebels infinitely easier; but the Egyptians alone could not have started a rebellion in Algeria, any more than the Greeks could have in Cyprus. Even more striking are the communist insurrections in South-East Asia. In Burma, Indonesia and the Philippines, local communists started unnecessary insurrections on orders from Moscow; because these movements had no basis of popular support and were demonstrably irrelevant in countries that were already independent, they were bound to fail and did. In Malaya, the insurrection was launched before independence was on the programme of the responsible colonial power. Accordingly, it took a deeper root than elsewhere; but it began to fail as soon as it became clear that Britain was preparing to hand over the country to the Malayans. In Indo-China, the independence movement was deep-rooted and amply justified; the communists managed to seize its direction, but they neither conceived nor created it.

My final conclusion is of more practical interest to rulers everywhere. Political opposition, where allowed, provides a visible warning of trouble ahead. It is better to act or respond *while* it is visible than wait until it has vanished out of sight. For that may be too late. The apparent absence of agitation after a long period of warning signs may be the deceptive calm before a storm. Calm may conceal conspiracy, and secrecy is often the prelude to violence.

PART IV

TERRORISM

I

A Limited Weapon

TERRORISM is a weapon of the weak. This is a factual observation: it does not exonerate those who use terrorism as a
weapon from any moral blame that may be put on them by their
victims or by outsiders. Nor, on the other hand, does it imply
that the weak are morally inferior to the strong. All acts of violence are open to criticism on moral grounds. The violence of
the strong may express itself in high explosive or napalm bombs.
These weapons are no less discriminate than a hand-grenade tossed
from a roof-top; indeed, they will make more innocent victims.
Yet they arouse less moral indignation around Western firesides.
The terrorist is an outlaw and—except when he deposits a time-
bomb—he is physically close to his victims. The airman is an
agent of established order and may be thousands of feet above
the roof-tops of those to be blasted by high explosive or seared
by fire. Often enough, the victims of terrorism are "us", whereas
the victims of bombing raids are "them".

I shall try, therefore, to avoid passing moral judgements. My
purpose is to examine the weapon of terrorism, to find out
whether it brings results, and to guess whether similar results
could have been achieved by other means, either at all or within
the same time. If I mention moral reactions, such as popular or
official indignation, it will be because such reactions have a
bearing on the efficacy of the terrorist weapon; not because I
agree or disagree with them. Emotion is a foe of impartiality.

I define terrorism, provisionally, as the threat or the use of
violence for political ends. As a weapon, it may be wielded by
rebels or by their opponents; in the second case, however, it
becomes counter-terrorism and belongs to a later chapter. It
comes in several varieties: it may be indiscriminate or selective: it

may be used against the enemy or against members of one's own side. If people in the terrorists' own camp are the victims, they are labelled traitors.

The purposes of terrorism are, likewise, several-fold. A common purpose is to make life unendurable for the enemy; another may be to eliminate traitors *pour encourager les autres*; a further purpose may be to extort money; in selected cases the victim may be a political leader whose removal is considered desirable. The methods favoured are more varied still : torture, mutilation, murder and massacre; the throwing or placing of bombs; arson; kidnapping. Some or all of these methods have been used in each of the rebellions I am examining.

The successes of terrorism are difficult to assess. In one or two of the examples I shall mention, the terrorist *side* achieved complete success. It does not follow, however, that these successes were due entirely to terrorist methods. It seems likely, on the other hand, that such methods did play an important part in them. In most of the other cases, success resulted from a number of factors, of which terrorism was only a minor one. And in at least one case the weapon was a boomerang, which contributed to the defeat of the terrorist side. Taken as a whole, my examples suggest that terrorism, at best or worst, is generally a useful auxiliary weapon rather than a decisive one. It may, however, be decisive under certain conditions, which I shall define with greater precision after examining the evidence.

I suggested in Part III that terrorism is the first active stage of violent rebellion, though it may continue after the later stages have come into play. It played an important part in the early years of the Indo-China war and a dominant one in the Malayan Emergency. It was the main instrument of the rebels in Cyprus and Kenya, and a major one in the hands of the Algerian FLN. It was an important contributory cause of the departure of the British from the Suez Canal Zone in 1954 and from Palestine in 1948. Between them, these examples span the scale of terrorism aims and methods, illustrate the kind of success terrorism can achieve and expose its limitations.

2

Terrorist Setbacks

In Indo-China, terrorism was a major weapon of the communist-controlled Vietminh from August, 1945. The situation could hardly have been more confused, but it can be reduced to simple outlines. The Japanese had just surrendered. Under the Potsdam Agreement, the Chinese Nationalists were to take over from the Japanese forces north of the 16th parallel and the British south of it. The Vietminh, which at that time did not by any means consist entirely of communists, was determined to turn the Japanese defeat to its own profit and to prevent the reinstatement of French authority. The first British and Indian troops, under General Gracey, arrived on September 12th. A French Commissioner for Cochin-China (south Vietnam) had been parachuted on to a rice-field. But the first French troops did not arrive until October 3rd; they were led by the famous General Leclerc. A few days earlier, the Vietminh forces, which surrounded Saigon, had massacred the French inhabitants of the Cité Héraud, a suburb on the outskirts. Throughout Cochin-China, huts and houses, crops and installations had been destroyed by the Vietnamese guerrillas, operating first against the Japanese then against the French.

From the day of Leclerc's arrival, it was clear that Vietminh terrorism had two purposes: to make life unendurable for the French, and to ensure the active support of the population by executing traitors and collaborators. Members of General Leclerc's forces soon became familiar with the Vietnamese term *Viêt giân*, which means "traitor" or "collaborator", and was applied to every Vietnamese who displayed friendship for the French or accepted French money. In the early stages (August–December, 1945) the terrorist machine had not been perfected. The usual Vietminh method, in effect, killed two birds with one stone. A village protected by the French Army would be selected as a target. The "protection" usually consisted of a handful of youthful French soldiers under a corporal. A burst of rifle fire after midnight would draw them in one direction; meanwhile, Vietminh insurgents would appear from the opposite side, set fire to huts or houses and kidnap or massacre those on the traitors' list.

At the turn of the year, the old anti-Japanese resistance movement in Cochin-China had broken up. It had consisted of a convenient alliance between the Vietminh—itself an uneasy coalition —and various bands pursuing private or semi-religious objectives. Communist brutalities alienated these groups, who went their separate ways. In the meantime, the returning French Commissioner in Tonking (north Vietnam), M. Sainteny, was negotiating with Ho Chi Minh and his provisional government of Vietnam. These negotiations resulted in an agreement on March 6th, 1946. Under this agreement, France recognised Vietnam as "a free state, having its government, its parliament, its army and its treasury, belonging to the Indo-Chinese Federation and to the French Union". The union of the three *ky*, or provinces, was to be subject to a referendum. In practice, this referendum was to decide whether Cochin-China was to join Annam (central Vietnam) and Tonking as part of a unified Vietnamese state.

I have, of course, already mentioned this agreement and the issue of Cochin-Chinese separatism. I recall them here because of their bearing on the second wave of Vietminh terrorism, from March, 1946, onward. After the March 6th agreement, the French thought that terrorism had ceased and would not return. This assumption was encouraged by a lull due to the breaking up of the old resistance movement, which I have mentioned above. "Security seemed to have returned," wrote Philippe Devillers, the able historian of those interesting years. "Once again, one could drive without escort on the roads, and in the ricefields the peasant's intensive work was starting up again."

The Vietminh, however, was reorganising its terrorist apparatus. One of its regional commanders in the south, Nguyen Binh, made this task his personal responsibility. This man was not a communist, but a militant member of the old nationalist organisation, VNQDD. He arrived in Cochin-China in November, 1945, and within weeks had organised an intelligence service, a network of informers and a corps of suicide volunteers. Later came "assassination committees". Despising the intellectuals of the Vietminh's Cochin-Chinese committee, Nguyen Binh believed in terrorism and military action to keep the population in line.

The French soon gave Nguyen Binh the pretexts he needed. Local French commanders interpreted the agreement of March 6th as unconditional surrender by the Vietminh. They ordered the guerrillas to hand over their arms. From the Vietminh Commander-in-Chief, General Giap, came the order to keep them. Other Frenchmen declared that the agreement did not apply below the 16th parallel. Vietminh suspicions of French intentions in Cochin-China were brought to a head on March 26th, when a prominent local personality, Dr. Nguyen Van Thinh, was elected head of the "provisional government of the Republic of Cochin-China". This was the signal for the second wave of terrorism.

Nguyen Binh's assassination committees sprang into action. By the dozen, village notables who had helped the French or accepted money from them were tied to posts and shot. Nationalists who disapproved of these methods shared their fate. Most of them had labels bearing the words *Viêt giân* pinned to their clothes after death. In the towns, particularly Saigon, terrorism was both specific and indiscriminate, and continued at least until 1952. Among the specific acts were the murders of two Cochin-Chinese separatist councillors on March 29th and May 3rd, 1946. The favourite indiscriminate weapon was the hand-grenade, casually tossed into a crowded café terrace by a running or cycling Vietnamese. The incident of the plastic bombs on untended bicycles, mentioned by Graham Greene in his novel *The Quiet American*, actually happened. Sometimes military targets were attacked, and terrorism overlapped into guerrilla warfare. The most spectacular of these cases took place on April 8th, 1946, when three of Nguyen Binh's men swam across a stream and blew up 4,000 tons of ammunition in Saigon's arsenal.

It is difficult to assess the returns of Vietminh terrorism, because the French consistently failed to take any advantage it might have offered them. On the one hand, Nguyen Binh undoubtedly succeeded, in the early stages, in rallying the peasants, who had greatly suffered from the scorched-earth policy and were ready to do what the village notables told them. Terrorism demonstrated the limited powers of the notables and branded many of them as traitors. On the other hand, it rapidly alienated the majority of the non-communist intellectuals. This circumstance might have been exploited by the French had they accepted the need to come to terms with Vietnamese nationalism. Instead, they provided the Vietminh with a justification for violence, while they discouraged the nationalists by stimulating Cochin-Chinese separatism and scarcely disguising their ultimate aim of reconquering Vietnam.

It is clear, however, that terrorism alone would not have defeated the French in Vietnam. They were defeated, on the political front, by the mistakes I have already analysed; and on the military front, by Giap's military genius and massive Chinese aid reaching his army by short lines of communication. Indeed, from 1952 on terrorism played a reduced part in the Vietminh offensive.

In Malaya, as in Vietnam, terrorism dominated the early stages of the communist insurrection. In spite of a deliberate policy decision to abandon indiscriminate terrorism, the Malayan insurgents were never able to dispense with it entirely. A comparison of the two situations, indeed, illustrates the truth of my first proposition: that terrorism is a weapon of the weak. It was a major weapon of the Vietminh until active Chinese aid began in January, 1950. Thereafter, it gradually ceased to play much part in Vietminh tactics; in the south, however, where the Vietminh was weaker than in the China border region of Tonking, terrorism continued unabated through 1951. In Malaya, on the other hand, the insurgents did not enjoy a comparable geographical advantage: denied heavy arms, they could never become a real army, for all their use of "regiments", "platoons" and other military terms. Moreover, in Vietnam the Vietminh exploited to the full the surge of Vietnamese nationalism. For Vietnam was a nation. Malaya, an amalgam of two major peoples and a substantial minority of Indians, was not. Anti-western sentiment existed, of course, but the Malayan Communist Party was never able to canalise it completely for its own ends. Inevitably, the insurrection was a minority movement. It was therefore weak, and continued to rely on terrorism as its principal instrument of policy.

The Malayan communists first displayed their capacity for terrorism during the hiatus of several weeks that occurred between the surrender of the Japanese in August, 1945, and the first landing of allied troops in Singapore. Emerging from the jungle with the British liaison officers of Force 136, they imposed a rule of terror. During those weeks, the communists dissipated most of the good-will they had gained as the spearhead of the anti-Japanese resistance. The beginning of the insurrection in the spring of 1948 was marked by a series of murders. Here, as in Vietnam, the terrorists struck against their own people as well as against Europeans. "Blood and Steel Corps" had been formed to extort and intimidate. The thugs of "Blood and Steel" raided Chinese-owned business places, seizing payrolls and takings. A Malayan Communist Party priority list for murder fell into the hands of the Special Branch: mine and estate managers shared top place with selected police officials, followed by district officers and government officers in Kuala Lumpur.

Murder and abduction were supplemented by the slashing of rubber trees and the destruction of estate telephone lines, the burning of buses and taxis and the extortion of food and supplies. Trains were derailed and police ambushed. The pace of terrorism was on the increase from 1948 to 1951. In February, 1950, there were 221 incidents; the village of Simpang Tiga, near Chin Peng's birth place of Sitiawan, in Perak, was set on fire and 1,000 people were made homeless. In May, the number of incidents rose to 534, and the higher figure tended to become the average: the total for 1951 reached 6,100.

If these tactics were calculated to make life difficult or unendurable for estate managers and their families, they might also have been purposely designed to alienate the ordinary Malay, Chinese or Indian. Certainly the three Asian races provided far more victims than the British. Likewise, terrorism affected civilians far more than army or police. Thus, until the end of 1951, 1,275 army and police were killed in action in the Federation of Malaya; but 2,319 civilians were murdered or abducted. The humble Tamil tapper or Chinese mineworker was treated as brutally as the "rich landlord", capitalist or "imperialist".

What return did these methods bring the communist insurgents? For Malaya, this question may be answered far more confidently than for Vietnam. The first effects of terrorism were devastating and brought the communists closer to victory than perhaps they realised. Although the violent strikes of 1947 had provided warning and the intelligence services were aware of communist plans, the British authorities were caught unprepared. The police force was inadequate for the extra burden suddenly placed on it; the army had only eleven battalions and an artillery regiment. Estates and mines were dangerously exposed. Moreover, in the highest places—in Kuala Lumpur and Westminster—there was a decided reluctance to believe that a major threat existed. When subordinates of the late Sir Edward Gent, the first High Commissioner of the Federation, warned him of an impending communist insurrection, he used to exclaim: "You people see a communist behind every bush." Sir Edward and the Labour cabinet in London seemed equally unwilling to take energetic action, and a state of emergency was not declared till June 18th, 1948, after several weeks of terrorism.

The communists thus started well. In the first two and a half years, they caused much havoc and disruption. And though the personnel of the estates and mines kept control of themselves, civilian morale was impaired. The climax of the terrorist campaign was the ambush and murder, on a winding road in thick jungle, of the High Commissioner, Sir Henry Gurney, in October, 1951. At that point, morale was at its lowest.

In military terms, however, the terrorist campaign ceased to be a vital threat after the first few months. On their side the guerrillas, despite their high-sounding "Malayan Races' Liberation Army", were unable to press home the initial advantages of surprise. About 8,000 strong, they were scattered throughout the peninsula. Their communications were primitive; it took up to a year for a central committee directive to reach the remoter units. In consequence, concerted actions were impossible. Terrorism hardly graduated to guerrilla warfare, much less to regular war. On all sides, the principles of the Chinese communist teachers, Mao Tse-tung and Liu Shao-chi, were violated: on the civilian front the people had been alienated, on the military front the communists had proved incapable of establishing a regular army in anything but name.

These shortcomings appear to have been pointed out to the Malayan Communist Party by the Chinese communist leadership at about the same time as it began to offer similar advice to the Vietminh. Owing to communication difficulties, Peking's advice —which probably had the strength of an order—was not translated into Malayan party policy until October, 1951, the month of Sir Henry Gurney's murder. The change of policy was enshrined in a 14,000-word directive to the communist guerrillas. Immediately afterwards, there was a drop in the monthly rate of "incidents", which the Federation authorities at first found puzzling. Some months later a copy of the directive fell into their hands; it then became clear that the apparent reduction in terrorist activity was the result of a deliberate change of tactics. The full text of the directive has not, to my knowledge, been published. The excerpts released to the press were not as explicit as might have been desired. Denis Warner, in *Out of the Gun*, says that the directive included an order to cease "all acts of sabotage, arson and intimidation calculated to alienate the masses". Military targets were defined and compensation was to be paid for murders or other outrages committed in the past. The directive thus implicitly, though not explicitly, admitted the futility of pure terrorism as a weapon of war. Indeed, the evidence was plain: the all-important Min Yuen, or food and supply organisation, had begun to report that terrorism was driving the people into co-operation with the Security Forces. As a corollary to military attacks, the directive prescribed greater efforts at infiltration of schools, trade unions and political organisations. In other words, terrorism was to be selective and military in intent; on the civilian front, it was to be replaced by subversion.

The new policy, though sound by communist military stand-ards, could have been carried out, however, only from mounting strength, not continuing weakness. But the party was caught in a vicious circle from which it was never to emerge. Terrorism had been alienating the people, but the abandonment of terrorism made the people believe that the rebellion was losing its impetus; infiltration therefore met with little success, and the party was driven back to terrorism; and by that time the "liberation" units were too weak to resume more aggressive methods. The decision to return to terrorism was taken about a year after the decision to abandon it; but the second wave of terrorism was feebler and far less effectual than the first. In turning full circle, terrorism had spent itself.

In the final analysis, terrorism in Malaya had proved itself effective only against an ill-defended population; as soon as re-inforcements arrived in sufficient number, its own inadequacy was exposed. From that point forward, it was able only to tie down a large security force (about 40,000 troops and 100,000 police of various grades) and impose a severe financial burden on the British and Federation Governments. But it was no longer a decisive weapon, as it almost had been during the first few weeks.

In Algeria, Kenya and Cyprus, we find again some of the fea-tures of Vietnamese and Malayan Chinese terrorism. Each, how-ever, has distinctive characteristics. In writing of terrorism in Algeria and tribal Kenya, it is hard to avoid emotive words like savagery; in Cyprus, for all its unpleasantness to residents and transients, terrorism was far milder than in North or East Africa. There is, however, a remarkable similarity in aims and emotional approach in all three countries. In all three, as indeed in Vietnam and Malaya, the objective of bullying the terrorists' own side into conformity gets priority over outrages against the enemy. The incitements to violence might almost have been drafted by the same hand; in the cases of Algeria and Cyprus, they often came from outside the country. For instance, the weekly *Ez-Zitouna*, organ of the students of the great mosque of that name in *Tunis*, addressed the following passage to its "brothers of the Aurès" (the Algerian terrorist) in its issue of August 26th, 1956:

> My brothers, do not kill only . . . but mutilate your adversaries on the public highway. . . . Pierce their eyes. . . . Cut off their arms . . . and hang them.
>
> Be certain that what you will do will strike fear and cowardliness into the soldiers of colonialism. They are not human beings, they are wild beasts, knowing only the law of the jungle. Be certain, my brothers, that the soldiers who will see their comrade hanging from a tree, minus an arm and a leg and with a blinded eye, be certain, I was saying, that these soldiers will in future allow the caravans of arms and supplies to pass and will take to their heels like rats.

Similarly, Athens radio, in January, 1955, repeatedly quoted, with manifest approval, from a Greek Cypriot terrorist pamphlet called *Enosis*. Particular emphasis was given to the following passage:

> It is a lesson of world history that no people can achieve their freedom without bloody sacrifices. . . . The Colonial powers and their organs understand only one language, the language used by all people who have won their freedom, the language of the Egyptians, Jews and Mau Mau [*sic*], the language of blood and sacrifices and of sabotage and dynamite. . . . Freedom or death is the eternal signal of Hellenism when black slavery covers the national sky.

In more specific terms, the second Mau Mau oath, bound members of the Kikuyu terrorist society in a brotherhood of murder:

> 1. If I am called upon to do so, with four others, I will kill a European.
> 2. If I am called upon to do so, I will kill a Kikuyu who is against the Mau Mau, even if it be my mother or my father or brother or sister or wife or child.

3. If I am called upon to do so, I will help to dispose of the body of the murdered person so that it may not be found.

4. I will never disobey the orders of the leaders of this society.

Though the Mau Mau oath put the killing of Europeans at the top of the list, ahead of the killing of Kikuyu, in fact the Mau Mau terrorists killed far more Kikuyu than Europeans. L. S. B. Leakey, the Kikuyu-speaking authority on that tribe, says in *Defeating Mau Mau* that the terrorists killed not only Kikuyu who gave information to the authorities but also those who attended second oath ceremonies but refused to take the oath. "No one will ever know," he writes, "how many of the thousands of 'missing' Kikuyu have died in this way." Thousands more were murdered because, having taken the oath, they repented of it and reported themselves to the authorities.

Similarly, Eoka, the Greek Cypriot terrorist organisation, consistently maintained a higher rate of elimination of "traitors" than of British Security Forces or officials. Indeed, in the early days of Cypriot terrorism, the population, easy-going by nature and tradition, showed signs of not taking the rebellion as seriously as its leaders had intended. Many Greek Cypriots seemed to be taking too long to break the habit of friendliness to the British. They were soon pulled up with a jerk, when the Eoka organisation circularised individuals with reminders that the penalty for traitors was death. The slogan "Death to Traitors", scrawled or painted on the white walls of Cypriot houses made the lesson visible. Selected murders of Greek Cypriot "traitors" drove it home.

Algeria conforms to the general rule that the victims of terrorism on the terrorist side outnumber those among the enemy. The insurrection had been highly organised. It broke out with simultaneous acts of terrorism in widespread places on November 1st, 1954. It was manifestly not, however, a spontaneous popular uprising of the (rare) Hungarian type. The Moslem mass of the population, whether Arab or Berber, though not necessarily pro-French, had no part in the rebellion. Its main concern appears to have been the desire to be left in peace. In the towns, many

Algerian intellectuals did not disguise their opposition to a policy of violence. Shopkeepers and artisans carried on as before. As in Cyprus, they were rudely awakened.

The aims of this terrorist campaign were varied: to enforce collaboration and to remove those who resisted coercion; to extort money; to ensure unanimity in strikes or the boycotting of schools. Heads of family, shopkeepers—including many Jews—caïds or tribal chiefs loyal to the French, gangsters or other criminals likely to be of use in terrorist activities: all these began to receive menacing letters from the FLN. I have seen photographic reproductions of many of these messages, both in Arabic and in French. I cannot judge of the Arabic, but those in French are crude and semi-literate. They are useful documents for the insight they give us into the mentality of terrorists at the executioner level. Here are some translated examples:

(*To a Caïd loyal to the French*)

Dear Caïd,

By order of the Army of National Liberation, I want to announce to you that your head will be chopped off. I swear it to you, you will never escape me, even if you go to the end of the earth.

You are reporting everything that happens to the Administration.

I shall marry your wife. But to escape death, you have five days' grace in which to resign.

Good-bye, dirty head.

Signed,
Political commissar,
FLN-ALN

(*To a Moslem of Algiers who had sent his son to school*)

If your son ——Mhd. is at school tomorrow at 7 o'clock, he will not come back in the afternoon.

(*To a Jewish shopkeeper in Algiers*)

Sir,

If on Wednesday you do not hand us the sum of 2 million francs, which must be deposited in the hall of the building situated at 1, Rue d'Isly, Wednesday 7th before 16.45 hours near the staircase at the end near the cupboard, your daughter will be abducted and will serve as a mattress for the Army of Liberation. Useless to put her in safety, we have our eyes on her.

If you do not follow our instructions, your shop will be blown up and we shall have your skins, yours and your wife's.

Such notes were always followed by ruthless action on the appointed day. Publicity, rather than secrecy, was sought: witnesses were not eliminated, rather were they spared so that they might spread the news. The French journalist Serge Bromberger, in his fanciful, tendentious but valuable book *Les Rebelles Algériens*, gives many examples of FLN methods. I shall borrow one, which took place in March, 1956, during the early days of the terrorist offensive in Algiers. The executioner was a young man known as Ali-la-Pointe, 26, a pimp and gambler recognisable by an intricate tattoo system including two slogans: "March or die" on the chest and "Shut up" on the left foot. The victim was a round little man, "king" of the Casbah's underworld, Abd el-Kader Rafai by name, but generally known, from his resemblance to an American comedian, as "Bud Abbott".

The FLN had acquired the services of Ali-la-Pointe by organising his escape from a detention camp where he was serving a sentence for attempted murder. "Bud Abbott", for his part, had just emerged from gaol at the natural term of his sentence. The FLN made several attempts to enlist his services. Each time he turned them down and boasted of it to his companions. One evening, in Bromberger's account, he is invited, with his mistress and a close friend, to dine with a neighbouring couple in their flat. They are scarcely seated when Ali-la-Pointe and another FLN man knock at the door. They are admitted, apparently without suspicion. Within minutes, the two terrorists have drawn revolvers and shot "Bud Abbott" and his mistress. The friend has taken refuge under a couch; he is pulled out and killed in his turn. The hosts, however, are spared. Thus they may spread the tale. The Casbah gangs are given a month to think things over, then another of their chiefs is murdered. That does the trick: some of the remaining bosses flee to Paris, the others join the FLN, followed by their rank-and-file.

The enforcement of conformity and obedience through fear: that is one aspect of terrorism. Another, the elimination of traitors, was always a major preoccupation of the FLN. Much hinges on the definition of "traitor". That the term applies to those collaborating with the "enemy", for instance by informing, is normal. The *caïd* who supplies the French with the names and addresses of terrorists ought, perhaps, to realise that his end is likely to be violent and sudden. But the FLN has always labelled as traitors those who pursue similar aims by different methods. In this they are not necessarily unique, but the practice is not universal among terrorist movements: in Palestine, for instance, between 1945 and 1948, the two Jewish terrorist organisations, Irgun Zvai Leumi and the Stern Gang, collaborated with each other and with Haganah, the more respectable para-military organisation of the Zionists. The FLN, in contrast, has expended a considerable portion of its energies and resources in exterminating the rival nationalist group, MNA (Mouvement National Algérien).

Messali Hadj, the oldest and best-known Algerian nationalist, had been left out of the rebellion. As we saw in Part III, the preliminary work was done by an inner group of militants, including Benbella and Belkacem Krim. Messali, kept in ignorance, condemned the insurrection at the outset. He may have supposed that it would not last much more than three months; and, indeed, the paucity of means on the rebel side would have encouraged this view. After three months, seeing that the rebels were not going to be crushed so easily, he announced the formation of the MNA, in tracts printed in Belgium. He then seems to have decided to make common cause with the rebels, but only on terms compatible with his dignity. Handicapped by house arrest in France, he sent two emissaries to Benbella in Cairo. Benbella, however, was not disposed to share his incipient power. He told Messali's envoys that they would have to accept the primacy of the new Army of National Liberation. They concurred, but shortly afterwards (says Bromberger) Benbella had them arrested by the Egyptian police. This was in May, 1955.

Messali, strong among Algerians in France but weak in Algeria itself, decided to create his own guerrilla forces. Many Algerians were brought back from France. Once in Algeria, they were formed into guerrilla groups. Most of these were in Kabylia. Although they took their orders from the MNA, they fought under the name of "Army of National Liberation" and wore ALN uniforms. The FLN, however, had not sanctioned this attempt to jump on to their bandwaggon. In the earliest days of the rival— or complementary—ALN, the lower grades of both organisations collaborated together and even shared in the buying and distribution of arms. But the honeymoon was short-lived. Abbane, one of the Kabyle (Berber) leaders of the FLN, wrote to his friends in Cairo on April 12th: "We have decided to strike down all the Messalist leaders." It was shortly after this that Messali's envoys to Cairo were arrested.

In Algeria and in metropolitan France, the new orders were executed with typical ferocity. "All through the spring and summer," writes Bromberger, "uniformed bodies of ALN men were found abandoned on the field: all were Messalists. The FLN chief of the Izerazen district, having persuaded one group to join him, spread its members out among his units, and three days later had their throats cut."

Bromberger may not be a reliable witness. But the evidence comes from many sources. In France, the settling of accounts between FLN and MNA continued for years. In Algeria, the MNA was swiftly reduced to impotence and, in most places, simply exterminated. So also were those who had helped the MNA. The most publicised incident, but by no means the only one, took place in May, 1957. Three hundred villagers of Kabylia, suspected rightly or wrongly of having helped the MNA, were herded together into the village of Kasba Mechta and knifed or shot to death.

Massacre or individual murder was often supplemented by mutilation before death, and sometimes by torture. Favourite methods of torture were red-hot pokers and boiling water poured from a kettle. Mutilation consisted of the amputation, by the knife, of nose, tongue, lips, ears or sexual parts. In many cases, the victims of mutilation were not killed off. In the massacres, neither women nor children, or even babies, were spared.

Although these methods were used far more often against fellow-Moslems than against the European settlers, the Europeans did, of course, come in for their share of terrorism. So did the Jews, equally infidels. The worst massacres of Europeans were those of August 20th, 1955. On that day, the ALN launched a general offensive in an arc extending from Collo and Philippeville on the Mediterranean coast to the mountains of Gounod. The military terminology is perhaps misleading. The only strictly military objectives were barracks and gendarmeries, where all weapons were to be seized. For the rest, the order was simply to kill every European in sight. Jacques Soustelle, who was then Governor-General of Algeria, has written a horrifying account of that day in his emotional, often wrong-headed but sometimes moving book *Aimée et Souffrante Algérie*. At Constantine, the first victim was not a European but Abbas Alloua, nephew of the nationalist leader Ferhat Abbas who, at that time, had not yet joined the FLN. His murderers were themselves killed within minutes by a French military patrol. On one of their bodies the soldiers found an FLN order for the execution of Abbas, who belonged to a rival nationalist organisation. M. Soustelle reproduces the order in an appendix, together with the text of an FLN statement disclaiming responsibility for the killing and for many other acts of terrorism. The worst of the massacres took place at the mining settlement of El Halia, where the European miners, together with their families, were killed to the last infant.

In Algiers and the larger towns, home-made bombs and hand-grenades were the favourite weapons of terrorism against the Europeans. The most spectacular incidents were the bomb explosions in two restaurants in Algiers on September 30th, 1956 (four killed, sixty wounded), and a series of bomb explosions in the same city in November of the same year.

In Algeria, as in Malaya and Indo-China, terrorism was not a decisive weapon of rebellion. Its effects, however, were far from negligible, particularly in the early stages. In this respect, too, the Algerian experience conforms to pattern. Soustelle has this to say about it: ". . . terror is a psychological lever of unbelievable power. Before the bodies of those who throats have been cut and the grimacing faces of the mutilated, all capacity for resistance lapses: the spring is broken." It is certain that the FLN's methods achieved conformity among the Moslems and sowed disarray among the French. It is not clear whether Soustelle's remarks applied to Moslems, or to Europeans, or both. In any event, terrorism brought diminishing returns, in Algeria as elsewhere. It is naturally easier, however, to substantiate the truth of this statement in relation to the French than in relation to the Moslems. All accounts agree that the settlers in Algiers were thoroughly unnerved by the terrorist offensive of 1956. But they were never on the point of surrendering. In itself, the dramatic nature of the terrorist challenge ensures a dramatic response to the call for counter-action. The effect of FLN terrorism on French policy was to strengthen the resolve to stamp out the rebellion, indeed to make it politically impossible to follow any other course. The massacre of Kasba Mechta, in particular, by its impact on French and world opinion, was a major setback to the rebel cause.

It is of course difficult to disentangle terrorism from guerrilla war in Algeria. Once the FLN's army had been established on a regular basis in 1957 there was less need of terrorism. In Algiers itself, and in the larger cities, the terrorist machine had, in any case, been dismantled. Terrorism having failed to bring victory, the rebellion settled down as a war of attrition, in which the rebels' capacity to ruin France financially through ever-mounting costs played as great a part in their calculations as military strategy.

As for the Moslem population, it remained terrorised, and therefore obedient, wherever the ALN was stronger than the French Army; in many places, like the Vietminh in the Red River delta of Tonking, it was stronger by night and weaker by day in the same locality. The overwhelmingly youthful population of Algeria solved all recruiting problems automatically. But the allegiance of the population was probably never universal. The referendum on General de Gaulle's constitution in September, 1958, provided an interesting test-case. More than 87 per cent of Moslem votes were cast in favour of the constitution, or, more accurately, of the General as potential saviour and peacemaker. As a popular consultation, the value of the referendum was open to doubt; without the French Army's protection, the Moslems might not have voted at all. But on any reading of the result, it was a defeat for the FLN, which had ordered a boycott and threatened reprisals for the disobedient.

* * *

The only outbreak of rebel terrorism that competes in savagery with the Algerian methods—and indeed outdistances them—is the Mau Mau insurrection in Kenya from 1952. I have already quoted from the second of the series of oaths which initiates of the society were required to take. This was a simple murder oath. Conceivably, this oath would have been only partially effective in a community with centuries of civilisation behind it. In a tribal community where magic and witchcraft still played an important part, the oath was binding. To the extent that tribal superstititions might have proved inadequate, the gap was filled by fear of personal violence or death for defectors or the faint-hearted.

The murder oath was, however, complemented by several "higher" oaths. I have not read specific accounts of the more advanced Mau Mau oaths, but those who have are agreed that they entailed bestial and degrading practices. The object of them appears indeed to have been the degradation of those who performed these practices. Degraded, they became outcasts who shrank at nothing; the acts performed were intended to be so depraved that, in comparison, the mere disembowelling of pregnant women, for instance, would seem mild. Leakey, who takes refuge in some of the adjectives I have used, plus many others, tells us that Kikuyu law recognised two acts for which there could be no purification: incest with one's mother and sexual intercourse with a ewe. He adds that the higher Mau Mau oaths involved the performance of a whole series of still more revolting acts, designed to make it impossible for the performer ever to be accepted back into normal Kikuyu society.

It is, then, small wonder that Mau Mau violence outstrips even Algerian violence. In its objectives and in most of the incidents, however, Mau Mau terrorism is much the same as terrorism elsewhere. The population was to be intimidated; traitors were to be punished; and life was to be made unbearable for the enemy, the European settlers. Mau Mau methods, backed by an efficient organisation, ensured the hold of terror over the Kikuyu. The machinery for dealing with traitors was strengthened as time went on. Mau Mau courts were set up, at first to fine members who had not paid their dues, then to extort money from the wealthier members of the tribe who did not belong to the society. Those who refused to pay fines, sometimes running into hundreds of pounds, were sentenced to death. As with the FLN, Mau Mau executions were swift and brutal, mutilation or strangling being the favourite methods. Against Europeans, Mau Mau operations fell into two categories: "military" operations and harassing operations against the civilians. The first category consisted mainly of raids of various kinds aimed at seizing arms. The second category consisted of raids on European-owned farms, the massacre of people living there, the hamstringing of cattle, the burning of grain stores and other acts of this nature.

Like the communists in Malaya but with less justification, the Mau Mau leaders affected military ranks, with a particular predilection for the higher ones, including "field-marshal". Nevertheless, the society never emerged from the terrorist stage of rebellion. Its activities therefore provide useful material for the study of pure terrorism for political objectives. These objectives included the recovery of alienated Kikuyu lands, self-government and the expulsion or subjugation of the Europeans. None of them was achieved. Whether these objectives are achieved later by other means is irrelevant: terrorism alone did not achieve them.

As with the other examples I have mentioned so far, Mau Mau

terrorism, as such, achieved only short-lived successes. In the early months of the insurrection, a number of Europeans decided that Kenya had become a place without a future, packed up and left. They were, however, a small minority. Most settlers were unshakeably resolved to stay, and their resolve was further strengthened as the security forces gained strength. The effect of Mau Mau terrorism on the native population, though deep, was mainly confined to the Kikuyu tribe. Some members of the Kamba and Teita tribes were drawn into Mau Mau, as they had been in the old Kenya Africa Union, which preceded it. But Mau Mau influence was never very strong over the Luo, Masai, Kipsigis and Bantu Kavirondo. As for the Kikuyu themselves, terrorism did bring considerable returns, but not for long. The Lari episode of March, 1953, when hundreds of Kikuyu were butchered, burned alive or mutilated, pregnant women disembowelled alive and children cut to pieces, did the society no good. Leakey says of it: "As the news of the Lari massacre spread, Kikuyu, all over the country, including many who had previously supported the movement, were so revolted by what had happened that I believe it is true to say that Lari marked the turning-point in Mau Mau fortunes."

* * *

In comparison with the Algerian and Kenyan horrors, Cypriot terrorism seems almost gentle. Even more than Mau Mau, Eoka provides an example of "pure" terrorism, undiluted by military complications Eoka was never an army and never looked like becoming one. It was a small, well-knit terrorist pressure group, consisting of two elements: a hard core of trained saboteurs and, in the towns, murder squads. When I visited Cyprus in the spring of 1956, it was not thought that the total hard core membership of Eoka exceeded sixty. On the other hand, the activities of the murder squads and saboteurs were supplemented by cells in the secondary schools.

As with the Malayan Emergency, there was a tedious sameness about Eoka incidents. On the one hand, there were "military" operations, organised by the saboteurs in the hills, and consisting of attacks on police-stations and arms stores, ambushes of service vehicles and, of course, sabotage. On the other hand, there were the purely terrorist incidents. These in turn fell into two groups: bomb incidents of various kinds and individual murders. The murders were normally the work of the murder squads in the towns; in most cases, the victims were alone, unarmed and were shot in the back. The bomb incidents were often the work of teenagers.

If I have described Eoka's methods as comparatively gentle, I ought to emphasise the strength of the Algerian or Kenyan competition. It should not be supposed that the Greek Cypriot terrorists were any less fanatical than those of the FLN or Mau Mau; to the extent that they preferred bullets and bombs to torture, mutilation and disembowelling, they seemed gentler. The resulting deaths were no less permanent.

It is exceedingly difficult to assess the returns of terrorism in Cyprus. In strictly military terms, the campaign did not impede the usefulness of Cyprus as base, such as it was: during the Anglo-French expedition to Egypt in November, 1956, the airborne operations from the island were not hampered by Cypriot terrorism. On the other hand, the forces at Britain's disposal in Cyprus were never sufficient to pursue terrorists and mount expeditions simultaneously. The Suez expedition interrupted an intensive anti-terrorist drive by the security forces and gave Eoka a useful breathing spell in which to regroup and rearm. Moreover, while the terrorism went on, public opinion in Britain was exposed to the kind of pressures that had been felt during the period of Egyptian terrorism in the Suez Canal base and of Jewish terrorism in Palestine. On the one hand, Conservative MPs and newspapers repeated that there could be no surrender to terrorism. On the other hand, Labour MPs and left-wing or simply liberal journals argued that the base was useless anyway, that there was no point in staying in a place where one was not wanted and that the Cypriots ought to be given the right of self-determination. The Conservative arguments tended naturally to prevail during a period of Conservative government in Britain. The Suez expedition, however, exposed both the deficiencies of Cyprus as a base and Britain's reduced capacity for independent action as a great power. Until then, the government did not seriously seek an integral solution of the Cypriot problem. Thereafter it did. It cannot be said that terrorism was a decisive factor in this change of attitude. On the other hand, the Cypriot problem, which had existed in dormant state for several decades, would not have become acute without Eoka's intervention. To that extent, there was a link between terrorism and policy-making in Whitehall and Westminster.

In the sphere of morale, although terrorism could not fail to affect the nerve of the British in Cyprus, the remarkable thing is how little it was affected. The effect on the Greek Cypriot population—admittedly the major target—was much deeper. Outwardly, Eoka's methods achieved complete conformity. Even the Greek police became unreliable after some months of murders in which they were frequently the targets. The point is not whether Eoka was loved: it was certainly obeyed. There is an interesting concrete example of this fact. On October 28th, 1955, Archbishop Makarios publicly called for the resignation of all Greek village Mukhtars or headmen. The date was symbolically chosen, for October 28th, known as *Okhi* Day ("No" Day) is the anniversary of the Greek refusal to submit to the Italian ultimatum in 1940. Only about a fifth of the headmen had responded by the end of the year, however. Eoka then went into action by murdering three headmen. Within three weeks, resignations reached 80 per cent.

In the early stages of the campaign, the Turkish population of Cyprus was left unmolested. The murders of Turkish police constables in 1957 and 1958, however, provoked violent Turkish reactions, both on the Turkish mainland, where mass demonstrations and murders of Greeks took place, and on the island. From relative indifference, Turkish Cypriots turned to fanatical demands for partition. In relation to the Turkish minority, therefore, Eoka terrorism produced effects that were the opposite to those intended.

3
Terrorist Successes

IN every instance I have considered so far, terrorism has appeared to be an instrument of dubious value, at best of short-
lived potency, never decisive. I now submit two further examples
which suggest that in certain circumstances, terrorism may be a
decisive instrument of rebellion. Those examples are the events
in Palestine between 1944 and 1948, and in Egypt between 1951
and 1954. The evidence is perhaps not conclusive in either case;
but it is strong enough to indicate the circumstances in which
terrorism may decide a political issue.

This is not a history, and the events of Palestine and Egypt
need not be analysed in all their complexity. I confine myself to
those that have a bearing on the effectiveness of terrorism and to
the barest outline of essential background.

In Palestine there were two terrorist organisations and a
military one, and they need to be seen in relation to each other.
The military organisation was Haganah, the Jewish home defence force, founded in Palestine in 1917. It consisted of three
branches: a static force of settlers and town dwellers numbering
40,000; a field army of 16,000 based on the Jewish Settlement
Police and trained in mobile operations; and Palmach, a full-
time, mobile striking force of about 6,000. The larger of the
terrorist organisations was Irgun Zvai Leumi, with a secret command and between 3,000 and 5,000 members. The smaller was the
Stern Gang, consisting of 200 to 300 terrorists. Irgun was formed
in 1935 by dissident members of Haganah; the Stern Gang, in
turn, originated as a dissident faction within the Irgun, when the
parent body decided to suspend operations in 1939. There was
thus a progression in fanaticism from Haganah, through Irgun to
the Stern Gang.

That the three organisations were equally dedicated to Zionist
aims goes without saying; but Haganah's immediate objectives

did not coincide with those of Irgun and the Stern Gang during the first part of the period that interests us. Later, there were identity of objectives and practical co-operation between Haganah and Irgun on the one hand and between Irgun and the Stern Gang on the other. A lucid and impartial account of these changing relations was given by Harry Sacher in *Israel: The Establishment of a State* (1952).

Haganah was, of course, the militant arm of the Jewish Agency, whose policy was based on the Balfour Declaration of 1917 and on the League of Nations Mandate of 1922. The Mandate, which incorporated the Declaration, supported the establishment of a Jewish national home in Palestine. In 1944, when Jewish terrorism against the British started in Palestine, the Jewish Agency had a dual objective: to uphold the Mandate and to fight the British White Paper of May, 1939, which, by restricting Jewish immigration, in effect invalidated the Mandate. In 1944, as Sacher put it, "the Jewish Agency was still at war with the White Paper, not with the Mandatory Power". This war was fought on more than one front. On a diplomatic front, the Jewish Agency tried to enlist American support for increased Jewish immigration; on the militant front, it organised the shipment of illegal immigrants. The diplomatic initiative need not concern us here. The execution of the militant campaign was partly entrusted to Haganah, which was charged with neutralising the British administration's efforts to keep the illegal immigrants out. At this stage, however, Haganah's operations were not aimed against the British forces; and its orders were to avoid, as far as possible, bloodshed.

The terrorist organisations, on the other hand, made no distinction between British policy and British nationals. From the beginning, Britain was the enemy and British citizens or property were legitimate targets. The Stern Gang's most notorious exploits spanned the entire period of terrorism; they were the murders of Lord Moyne, the British Minister Resident in the Middle East, in Cairo on November 6th, 1944, and of Count Bernadotte, the United Nations mediator, in Jerusalem on September 17th, 1948. Irgun, on the whole, was less interested in the

individual murder than in the mass outrage. Its most spectacular
operation was the blowing up of the Palestine Administration's
headquarters in the King David Hotel in Jerusalem on July 22nd,
1946. But the range of terrorist activities in Palestine was fairly
wide: trains were derailed and robbed; police officers and army
personnel were kidnapped; Royal Air Force camps, army and
government establishments were attacked. In two respects, however, the Palestine terrorists differed from some of the other
terrorists I have mentioned. The more blood-curdling methods
of terrorism—such as torture and mutilation—seem to have been
avoided; and terrorist activities were not, or virtually not,
directed against the terrorists' own side. The incident that most
shocked British public opinion was the kidnapping and murder
by hanging of two British sergeants whose bodies were found on
July 31st, 1947; booby-trap mines had been placed under the
swinging bodies. But this incident, though calculated to outrage
public feelings, scarcely competes in horror with Algerian or
Kikuyu terrorism. The absence of a "death to traitors" movement
is important: it suggests that such a campaign was unnecessary
because mass support existed anyway. In fact, however, it would
be misleading to speak of mass support of terrorism in the early
stages; but neither Irgun nor Stern members seem at any time to
have been in danger of betrayal to the British. The nearest approach to a "death to traitors" campaign came in September,
1946. On the 15th, the Jewish Agency had condemned Irgun's
money-raising methods: robberies of banks and government
institutions and levies on the Jewish population. Three days later,
a Haganah pamphlet attacked Irgun and Stern for gangsterism
and armed robbery, drug trafficking and black marketeering, and
announced measures to stamp out terrorism. Irgun's reply was a
threat to shoot any Haganah member who betrayed them. But as
Sacher points out, Haganah had no such intention.

The relationship between the terrorist organisations on the one
hand and the Jewish Agency and Haganah on the other was by
no means consistently antagonistic. The Jewish Agency was
divided into moderates like Mr. Ben-Gurion, who wanted no

truck with terrorism, and extremists like Dr. Sneh, who favoured a tactical alliance with the terrorists. It was Dr. Sneh who was in control of Haganah. In December, 1944, as a reaction to the murder of Lord Moyne, the Jewish Agency decided to fight terrorism by driving terrorists out of work, denying them shelter, resisting threats and co-operating with the government.

By the autumn of 1945, because of disappointment at the attitude of the new British Labour Government, the anti-terrorist policy was discarded. In October, Dr. Sneh, on behalf of Haganah, reached a working arrangement with Irgun and Stern, under which the terrorist groups were to carry out tasks assigned to them by Haganah. The British White Paper on terrorist activities in Palestine (Cmd. 5873), issued in July, 1946, was thus right, but probably premature, in alleging that the three militant organisations were working together.

Active co-operation continued for about a year, and Haganah acquiesced in the King David Hotel outrage. In consequence, Ben-Gurion, from his exile in Paris, removed Haganah from Dr. Sneh's control. In September, 1946, as we have seen, the Agency and Haganah again declared war, though not total war, on terrorism. After a further fifteen months of intensified terrorist activity, Haganah resumed its co-operation with the terrorists. This brings the story to December, 1947. On the 11th, the Colonial Secretary, Mr. Creech Jones, had announced in the House of Commons that Britain intended to terminate the Mandate not later than May 15th, 1948, and to evacuate its troops from Palestine by August 1st, 1948. This was the situation when the Agency and Irgun opened negotiations with a view to co-operating in the impending struggle for the establishment of a Jewish state.

Thus for nearly half the terrorist period, the terrorists enjoyed an alliance with the militant mass organisation, and therefore the active support of the Jewish population; for the remainder of that time they enjoyed at least a measure of passive support and immunity from betrayal. The terrorists were consequently stronger in Palestine than they were in Vietnam, Malaya, Cyprus, Algeria or Kenya.

In the light of this factual background, it is possible to assess the returns of Palestinian terrorism with greater precision than in my previous examples. Whereas elsewhere terrorism brought rapid but diminishing returns, in Palestine the returns were meagre at first and increased later on. The assassination of Lord Moyne in the early period worked against the terrorists' own interests in two ways. In the first place, it was the signal for the first anti-terrorist campaign launched by the Jewish Agency under Ben-Gurion. In the second place, it caused Mr. Churchill, then Prime Minister, to defer indefinitely his plans for Palestine. The choice of Lord Moyne as a victim was indeed doubly unfortunate: not only was Lord Moyne a close friend of Mr. Churchill, but Churchill's attitude was known to be friendly towards the Jews; the murder caused a revulsion of feeling which, for a time, led to a marked setback for Jewish aspirations.

Similarly, the King David Hotel explosion led to the second Agency campaign against terrorism and to the removal of the extremist Dr. Sneh as controller of Haganah. These two incidents marked the precise point at which terrorism ceased to bring returns.

On the whole, however, Jewish terrorism must, in retrospect, be accounted as one of the decisive factors in Britain's decision to abandon the Mandate, and therefore in the establishment of Israel as a state. Once again, as in Algeria and elsewhere, one of the effects of terrorism in Palestine was to force the responsible power into ever-mounting expenditure on security. On May 20th, 1947, the assistant Secretary for Economic Affairs in the Palestine Administration announced that expenditure on security would rise to an estimated £8 million in 1947, compared with £4·5 million in 1945. Mounting costs might have been borne, terrorist harassment withstood and American pressure resisted *if retention of the Mandate had been essential to Britain's security or economic survival.* But demonstrably, it was not. When Mr. Creech Jones announced the decision to quit, in the parliamentary debate on December 11th, 1947, he put the situation succinctly: "The perpetuation of the Mandate régime implied increasingly

active and costly military commitments, and a situation deterior-
ating by lawlessness, terrorism and non-co-operation by the Jewish
community with the government." More succinctly still, terrorism
had won.

*   *   *

In the Suez Canal Zone, Egyptian terrorism was equally successful. The signal was the unilateral abrogation by Egypt on October
15th, 1951, of the 1936 Treaty with Britain. Two weeks earlier,
Iranian agitation had forced the Anglo-Iranian Oil Company to
evacuate the Abadan refinery. No British Government would
have found this an appropriate moment for appeasement. Labour
was in power. Speaking in the House of Commons about eighteen
months later—on May 11th, 1953—Sir Winston Churchill, himself back in power, outlined the actions of his predecessor, Mr.
Attlee, and the Labour Foreign Secretary, Mr. Herbert Morrison.
They had, said Sir Winston, ordered British troops in the Canal
Zone to protect themselves and prepare to protect British civilians
from outrage and massacre. "A kind of guerrilla war" had broken
out.

The "kind of guerrilla war" had, in fact, started during Labour's
last few days in power. On October 25th, 1951, Churchill's
government took over and carried on where Labour had left off,
for this was a national, not a party, matter. Yet three years later,
the same government had signed an agreement with Egypt providing for the evacuation of the Canal Zone base.

What had happened in those three years? There were three
waves of incidents: from October, 1951, to July, 1952, when a
period of calm followed the young officers' revolution; from
July, 1953, till the end of the year, with a lull in September; and
from March, 1954, till the end of May. There were two unusual
features about the Canal Zone terrorism: it was relatively mild,
and it was fairly evidently carried out under the orders of successive Egyptian governments or, at the least, with their connivance.

To say that the terrorism was mild is not to deny its unpleasantness for those who bore the brunt of it; and indeed there

was a ration or murders. Mr. Anthony Nutting, then Under-Secretary at the Foreign Office, gave the House of Commons some figures on June 16th, 1954: between October 16th, 1951, and June 1st, 1954, he said, forty-seven British service-men had been killed in the Canal Zone; there had been ten cases of sabotage by arson and 3,297 thefts of official property. This amounted to a fairly continuous harassment, perhaps, rather than "a kind of guerrilla war", although men lost their lives.

The responsibility of the Egyptian Government is hardly in question. The Nahas Pasha government, on October 13th, 1951, had demanded the immediate and unconditional withdrawal of the British forces in the Canal Zone. The unilateral abrogation of the 1936 treaty (which still had five years to run) took place on the 15th, and the incidents started the next day. The government withdrew the whole Egyptian labour force from the Zone, and encouraged the recruitment of students and strong-arm men for "liberation units" to fight in the Zone. All this was done to an accompaniment of anti-British propaganda in press and radio. The Nahas government was dismissed by King Farouk after the uncontrolled anti-British riots in Cairo on January 26th, 1952, in which tens of thousands of unemployed Egyptian labourers from the Canal Zone played a major part. But the incidents in the Zone continued under Nahas's successor, Aly Maher Pasha. They were resumed under the Revolutionary Junta after it had consolidated itself in power, although General Nagib agreed that Egypt should pay Britain £96,000 compensation for damage during the Cairo riots. On May 25th, 1953, Nagib announced a plan for the expulsion of the "imperialist forces" from the Canal Zone. The first stage was to be a boycott against the occupation forces and everything British. Although Nagib said nothing about force, he did say that the British could easily be dislodged at any chosen moment. In Britain, it was generally accepted, by those who had investigated the matter, that the incidents were organised by the Egyptian Government; more specifically, that they were directed by an officer of the Egyptian Army's intelligence service. Certainly, the Egyptian Government was able to stop them whenever it thought fit or whenever they showed signs of getting out of control. Three instances may be given. On May 30th and 31st, a few days after announcing his plan to expel the British, Nagib had fifty Egyptians and foreigners arrested in the Zone; the Egyptians were said to include some "super-patriotic hotheads". A second instance occurred during the same year, in December, when the Nagib government transferred additional police to the Zone. The number of incidents immediately decreased; it increased again in January when the reinforcement were withdrawn to deal with the anti-Nasser Moslem Brotherhood in Cairo. There was a further lull after Colonel Nasser had seized power on February 24th, 1954, when more "hotheads" were arrested in the Zone.

For the Egyptian Government, the dilemma was how to use enough terrorism to make it difficult, expensive and uncomfortable for the British to remain in the Canal Zone, yet not so much as to make it politically impossible for the British Government to withdraw. The British Government's dilemma was the converse of the Egyptian one: how to reach a negotiated solution without appearing to negotiate under duress. The pressure of the right-wing Conservative MPs against negotiations exerted itself increasingly with each wave of incidents. By March 22nd, 1954, the government had evidently made up its mind to withdraw, but Mr. Eden, then Foreign Secretary, told the House that the incidents in the Zone made the resumption of the Anglo-Egyptian talks impossible. The talks were in fact resumed in July, after the incidents had ceased. The previous series of talks had taken place in Cairo, on an informal basis, between July 30th and October 21st, 1953. Apart from the lull in September, this was a period of continuous incidents; the lull suggests an Egyptian response to a British threat to break off the talks; the resumption of terrorism in October suggests, in turn, an Egyptian attempt to force the issue.

In the final analysis, it seems probable that the Egyptian terrorism was the principal cause of Britain's decision to withdraw from the Canal Zone. It was not, of course, the only one:

there is general agreement among observers of these events that a major factor was the unremitting pressure in favour of withdrawal exerted by the United States through its Ambassador in Cairo, Mr. Jefferson Caffery. Captain Waterhouse, leader of the Conservative MPs who rebelled against the Anglo-Egyptian settlement (the "Suez rebels") made a sarcastic reference to the Ambassador in the House of Commons debate on July 29th, 1954: "For many years we have had a little American lamb bleating in Cairo, not helping and if anything hindering in most things."

The government itself gave further reasons in the same debate. Mr. Anthony Head, Secretary of State for War, who had initialled the heads of agreement in Cairo two days earlier, gave three reasons: the advent of the hydrogen bomb had diminished the usefulness of the base; Turkey's decision to join Nato had made the British presence less necessary and the base was, in any case, remote from the area in which fighting was most likely to occur in the event of war; and the British forces were "overstretched and overstrained" (there were at that time 80,000 British personnel in the Zone, including 60,000 troops). The third of these carried more conviction than the first two; but the War Secretary came nearer the probable truth in a parenthetical remark that the Canal Zone "facilities would be of little or no use to us in peace or in war with a hostile Egypt". He went on: "Unless there is a better spirit and more co-operation in Egypt, it will be vain to expect that we can take any useful advantage of these facilities."

The cat was out of the bag. And it scampered figuratively across the floor of the House as Mr. Head went on to argue that to stay put "would be provocative and would result in an increase of banditry and terrorism". What, he asked, would happen to the lines of communication of the Canal Zone force in that event? "One could either supply that force by air," said Mr. Head, "as in the case of the Berlin airlift—but surely one would look rather stupid with a beleaguered garrison in Egypt being supplied by air; or one could reinforce with more troops in order to safeguard one's lines of communication." This, he concluded, would be not only provocative but militarily and politically unacceptable.

In other words, once again terrorism had won.

* * *

Where do the facts lead us? Every example I have given confirms my initial proposition that terrorism is an instrument of the weak. Equally, every example makes it clear that the terrorists cannot hope to succeed unless they enjoy a ready supply of arms and the support of the overwhelming majority of the population. The need for arms is self-evident: it is underlined by the fact that almost the only "legitimate" activity of terrorists everywhere is the raid on places likely to provide a supply of arms. As for the support of the population, it is unlikely to be by coincidence that the places where terrorism apparently succeeded—such as Egypt and Palestine—were those where the terrorists did enjoy unquestioned support. In places where this support is half-hearted or confined to a minority, the terrorists are forced to dissipate their energies—and waste their ammunition—in efforts to keep their nominal supporters in line. In such places, though terrorism may win spectacular successes for a time, it does not appear to be a decisive instrument of rebellion. Beyond a certain point, the horror of terrorist deeds is likely to work against the interests of those who order or perform them. Continuous harassment, coupled with murders, appears to bring greater returns than unrestrained savagery. Finally, the success of terrorism probably depends less on the actual outrages committed than on the mounting expenditure forced on the "enemy" for purposes of security. This expenditure, particularly in parliamentary democracies, is subject to scrutiny by politicians and in the press. When the question "Is it worth it?" begins to be asked, the terrorists are winning. When the answer is "No", they have won.

PART V

REPRESSION

I

Official Violence

WHEN the Russian peasants resisted collectivisation, Stalin allowed five million of them to starve to death. When he was consolidating his power and industrialising the Soviet Union in the 'thirties, he sent unnumbered millions to forced labour camps and nearly wiped out a generation of administrators. When the Nazis invaded Russia he deported an entire people, the Chechen-Ingush, from the Caucasus to Siberia, because he thought they might have collaborated with the Germans. During the great purges, he caused seven presidents of "sovereign" republics of the USSR, and six prime ministers, to be shot, as John Gunther, that great compiler of facts about countries, has pointed out.

These are random and well-known examples of a terror that lasted more than twenty years. Together they constitute repression on a scale and of an intensity unique in the twentieth century. For a student of rebellion, the Stalinist example is compelling: it will always stand as the ultimate instance of the repressive power of the state, the criterion by which other attempts at repression must be judged.

It must be allowed that Stalin's repression was successful: he did impose collectivisation on the peasants, he did wipe out all rivals, he did industrialise Russia, and he managed to die in his bed at the reasonable age of 73, whether or not the cause of death was natural. We shall never know whether he forced the Russian people to pay too high a price, by his own concepts, although the Chinese experiment, so far, does suggest that he could have accomplished all he did while exterminating only a fraction of the Soviet citizens who met their deaths during his reign. The Chinese communists, in contrast, set out deliberately, in their early years of power, to liquidate various categories of people who, they believed, would never play a useful part in the society they were planning to impose on the Chinese people. The numbers thus liquidated were certainly not as small as the 50,000 C. P. Fitzgerald mentions in *Flood Tide in China*; nor, on the other hand, as large as the 25 million claimed by the Chinese Nationalists. For reasons that have no relevance to this book, I believe the actual figure to have been somewhere between 800,000 and 900,000. The point is that once these people had been executed, the Chinese communists set about accomplishing by massive persuasion what Stalin had accomplished by physical terror. But when faced with a real rebellion, as in Tibet, they adopted the techniques of repression that had been used by Stalin's successors in Hungary in November, 1956.

From their own point of view, I have no doubt that the Chinese communists were right to attempt to impose their ideas with a minimum of physical violence. In any case, violence was kept in reserve, and the official capacity for using it had been demonstrated during the period of the executions, which took place in public.

The Soviet and Chinese examples illustrate contrasting methods of ruling a people against its will. On the one hand, a constant official terror, suppressing rebellion before it has taken root. On the other hand, a nation-wide mobilisation of the techniques of persuasion and propaganda, designed to make all sections of the people participate, apparently of their own free will, in the revolution. But the two major communist systems have this in common: when terror or persuasion has failed and an insurrection nevertheless breaks out, it must be ruthlessly and violently crushed.

It is patent that the democratic countries—at any rate since the war—have been far less successful in crushing rebellions than the communist countries. True, the Mau Mau insurrection was crushed, but, as we have seen, the authorities had many things in their favour: the Kikuyu are only one of the tribes of Kenya, and the other tribes did not support Mau Mau; the revolting practices of Mau Mau alienated many of the Kikuyu themselves; the rebels were primitive and the security forces had contemporary techniques of repression at their disposal. But most other cases of attempted suppression failed. When these words were being written, the Algerian rebellion had lasted about four and a half years. The French were driven out of Indo-China. The British failed to crush the Zionist rebels in Palestine or the Egyptian saboteurs in the Suez Canal Zone. The Indonesian Republic failed to crush the Darul Islam Movement or the major rebellion of 1958 in the decisive way that it had crushed the communist uprising at Madiun ten years earlier. The Burma army was still fighting the Karen rebels ten years after independence. In all these instances, to a greater or lesser degree, the authorities put their main reliance on pure suppression: the official use of force. Political concessions either came late, were inadequate or did not come at all.

Perhaps the most interesting example of the failure of a policy of suppression was that of Cyprus. That Eoka, the terrorist movement, was itself unsuccessful does not affect the point: it was still fighting and its organisation more or less intact when the political settlement of the Cypriot problem was reached in London in March, 1959. The settlement itself, and the ending of the insurrection, were due entirely to political initiatives that had nothing to do with repression. It happens that these initiatives were taken after the replacement of Field-Marshal Sir John Harding by Sir Hugh Foot, as Governor of Cyprus. But though Sir Hugh ably and nobly played his part in helping to make the settlement possible, the initiatives that led to it resulted from a change of policy in London, not from Sir Hugh's administration of the island. Indeed, Sir Hugh's appointment was itself the effect, not the cause, of this change of policy. Conversely, Field-Marshal Harding failed not because of shortcomings in his administration but because he was required to administer a policy that was doomed to failure from the start. It has often been said of this delightful and much-maligned man that he was too ruthless in Cyprus; "Butcher Harding" was a label which the Greeks tried to pin on him. But this is the sheerest nonsense: given that Sir John was required to suppress a rebellion, without simultaneous political advance, he was surely far too *soft*.

I should not like my readers to misunderstand me. Pure repression must be judged by Stalinist standards. The British, however, are not Stalinists or even communists of milder persuasion. Sir John Harding, a kindly man of great charm whom I met at Nicosia when he was Governor of Cyprus, was no Stalin; nor even, for that matter, was he a mere Khrushchev. The unpleasant measures he felt obliged to take aroused enough outcry, even in Britain, for the government to be seriously embarrassed; yet how much worse it would have been had he behaved as the Nazis did in Poland or the Russians in Hungary. It was foolish in the first place to ask him to crush a rebellion, in the knowledge that he could not be completely ruthless, or alternatively, in the knowledge that no further constitutional advance was contemplated in Cyprus. Repression, as I have pointed out, is indivisible.

What Harding did, with every encouragement from the British Government, was to fall neatly between two stools. When I visited Cyprus at the end of May, 1956, he was, for instance, inflicting collective fines on villages where terrorist outrages had taken place. This kind of measure was doubly futile, doubly self-defeating: because it inevitably alienated many innocent people who saw no reason why they should be punished for other people's crimes; and because everybody would rather pay a share in a collective fine than receive a bullet between the shoulder-blades. And that was precisely the choice they faced: if they did not tell the security forces what they had seen, they were fined; but if they had told, they would have been shot by Eoka. If official terror is to be pitted against rebel terrorism, it must be made competitive.

Ruthlessness is not, however, the only way to defeat a rebellion, although governments often misguidedly think it the easiest since it appears to obviate the necessity for thinking. Since the war, some rebellions have been defeated by democratic governments, by a judicious combination of repressive measures and political advances. This is how the Malayan terrorists and the Hukbalahaps of the Philippines were defeated. Both happened to be communist insurrections. There is a touch of piquancy in the thought that though the communists, since the war, have shown themselves the most accomplished suppressers of revolts, they have also displayed a remarkable ineptitude for revolution—their own chosen stock-in-trade.

There are conclusions to be drawn from the examples I have mentioned and from others I have kept in reserve. But I prefer to withhold the conclusions until the evidence has been examined more carefully. We have seen how the major post-war rebellions broke out and tried to find out why. We have found, among other things, that at least some of the frustrations that caused rebellions resulted from official shortcomings. We must now try on the shoes of prime ministers or heads of state, and see what we should do if we were asked to wear them. Despite all our wishes and last-minute measures, a rebellion has broken out. We wish to defeat it. How shall we set about it?

We cannot do better, I suggest, than to look at a few case histories of rebellions that were successfully defeated. From these, we shall attempt to extract principles of general application.

2

The Old Way

IN the flood-tide of British imperialism, the British did not hesitate to shed rebel blood in quantities sufficient to ensure victory for the forces of order. One need only mention the Indian Mutiny, which independent India knows under another name. Since the second world war, they have been engaged, under successive governments, in transforming the Empire into a Commonwealth of many hues. This operation has proved incompatible with total repression. The idea of transforming colonies into partners had not made any headway among the Dutch or the French at the end of the war, and both attempted to re-establish themselves in their Far Eastern territories. Neither was successful, though the French understandably held on much

longer than the Dutch. In Africa, moreover, the French scored
certain limited, but definite, successes. Since they are the best
examples I can find of successful repression by a Western
democracy, I shall turn to these relatively recondite rebellions. I
have in mind the Sétif uprising of May, 1945, and the Malgache
insurrection of March, 1947.

That they *are* recondite is an important point, to which I shall
return. The only full account in English of the Sétif disturbances,
as far as I know, is an article by the American writer Manfred
Halpern, entitled "The Algerian Uprising of 1945", which appeared in *The Middle East Journal* in April, 1948. This account,
from which I borrow some of the facts that follow, in turn bor-
rowed from newspaper reports which I too shall acknowledge.

There is no need, however, to tell the story in the fullest detail.
Sétif is a town of 34,000 in the Berber country of Algeria. The
local French authorities decided to allow a Moslem procession
through the town to celebrate VE-Day, on condition that it was
not to have a political character and that the demonstrators refrained from carrying placards or displaying banners. In the
event, the demonstrators violated both conditions. Between 8,000
and 10,000 strong, they marched down the Rue Clémenceau,
waving French, British, Russian and American flags and trailing
banners that called on the French to free the nationalist leader
Messali Hadj, then under detention, and saying: "We want to be
your equals." Shots were fired and the demonstrators began to
riot. The disturbances soon spread to Kerrata and Guelma, where
200,000 Europeans were living in the midst of 3,400,000 Berbers.

There is no doubt that many of these Europeans were killed,
often in atrocious circumstances. But we are concerned with
repression, and there, it must be said, the evidence is conflicting.
According to one of the newspapers cited by Manfred Halpern,
French ground and air forces killed or wounded more than
10,000 rebels in a nine-day campaign. Bombers were said to have
smashed villages around Constantine and to have made up to 300
sorties in one day: "Entire communities of thatched and dirt
homes were levelled." Ninety-seven Europeans, mostly colonial

administrators, were said to have been killed. This account appeared on May 31st, 1945, in a Casablanca dispatch to the Rome edition of the American Forces newspaper, *Stars and Stripes*.

Another newspaper report appeared nearly a year after the event, in the *New York Times* of April 29th, 1946. "The French," it said, "used not only troops but bombers and gunboats in suppressing the uprising with the utmost severity." The cruisers *Dugay-Trouin*, *Tigre* and *Tempête* were said to have taken part in the pacification; Senegalese troops, Spahis and the Foreign Legion had joined in. By May 16th, eight days after the original demonstration at Sétif, many thousands of rebels had surrendered. The French Minister of the Interior, M. Tixier, in a statement on the Algerian radio on June 29th, said that 5,000 had taken part in the uprising; 88 Frenchmen and women had been killed and 150 wounded; on the Moslem side, between 1,200 and 1,500 had been killed and 2,400 arrested, of whom 517 had been released by June 26th. Later, 170 Moslems were convicted by military courts on charges arising out of the disturbances and 28 of them were sentenced to death. Not all of them were executed. (Mazerna, a follower of Messali Hadj, alleged after being released that he and others had been tortured while in prison.)

M. Tixier, then, had said that between 1,200 and 1,500 Moslems had lost their lives, compared to 88 on the French side. Cyrus L. Sulzberger wrote in the *New York Times* of December 25th, 1946, that the figures were between 7,000 and 18,000 Moslems killed and 200 French. Messali Hadj's estimate was 40,000 and 100 respectively. Later, the Algerian rebel organisation, the FLN, raised the figure of Moslem deaths to 45,000; and on October 13th, 1958, *Time* quoted a French politician as having estimated that "the actual figure was closer to 20,000". Arab defenders of the FLN are fond of attributing to Mr. Pinkney Tuck, former American Ambassador in Cairo, the remark that, according to the State Department's own reports, "well over 40,000" Moslems had been killed. Finally, since this choice of figures must end some time, the report of the official French commission of inquiry estimated the Moslem deaths at not less than 1,020 and not more than 1,340. Dealing with Moslem atrocities, the report said that 103 Europeans had been murdered and several women, including one aged 84, raped by the rioters. It is only fair to add that the commission of inquiry was chaired by a man of liberal views, one of whose collaborators was a Moslem and the other an advocate-general of the Court of Appeal in Algiers.

Let us agree simply that the affair was sanguinary and that repression was whole-hearted. The point is, however, that probably neither Mr. Manfred Halpern nor Mr. Cyrus L. Sulzberger nor I would care to state on oath that this figure or that figure was true beyond all doubt. The revolt took place at a time when the attention of most of the world was concentrated on the allied victories in Europe. The news of it was kept out of the French press, and indeed only barely trickled beyond the borders of Algeria. In a democracy, turmoil and secrecy are the friends of repression.

Admittedly, the same conditions did not apply at the time of the insurrection in Madagascar in March and April, 1947. The events were indeed reported in the press at the time, but for various reasons they aroused relatively little interest or indignation. True, the war was over, but the French public was far too concerned with the more important rebellion in Vietnam to shed as many tears over Madagascar. In Britain, public opinion was infinitely more exercised by the mounting rhythm of terrorism and repression in Palestine. The United States was busy with the opening campaigns of the cold war and with the problem of setting Europe on its feet again after the war. In any event, Madagascar was remote from the main points of world conflict and played no part in the international struggle for power. In brief, not many people cared about what was going on in a large but mysterious island off the eastern coast of Africa.

The French Government of the day did, of course, care, for the insurrection was avowedly aimed at the overthrow of the French administration and the establishment of an independent Madagascar. It was launched on March 29th, 1947, by the *Mouvement Démocratique de la Révolution Malgache*. The planning had been thorough, even if the means turned out to be inadequate.

The day began with concerted attacks on towns, military depots, railways and telegraphic installations. On April 3rd, M. de Coppet, the High Commissioner, declared martial law in a number of districts. About a week later the leaders of the movement were arrested. They included two Malgache deputies to the French National Assembly. It was officially stated at Tananarive, the capital of the island, that they had signed a document ordering the insurrection, and that they were aiming at the restoration of the power of the Hovas, the land-owning class that had ruled Madagascar before the French conquest. In Paris, M. Ramadier, the Prime Minister, attributed the insurrection to France's loss of prestige after the collapse of 1940, further accentuated by the British invasion of Madagascar in 1942, and to the French inability, partly due to lack of shipping, to meet the economic needs of the island. But in a debate in the National Assembly on May 7th, various colonial deputies came a little nearer the deeper cause of the trouble when they accused France of failing to implement the provisions of the constitution conferring self-government on constituent parts of the French Union.

Meanwhile, the insurrection had settled down to intermittent guerrilla warfare. The rebels attacked the gaol at Farafangama, burned private houses and granaries, sabotaged railways and other communications, and destroyed the coffee and tapioca plantations. General Pellet, director-general of military affairs in the French Ministry of Colonies, was appointed Commander-in-Chief in Madagascar and sent there with large reinforcements. On June 25th, he made a final appeal to the insurgents to lay down their arms. It went unheeded, and he then struck with all the force at his disposal.

French accounts of these events, such as Henri Benazet's *L'Afrique Française en Danger*, have been generous with details of rebel atrocities, but reticent about rebel casualties inflicted by the French Army. A British account, which appeared in the review *African Affairs* in April, 1949, quoted an estimate of 20,000 "sympathisers" and 80,000 rebels *killed*, in comparison with European deaths numbering not less than 100 and not more than

800. The author, John T. Gordge, went on to say that the figures quoted for rebel killed were probably greatly exaggerated. There seems little reason, however, to doubt that the Malgaches lost some tens of thousands of insurgents and supporters—though perhaps no more than the 30,000 mentioned in various British newspapers at the time.

Technically, the repressions of 1945 and 1947 were thorough and successful. Politically, though they solved nothing, they were not without value in that they removed the threat of violence against the established authority for several years. The only justification for pure repression ought surely to lie in the use that is made of the years so gained. But in practice an abortive rebellion is rarely followed by political advancement. This is, I think, deplorable, but easily understandable. The people in whose interests the rebellion has been crushed refuse to allow that the people in whose interests the rebels acted should benefit from the rebellion. It was thus in Algeria after the Sétif rebellion. The members of the commission of inquiry were enlightened enough to see the need for conciliation and reconciliation after the bloody incidents of May, 1945. Their report noted the necessity for reassuring both the main communities of Algeria, and added: "It seems also that it is necessary, without delay, to define with clarity and sincerity the political and economic programmes which the authorities will decide to apply in Algeria."

These wise words were not lost on the then Governor-General, M. Chataigneau, but the European community had been unnerved by the events of May and fiercely opposed all his efforts to conciliate the Moslems. I have already traced the sequence of events that led, almost fatally, to the much larger insurrection of November, 1954. The events of May, 1945, ought to have been a warning and a signal for action; instead, they ushered in nine wasted years.

*   *   *

We have seen, in our chapters on terrorism, to what a pass the city of Algiers had been brought by the beginning of 1957. But the events of that period also provide an interesting example of successful official repression. For various reasons, these events may usefully be considered in either of two ways: as part of the wider hostilities in Algeria, or in isolation. At this point in our argument, it is more rewarding to consider the "battle of Algiers", as these events have come to be known, in isolation. From the rebel point of view, Algiers was indeed an isolated sector. It was known to them as the "autonomous zone of Algiers", and during the latter stages of the battle it was completely cut off from other sectors and from the central command of the Army of Liberation. This isolation was indeed one factor in the French success.

The student of terrorism will find in the battle of Algiers an extreme example of the havoc that can be wrought by limited means. According to Serge Bromberger in *Les Rebelles Algériens*, not more than 1,500 to 1,700 people, including casual collaborators, took part in the "battle" on the rebel side. The true terrorists were divided into political, military and information sectors, and subdivided into secret cells. Men and women, youths and girls, including at least one French girl, helped by running messages and carrying home-made bombs.

The student of repression, on his side, will find in this battle for a city a perfect example of what can be accomplished by authority when it concentrates overwhelming strength and skill in a limited area, and when it shrinks at nothing. Both successes— the rebels' and the authorities'—would have been impossible in rural surroundings. In the early stages, the terrorists caught both the authorities and the civilian population unawares and gained the success of terror by the violence and concentration of the blows they struck. The local police had neither the organisation nor the training to deal with terrorism on that scale. By January, 1957, they were completely submerged and the rate of civilians killed had reached 200 a month. In the second half of February, four regiments of paratroops were recalled from normal operational duty, and their commander, the famous General Massu, was given the job of cleaning up Algiers—no holds barred. He began in March, started gaining the upper hand in July and August and completed the job on October 15th with the arrest of the last active sector leader.

It was the combination of military and police methods, ruthlessly applied, that won the day. The traditional *passage à tabac*, or third degree, of the French police was carried by the paratroops to its logical refinement of torture by electric current. Applied at sensitive spots, such as the nipples or genitals, it left no traces and brought results. Those treated in this way included the young Algerian woman Djamila Bouhired and the French communist writer Henri Alleg. Their cases, and a handful of others, became *causes célèbres* through the books they wrote or that were written about their experiences. Public opinion was aroused, both in France and abroad, but by the time the details were known, the battle of Algiers had been won.

Information obtained, whether or not by torture, was immediately acted upon, by troops kept in a constant state of alert, ready and able to do without sleep or rest whenever duty called. Roof-top chases, staircase battles, running gunfights became their normal routine. Often the paratroops, having intercepted a terrorist courier, would be at a rendezvous at the moment when the person for whom the intercepted message had been intended was expected. Speed, surprise, initiative and the sudden concentration of strength on an objective—these were the weapons that smashed the autonomous zone of Algiers, as well as official violence and cruelty. All these and—I think unquestionably—the support of the whole European population of 300,000 and even of the great majority of the Moslems. For pro-French or not, the Moslems were certainly anti-FLN after close acquaintance with its methods. Unquestioned obedience to its dictates was forthcoming only during the period of terrorist ascendancy; it did not last into the period of rebel misfortunes.

3

The Communist Way

THE world of 1956 was already not the world of 1945. In the
intervening eleven years, the subject nations of South-East
Asia had won their independence; the exception, Malaya, was
about to gain it. By October, 1956, Africa was moving in the
same direction. Tunisia and Morocco had become independent
and Ghana had only six months more to wait. The Bandung conference of April, 1955, had given expression to a vague but
powerful feeling of Afro-Asian solidarity against the fast-vanish-
ing force of Western imperialism. Despite French brutalities in
Algeria—a special case because of the large settler population—
it was no longer possible for the Western colonial powers to
resort to pure repression as an instrument of policy. The climate
of world and domestic opinion was against it; and in any case it
had become deliberate policy, particularly in Britain, to avoid it.

No such restraints hampered the communist powers. Repression was a built-in instrument of government, for it was inherent
in the concept of the "dictatorship of the proletariat", expressed
through the "power of the people"—in practice, the power of the
Communist Party. The communist powers were not of course
entirely insensitive to outside opinion, and particularly to the
opinion of communist parties outside the communist bloc. But at
home, particularly in the communist imperialist countries—
Russia and China—all media of information remained firmly in
the hands of the party, which comprehended the government and
the state. Domestic public opinion might have been a factor in
issues of domestic policy, in which the people might be guided by
the evidence around them, but could safely be ignored in foreign
policy, where only officially approved information was available.
These facts are simple but fundamental. They explain why it was
possible for Russia to suppress the Hungarian revolution, and why,
in the last analysis, it proved impossible for Britain and France to

impose their will on President Nasser of Egypt through the Anglo-French military expedition.

The Russian repression of October–November, 1956, was as thorough-going an example of repressive technique as any in modern history, and it is as such that I propose to consider it. Here again the main facts are simple enough. The Soviet Army intervened twice in the revolution: from October 24th to October 29th, and from November 4th to November 11th. In the brief interval, the revolutionaries and their supporters—together constituting almost the entire Hungarian people—had tasted five days of freedom and apparent victory.

Until the Russians intervened, the Hungarian freedom fighters had been opposed by only 30,000 to 40,000 armed members of the notorious political police, the AVH. The Hungarian Army, either openly sided with the insurgents or at least provided them with arms. During the night of October 23rd, the people of Budapest had been fighting the AVH. As dawn broke, they found that they were up against the Soviet Army as well. The Russian tanks entered the capital from several directions between 2 a.m. and 6 a.m. It was at six o'clock that a column of armoured vehicles opened fire without warning near the People's Park. The intervention had begun.

As the United Nations report pointed out, the Soviet forces had been told they were to liquidate counter-revolutionary gangs. On finding that the "gangs" consisted of the entire people, except the political police and the hard core of the rapidly disintegrating party, some of the Russians were embarrassed. Those who had been stationed in Hungary for some time were able to hear the truth from the prisoners they took, and indeed some of the younger freedom fighters spoke Russian, which they had been taught at school. A few Russian officers and soldiers joined the insurgents.

For the majority of the Russians, however, they were in the fight for better, for worse. The Molotov cocktail was the most useful anti-tank device available to the Hungarians. Loosely corked bottles were nearly filled with petrol with towelling around the cork; the bottle was then tilted till the petrol seeped into the towelling; a match, a well-timed throw and another tank would be out of action. Faced with these tactics, the Soviet tanks fired indiscriminately through windows or at people in the streets.

On October 25th, the Soviet leaders, Mikoyan and Suslov, had flown to Budapest. They arranged for the replacement of Gerö by Kadar as Secretary-General of the Hungarian Communist Party. On paper, this move seemed calculated to placate the revolutionaries, for Kadar had spent most of the Rakosi period in prison, where he had been severely tortured by the AVH. It soon became apparent, however, that his loyalty was to the party, right or wrong, and not to the Hungarian people. In contrast, Imre Nagy, called in as Prime Minister, spent most of his brief period of office desperately trying to satisfy popular demands. His first concern was to get the Russian troops, which Gerö had invited in, back to their provincial barracks. Early on October 28th, he announced that the Soviet Government had agreed to withdraw its troops. On October 29th, the Minister of the Interior announced the dissolution of the AVH. On October 31st, Hungary's withdrawal from the Warsaw Pact was declared, and on November 2nd, Nagy formed a coalition cabinet with the participation of the Social Democrats and the re-formed Peasant Party. The Hungarian people appeared to be victorious.

The Soviet troops had indeed withdrawn from Budapest, but it was the clearest case of *reculer pour mieux sauter*. While they were withdrawing, new forces were moving in from the east. They included heavy armoured units manned by troops of Mongolian origin who knew nothing of the Hungarian revolution and had no common language with the local people. Some of them, it appears, thought the Danube was the Suez Canal and that they were fighting against the British and French.

Against this second and more massive intervention, the Hungarians held out, not only in Budapest, but in towns and villages all over Hungary, for six days. Once again but in more systematic fashion, the Soviet tanks drove down the boulevards, firing right and left at every house. The insurgents fought to the end from behind improvised barricades. By November 9th, some 4,000 buildings had been completely destroyed and more than 20,000 damaged; about 35,000 Hungarians had been killed.

Politically, the advancing Russians deposed Nagy and replaced him by Kadar who, for some weeks after the fighting had ceased, continued to rule through the Soviet Army. Nagy himself, who had taken refuge in the Jugoslav embassy, was later abducted by the Russians, tried and executed.

The task of repression had, in effect, been delegated to Kadar. But before he was in a position to pursue it, the Russians had begun to supplement their military massacres with mass deportations of civilians. At first, the procedure was for tanks to seal off each end of a street, while people were rounded up in the streets. The arrests were quite indiscriminate. In one case, fifty people were liberated after being placed in trucks; they were promptly replaced by fifty others, arrested at random. In many cases, shoes and top clothing were removed and the deportees made to travel in unheated trains or lorries, in bitterly cold weather. Although most of the deportees were captured by Soviet troops, many were seized by former members of the AVH, who were collaborating with the Russians. Those seized by the AVH were usually tortured and forced to sign documents confessing that they were "counter-revolutionaries".

On taking over "power" from Nagy, on November 4th, Kadar had stated that "the government will not tolerate the persecution of workers on any pretext for having taken part in recent events". This promise was soon forgotten as he settled down to the business of long-term repression. A series of decrees was passed, establishing a régime of summary jurisdiction against "counter-revolutionary elements, professional criminals, irresponsible trouble-makers and other persons not entitled to possess arms". A new security police was established, under Colonel Laszlo Matyas, who had once shared a cell with Kadar in AVH prisons. But just as Kadar himself, who had suffered from Rakosi's repression, initiated a new repression, so Matyas, who had suffered under the AVH, turned to former AVH members for his recruits.

The revolutionary committees and councils were abolished. Un-authorised public meetings and parades were banned. A State Information Office was established, to supervise the press and information services. Members of the Students' Association were arrested; so were several young university professors and many journalists and writers. The Writers' Union and the Journalists' Association were suspended. The right to strike was abolished; students were deprived of the freedom to choose the language they wished to study. All religious appointments, dismissals or transfers were made subject to the approval of the party praesidium. Finally, on February 6th, a decree was passed increasing the penalties for encouraging or assisting persons attempting to cross the frontier illegally.

It had taken only three months for Mr. Kadar's régime to turn the wheel full circle back to the darkness of the Rakosi era, under which he himself had suffered. The repression was complete.

4

The Sensible Way

IN Malaya and the Philippines, communist challenges of strength were defeated after a bad start, and in conditions that favoured the aggressors. In both countries the tables were turned by the adoption of enlightened methods, leading to a combination of military toughness and political and social progress. In each country—though even more in the Philippines than in Malaya—one man must be accorded the major credit for redressing morale and transforming defeat into victory. These men were Field-Marshal (then General) Sir Gerald Templer, High Commissioner in Malaya, and President Ramón Magsaysay of the Philippines.[1] Both countries provide nearly perfect examples of the kind of repression that a democratic authority may practise without ex-cessive hurt to its public conscience, and therefore with success.

In Malaya's case, the democratic authority I have in mind was

[1] Some observers, however, attribute Magsaysay's successes to his American advisers.

of course the government of the United Kingdom, to which General Templer was responsible. And it is as well to acknowledge straightaway that Templer often did hurt at least a part of the public conscience with the kind of action for which Harding of Cyprus was so bitterly attacked. Like Harding, Templer more than once imposed collective fines on villages which refused to give information about terrorist activities in their midst; on limited occasions, he carried the punishment as far as mass detention and reduction of rations. And it must be seriously doubted that these methods were of any greater value in Malaya than in Cyprus, for in the one as in the other these collective punishments could not compete with the selective terrorism of the rebels. But there was a fundamental difference between the two situations. As we have seen, Sir John Harding in Cyprus was forced to apply a policy of pure, and therefore self-defeating, repression, without parallel political progress. In Malaya, however, Sir Gerald Templer was charged with leading the country as rapidly as possible towards self-government, *while* combating the insurrection. It is not surprising, therefore, that his technique of repression seemed more successful than Harding's.

I "covered" the installation of Sir Gerald Templer as High Commissioner in the Federation of Malaya, for Reuter-Australian Associated Press. It was February, 1952, and terrorism was at its height. I met Sir Gerald, whose martinet tongue and manner impressed me unfavourably at the time, and his gentler successor, Sir Donald MacGillivray. My first impression was shared by most of the journalists present, but was quite unimportant; on the record, Templer was an outstanding success. The situation demanded a martinet. Besides, he showed himself intelligent as well as ruthless.

Templer had brought with him a directive of which the most important passages are these:

> The policy of His Majesty's Government in the United Kingdom is that Malaya should in due course become a fully self-governing nation. His Majesty's Government confidently hope that that nation will be within the British Commonwealth. . . .

Communist terrorism is retarding the political advancement and economic development of the country and the welfare of its peoples. Your primary task in Malaya must, therefore, be the restoration of law and order, so that this barrier to progress may be removed. Without victory and the state of law and order which it alone can bring, there can be no freedom from fear, which is the first human liberty. . . .

You may assure the Malayan peoples of all communities that they can count on the powerful and continuing assistance of His Majesty's Government not only in the immediate task of defeating the terrorists but in the longer objective of forging a united Malayan nation. His Majesty's Government will not lay aside their responsibilities in Malaya until they are satisfied that this Communist terrorism has been defeated and that the partnership of all communities, which alone can lead to true and stable self-government, has been firmly established.

This enlightened directive, which Sir Donald MacGillivray inherited on Templer's departure late in 1954, thus stated a desirable goal, defined the major obstacle and pledged help to overcome it.

It is no less tempting to oversimplify the Malayan situation than other situations of comparable complexity. And indeed in a work of this kind, oversimplification is scarcely avoidable. But it will help to keep the sin within limits, and Templer's achievements within their correct perspective, if I briefly describe the bad start that had been made in fighting the insurrection, and the beginnings of progress under Templer's predecessor as High Commissioner, Sir Henry Gurney.

As I have pointed out in earlier chapters, the terrorists struck at a country that was inadequately protected. But this chapter is concerned with methods rather than means. J. B. Perry Robinson, whose *Transformation in Malaya* admirably describes those methods, quotes "a senior and very shrewd Police officer" who, asked what was the biggest difference between the Emergency in 1954 and the Emergency five years earlier, replied: "Less beating up." Those were the days of frustrating visits to Chinese squatters' villages, where blank incomprehension invariably met security force patrols inquiring about the authors of incidents committed under their noses. Frustration bred violence, and the squatters, for their part, preferred the flying fists of exasperated police to the savage reprisals of the terrorists. In any case, the squatters were confused by one of the more stupid pieces of self-defeating legislation in the first phase of the Emergency: a special regulation that made "consorting with terrorists" punishable by death. The rural Chinese, in particular, could scarcely avoid consorting with the terrorists, who sought them out. In the conditions then prevailing, this seemed to give them a choice between death for consorting, and death for not consorting, with the terrorists. The temptation to see, hear and speak nothing must have been overwhelming.

Those were also the days of fruitless searches in the jungle on the improbable chance of finding a communist or two. The notion that searches were futile unless they were based on precise information came only later. In short, nobody knew what to do. The communists struck where and how they pleased. The population was terrorised and the security forces were powerless to protect it. The communists had all the supplies they needed, and the authorities were unable to stop the flow. The communists knew when and where they might be sought and in what strength, and nearly always got away in time; on their side, the security forces had no idea where or when the communists would strike next.

In the earliest days of the insurrection—before the state of emergency had been proclaimed—hardly anybody in authority either realised the magnitude of the challenge or had an inkling of how to meet it. Sir Edward Gent, the High Commissioner, unwilling as ever to admit that peace was being disturbed, considered that the rubber and tin industries were not endangered. The Commissioner of Police thought the CID could cope on its own. The army leaders thought the troops would soon catch up with the bandits in the jungle. The Malay rulers thought that the activities of five or six thousand bandits were hardly an occasion for lost sleep. As Robinson points out, the only man who realised the scale of the communist effort and saw it in its South-East Asian perspective was the Commissioner-General, Mr. Malcolm MacDonald. In later years, Mr. MacDonald was accused, I think with some justification, of complacency over the turn of events in Indo-China; but in June, 1948, he alone seemed to realise what the situation demanded. At a heated conference in Kuala Lumpur, he talked the less realistic higher officials into raising a Special Constabulary of 25,000 to 30,000 men, to guard estates and mines. By September—three months after the Kuala Lumpur conference—there were 24,000 of them: ill-trained, or untrained, a rabble in need of target practice, they nevertheless did much to save what might have been a desperate situation.

The raising of the Special Constabulary was a solitary bright spot in a phase of fumbling in the dark. It was obvious from the beginning that the squatters—who lived on the fringes of the jungle and supplied the bandits—must be separated from them, but it was easier said than done. A "squatter committee" was appointed in September, 1948, but it did not get down to work till November and did not produce its report till the following May—nearly a year after the Emergency had begun. And a year after that, when General Sir Harold Briggs took up his post as the first Director of Operations, practically nothing had been done, largely owing to the reluctance of the Malay rulers to play their part in a tiresome and unpopular operation. Gurney himself, who had succeeded Gent, was well aware that no progress could be made until the contact between the squatters and bandits had been broken, and that only a Director of Operations with powers to overrride local objections could accomplish the task. Briggs, given the powers, readily concurred, and the resettlement project, which was initiated during his period in office, is known as the Briggs Plan.

Sir Harold Briggs brought to the situation the first touch of the ruthless efficiency which it demanded. His method was dramatic. In the darkness before dawn troops would surround a squatters' village. As the first light shone, they would close in. There were lorries on the nearest road to remove the inhabitants and their possessions; there were Chinese-speaking state government officials, police and agricultural officers, medical and welfare specialists. While the Chinese-speakers gave instructions, the agricultural experts assessed the value of the crops and of machinery that could not be removed, for compensation purposes. These were no deportations to Siberia, on the Chechen-Ingush model: the sites of the New Villages to which the squatters were removed were often enough only a couple of miles from the "old villages" which they had left. If the villagers were mine-workers, they worked in the same mine; if they were tappers, they worked the same trees. The New Villages were on flat ground and astride main roads; they had guarded gates and were wired in. In most cases—though there were bad exceptions—amenities were better than those that had been left behind, and standards of nutrition, welfare and health rose appreciably.

Other things of value were initiated during the Briggs-Gurney period. A Home Guard was built up in the kampongs (villages); detention camps were created, in which suspects were sorted out into various categories, and rehabilitation camps in which former detainees were trained for a useful civilian life; the police, army and civil administration were integrated under a State War Executive Committee, with a Federal War Council to co-ordinate planning. All this was in existence *before* Templer arrived. What Templer did was to make maximum use of the existing machinery and improve it; to galvanise civilian morale by ubiquitous personal appearances and pep-talks; to set an example of unsparing toil; to *make* an example of those who supported the terrorists whether actively or passively; to show confidence in those under his orders; to speed the pace of self-government; in brief, to lead. It is not easy to explain Templer's impact in words; it was tangible during the seventeen months I spent in Singapore and Malaya, and must have been comparable to that of the late Marshal de Lattre de Tassigny, who died shortly before I arrived in Vietnam. Templer was determined to make his presence felt throughout the Federation and to interest himself personally in every aspect of the vast combined operation he was directing. It was in this spirit that he visited every one of the 500 New Villages, in which more than half a million squatters had been resettled. It was by such ceaseless outpouring of energy, by honesty and by ruthlessness, rather than by any startling innovations, that Templer transformed the situation.

Gradually, the terrorists were driven deeper into the jungle. There they bullied the aborigines into working for them. Gradually, under Templer and his successor as Director of Operations, Lieutenant-General Sir Geoffrey Bourne, the aborigines were won over to the anti-communist side. Dyak trackers were imported from Borneo; helicopters in increasing numbers dropped patrols into the jungle, no longer at random but directly on to terrorist camps; the foot patrols knew where they were going: they were no longer ambushed by terrorists, it was they who did the ambushing. Another thing Templer understood was the need for psychological warfare when dealing with an enemy who was kept going by an ideology. It was more than simply offering rewards for captured terrorists—although very substantial rewards were offered and frequently claimed. It was a question of telling the public what was being done, and of drafting the kind of leaflet that induced men to surrender. The sceptics, who were many, were confounded by the results of this major war for men's minds. Gradually, the rate of surrenders increased and the great majority of the 1,500 who gave themselves up in the first seven years of the Emergency did so after reading government leaflets or hearing official broadcasts. In terms of money spent, it was good value.

But it is doubtful that even these enlightened tactics would have been so effective if they had not been accompanied by consistent progress on the political front. Templer was a great believer in education for democracy from the base upward. There were village elections in the New Villages; local council elections that grew out of the election of village committees, and municipal elections in Penang, Malacca and Kuala Lumpur, all in Templer's time. State Council elections followed under Sir Donald MacGillivray in 1954 and 1955, then the final stage of nation-wide general elections in 1956, leading, as the British Government had promised in Templer's directive, to full independence. The first Prime Minister of independent Malaya, Tunku Abdul Rahman, inherited the remains of the Emergency and at the time of writing, the last hard core of terrorists had still not surrendered. But the insurrection was defeated long before that. Even while Templer was in office, he had been able to declare certain areas "white"— that is, clear of terrorists. For the people living in those areas this was a true liberation, from the fear of terrorism and from the restrictions of food control and barbed wire.

When one recalls the desperate autumn days of 1951, after the murder of Sir Henry Gurney, and the state of public morale at the time of Templer's installation, one must concede that he wrought a spectacular change. Neither the sound organisation of Sir Harold Briggs nor the mistaken tactics of the communists can detract from this achievement.

* * *

In some respects, the Philippines are a more illuminating example than Malaya. Both countries faced communist insurrections; that is, in the last resort, challenges to their sovereignty from alien enemies. But in Malaya, the picture was blurred because the repressive machinery was controlled by a colonial power; although it was not an old-fashioned colonial war, it could be so labelled by the communists. The Philippines, on the other hand, had been independent for two years by the time the Huks launched their second insurrection in 1948. In one sense, therefore, the issue seemed clear-cut: an internal challenge to the legally constituted authority, initiated at the instance of a foreign power through its conspiratorial international network, the communist movement. Given these circumstances, one might have expected the repression to be as swift and totally successful as, say, in the Madiun affair in Indonesia. That it was not is one reason why the Philippine example is so arresting.

In the end, indeed, the Huk rebellion was more satisfactorily suppressed than the Malayan communist uprising. And once the right methods were adopted, success came rapidly. In the early stages, however, the repressive technique was not merely inept, it was an invitation to disaster. Moreover, in all respects except the fact of Philippine independence, conditions favoured the rebels. The peasants had no knowledge of communism apart from the teachings of the rebel leaders, who presented themselves as their champions and communism as their salvation. It was not difficult for the peasants to accept these claims. It was natural for them to regard the Huks as the legitimate successors of the peasant uprisings of the 'twenties on Luzon and Mindanao, or of the Sadkal rebellion of 1935. The Huk rebellion seemed equally an expression of agrarian discontent. In the 'twenties, agrarian secret societies had incited the peasants to revolt against their absent landlords, to kill members of the brutal local constabulary, who oppressed the peasantry in the name of law and order, and to burn land records and titles. Several million landless tenants and labourers had risen in 1935 at the bidding of Benino Ramos and his Sadkal movement. Luis Taruc naturally appeared to be the linear descendant of Ramos and earlier peasant insurgents. Moreover, the earlier uprisings had been suppressed without thought of reform, or, at best, had been followed by paper reforms that were never put into operation. In the independent Republic of the Philippines in 1948, the gap between landlords and tenants, or between the impoverished mass of Filipinos and the dominant business class of Americans, Chinese or Spanish-Filipinos, was greater than ever.

Nor was the administration setting an example likely to encourage a respect for law and order. Inflation, corruption, inefficiency and profiteering from American aid aggravated the legacy of the war, which the first President of the independent Philippines, Manuel Roxas, had described in these words:

> There is hunger among us . . . Plagues of rats and locusts gnaw at our food supplies. Public health and sanitation have been set back a quarter of a century. Housing . . . is shocking in its inadequacy and squalor. Our communications are destroyed, stolen or disrupted . . . Schools have been burned and teachers have been killed.

President Roxas, who died in office on April 15th, 1948, was succeeded by Vice-President Elpidio Quirino. Things went from bad to worse. In the words of Professor Claude A. Buss in *The Far East*: "His administration was marred by scandals and presented an unsavoury record of inefficiency and corruption." The Huks had been outlawed a few weeks before President Quirino came to power. As we have seen in Part III, his first official act was to proclaim an amnesty and invite the Huk representatives to take their seats in Congress, on condition that the rebels registered with the government and surrendered their arms. By that time, of course, the Philippine communists had received their orders from Calcutta and were bound to disregard the amnesty offer. But the policy of pardon was probably doomed to failure in any case, for the great mass of the peasantry was utterly divorced from its elected rulers. Both the governing Liberals and the opposition Nacionalistas were identified with absentee landlords and foreign, or part-foreign, business interests in a way that seemed providentially to confirm the Marxist analysis of "bourgeois democracy".

In the countryside, the agencies of repression—the army and constabulary—were seen to be the oppressors, not the protectors, of the peasants. William O. Douglas, in *North from Malaya*, records two examples of oppression which, even if they were extreme cases, could have occurred only in a general context of official brutality. "One night in Laguna," he writes, "50 farmers who were attending a dance were lined up and shot by the constabulary because they were *suspected* of being Huks. On Good Friday 1950 the army, in revenge for the killing of an officer, massacred 100 men, women and children in Bacalor, Pampanga, and burned 130 houses." By such methods and against the background I have described, the government had made it possible for the Huks to gain control of large areas, levying their own taxes and often usurping the police functions of the constabulary. That was the situation in September, 1950, when Ramon Magsaysay was appointed Minister of Defence.

By that time, President Quirino was firmly in the saddle, having succeeded himself in 1949 by means of elections in which fraud and intimidation ensured a Liberal victory. A few months later, in the conditions we have seen, the Huks, with a little more boldness, might have seized power. At that time, a strong group of Liberal senators, some say in response to American suggestions, began to campaign for the appointment of Magsaysay as Defence Minister. This remarkable man was born in 1906 in Iba, provincial capital of the hilly province of Zambales, in western Luzon. Some authorities say he was the son of a trade-school teacher, others say his father was a blacksmith; it is certain, in any event, that he did not belong to the privileged ruling group. Of mixed Tagalog, Ilocano, Spanish and Chinese blood, he worked his way through the University of the Philippines as a mechanic. During the war he captained a guerrilla band, and after it he was elected to Congress as a Liberal.

As Defence Minister and later as President, Magsaysay displayed much the same restless energy and ruthless overriding of obstacles as Templer in Malaya. He cleaned out and reorganised the constabulary and army from top to bottom. He made examples of servicemen who accepted bribes, shot villagers on suspicion of aiding the Huks or in any other way misbehaved. Weeding out the inefficient, the corrupt, the unsuitable, he attended to the grievances of soldiers or constables, promoting officers of his own choice. Like Templer two years later, he stumped the country on unheralded trips, seeing for himself. His new constabulary protected instead of oppressing; his new army pursued the Huks into their fastnesses. He trained dogs to hunt them, he used surrendered Huks to guide the army. He talked captured communists into supporting him, and put prices on the heads of the more stubborn or elusive leaders. By radio or through the printed word, he offered a pardon and a job to Huks who surrendered, excepting only those guilty of certain crimes. By 1951, the Huks were on the run, and the peasants, if not exactly pro-government, were at any rate no longer hostile to the central authority. A further effort was needed, and Magsaysay furnished it. He put army lawyers into the courts to defend tenant farmers against prosecution by landlords. Such cases were not infrequent: though the law limited farm rents to 30 per cent of the value of the crop, landlords were evicting tenants who refused to exceed the legal ceiling. Before Magsaysay the whole judicial apparatus had been weighted in favour of the landlords. Under Magsaysay, the concept of justice was given meaning. It was the turn of the tide: supporters flocked to the side of Magsaysay "the liberator" and melted away from the communists. Those who rallied to him had no cause for regret. Paroled to Magsaysay, or while serving their sentences, they were taught a trade. Later, small loans set them up in business. On the land, a rural rehabilitation programme provided land for ex-Huks. Repression had become enlightened.

The man who makes friends by the thousand inevitably makes enemies by the hundred. Magsaysay was no exception. Appalled by the corruption within his own party and by the methods that had ensured its electoral victory, he set out to guarantee fairness at the polls in the congressional elections of 1951. In charge of the armed forces and with a renovated constabulary loyal to him, Magsaysay prevented government candidates from using force to intimidate opponents and secure election. The outcome was a victory for the Nacionalista opposition. Thereafter, Magsaysay had to contend with the organised hostility of the governing Liberal executive. The constabulary was removed from his control and operations against the communists were held up while new and abortive negotiations with the Huk leaders were conducted. These actions convinced Magsaysay that he could not hope to complete his task from within the Liberal Party. He resigned as Minister of Defence, joined the Nacionalistas and was adopted as their presidential candidate. On December 30th, 1953, after campaigning on a platform of social justice and honest government, he was swept into power as President of the Philippines.

That he soon ran into the opposition of the Nacionalistas, as he had earlier with the Liberals, was inevitable, but scarcely relevant to this narrative. No less than the Liberals, the Nacionalistas were the party of landlords and business-men. No less than his former patrons, his new ones resented the implementation of a programme that had served its purpose in winning the presidential elections. Equally, they resented his attempts to fulfil the promises implicit in his much-quoted campaign statements: "I will get officials and bureaucrats out of their offices and into the barrios where people need their help"; or "I shall welcome you into Malacanan [the Presidential palace] even if you have no shoes for your feet." It is true that internal opposition frustrated or slowed down Magsaysay's legislative programme. But the essential job was accomplished: on September 17th, 1954, less than five months after Magsaysay had become President, the Huk leader Luis Taruc surrendered.

Outside the United States, the Huk rebellion has had understandably less publicity than the insurrections against British or French rule. But the student of rebellion cannot afford to neglect it, for it is an object-lesson, a compendium of all the rules. Neglect or misrule had created the conditions of frustration. Because genuine grievances existed, the alien communist insurrection took root. Pure repression was ineffectual; so was a presidential amnesty against a background of administrative chaos. In the end, "enlightened repression"—efficient operations combined with visible reforms—did the trick. The sensible way had prevailed.

5

The Lessons of Repression

WE have surely not exhausted the list of possible forms of repression. But I suggest that our sample has been reasonably varied. We have considered, in some detail, repressive campaigns that succeeded, and suggested why; in passing, we have glanced at other campaigns that failed, and found probable reasons for these failures.

In the long run, I am inclined to think that pure repression cannot succeed. But there is admittedly nothing to justify such liberal optimism in the short span of history since the second world war. There is no evidence, at the time of writing, that the Hungarians, left to their own devices, can hope to overthrow the tyranny that weighs over them by the methods of October, 1956. The Poles stopped short of trying to set up a non-communist state and proclaim their neutrality; as a result, their partial revolution brought them some gains, which had not been entirely eroded two or three years later. But the Hungarians allowed their revolution to get out of hand; total revolt brought total repression.

We have seen why the Russians could allow themselves this orgy of blood-letting, confident that they would get away with it. The democracies can never feel so free, though in special circumstances and on a limited scale, the French were able to repress the rebellions of 1945 and 1947 with totalitarian abandon. To be sure, they have killed far more people, including civilians, in Algeria, since 1954, than the Soviet Army killed in Hungary. But the blood-letting has been spread over several years, and the impact of it has been offset by the savagery of the rebels. A Christian minority may argue that two wrongs don't make a right; but to the great majority of half-believers they do. This is a help to governments, from President de Gaulle's to Fidel Castro's.

The British discovered the limitations of repression in Cyprus, where a curious attachment to obsolescent concepts of power blinded them to the lessons they had taught themselves in Malaya. What it comes down to is this: there is a profound difference between a successful repression and a freely consented settlement. By suppressing the Hungarian revolution, the Russians kept their hold on their satellite empire, for at any rate a few years. But they did not remove the causes of Hungarian discontent. By its very nature, the graveyard peace of November, 1956, is impermanent. The British, in Malaya and after all in Cyprus, made their peace with the local populations. From the British standpoint, Malaya and Cyprus are problems that have been solved. What the

of reasonableness and capacity beneath his front of fanaticism, he can, for instance, be invited to share in the business of government. This was the course chosen by the former Governor of the Gold Coast, Sir Charles Arden-Clarke, who brought Dr. Nkrumah out of gaol and gave him a job on the Executive Council. If, on the other hand, those in authority have grounds to believe that a rebel leader would lead his country to disaster or sell it to a hostile power (which must be the assumption when the rebel is a communist), then either of two further courses is open to them. They may decide on pure repression, particularly if they are convinced that their position is a vital one which must not, at any costs, be surrendered. This was the decision in Kenya and in Cyprus. In the latter, the British Government of the day nourished the delusion that Cyprus was a vital interest; the rebel leader, Grivas, was no communist, but he had this in common with communists, that he was acting in the interests, not of the Cypriots but of a foreign power—in this instance, Greece. If pure repression is the decision, then the established authority had better be quite sure that it has both the means and the will to carry out the job. Both were available in Kenya; neither quite was in Cyprus.

But if pure repression is not the choice, then another course is open: to find an alternative rebel to whom power may eventually be handed. It goes without saying that this course can be successful only if the established authority finds a genuine leader, able to steal the thunder of the rebel who has already turned to violence, and is prepared to carry out whatever political and economic reforms the situation demands. To find a dubious or incapable leader is worse than useless: he will be regarded as a traitor or collaborator. To find an able man and refuse him the tools needed for the job is equally useless. Both the man and the reforms are needed; the man without the policy is an invitation to defeat.

The best example I know of the failure of an "alternative leader" policy is the Bao Dai experiment in Vietnam. I have already suggested (in Part II) that the experiment was doomed to failure from the start because of a fundamental contradiction between the motives of the French and of the Vietnamese nationalists for desiring the ex-Emperor's return. The French thought that Bao Dai would not insist on the two demands of Ho Chi Minh—the unity and independence of Vietnam—which had wrecked earlier negotiations. The nationalists hoped he would succeed where Ho had failed. I went on to suggest that the French and Vietnamese nationalists could have won the war against the Vietminh if the French had given Bao Dai the substance of power and Vietnam the substance of independence.

This hypothetical argument calls for elaboration. The great majority of observers, before, during and since the Bao Dai experiment, have expressed the view that the ex-Emperor's defects of character precluded him from ever exercising the kind of leadership that would have caused the Vietnamese people to desert Ho Chi Minh and rally to his side. The events of 1949 to 1954 appeared to justify this view. It seems hard to defend the "roi fénéant" who preferred hunting tiger in the jungles of Annam to handling affairs of state in Saigon, who drew a huge allowance while his country bled, who handed over control of Saigon's police to a gangster who controlled its gambling and prostitution, who lounged in his castle at Cannes during the long agony of Dien Bien Phu, and later during the difficult first months of the Ngo Dinh Diem administration which took office after the Geneva settlement of 1954. These things were true but they were only part of the truth, and some of them, as we shall see, were defensible. (The least defensible was the appointment of Le Van Vien, or Bay Vien, boss of the Binh Xuyen gang, as chief of police. I reproached Bao Dai with this at our last meeting in Paris in the spring of 1955, and he remarked: "You know, Bay Vien has never squeezed the people.") On the whole, however, they are incompatible with the example required of national leadership. It does not follow, however, that it was Bao Dai's character alone that wrecked the Bao Dai experiment, for there was a clear correlation between the deterioration of the man and his treatment by the French. Differently handled, Bao Dai might never have become the execrated personality whom Diem deposed—in an admittedly unfair referendum—in October, 1955. And under certain conditions, which were never realised, the experiment might have succeeded.

This exercise in hypothesis is, I suggest, worth making, for without it the true lessons of the Bao Dai experiment do not clearly emerge.

A man of luminous intelligence, Bao Dai was not by nature either a rebel or a political leader. (Ex-King Norodom Sihanouk of Cambodia was both.) He was, on the other hand, well qualified by birth, education and modernity of outlook to exercise the supra-political functions of head of state. Politically, his life at all stages was compounded of frustrations. Had he been a rebel, he would have revolted; had he been a political leader, he would have turned circumstances to his advantage. At best contemplative, at worst indolent, he took refuge in play or inactivity.

The young Emperor returned to Vietnam on September 8th, 1932, after ten years in France. The first Vietnamese sovereign to have been educated in Europe, he planned a radical modernisation of his country's society and monarchy. On May 2nd, 1933, still only 20, Bao Dai announced that he was taking over "the direction of the country's affairs". He dismissed most of his French-approved ministers, abolished the post of Prime Minister, and appointed as Minister of the Interior a young Catholic mandarin, renowned, as Devillers observed, "for his perfect integrity, his competence and his intelligence". Twenty-two years later, this man, whose name was Ngo Dinh Diem, had Bao Dai removed and himself proclaimed Chief of State. But in those days the two men were partners, first in enthusiasm, very soon after in frustration.

Every one of their joint efforts at reform was blocked, both by the French officials and by the Vietnamese traditionalists; the first were determined to squash any manifestation of independence, and the second were bent on defending their privileges. Mr. Diem who, even in those days, was not a man to compromise on matters of principle, told the Emperor in September, 1933, that he would have no part in the comedy that was being played, and resigned. Bao Dai, never a fighter for his beliefs, withdrew into his shell, avoiding the society of the French, relieving his boredom with hunting and sport, and limiting his official activities to the signature of documents and to ceremonial functions.

Bao Dai emerged from his obscurity only on March 11th, 1945, when, two days after the Japanese *coup de force* that overthrew the Vichy French administration in Indo-China, he proclaimed the independence of Vietnam. He was, in fact, entering his second period of frustration. In August, after the Japanese capitulation, the communist-led Vietminh rapidly gained control of north Vietnam; on the 18th, Bao Dai sent letters to President Truman, the King of England, Marshal Chiang Kai-shek and General de Gaulle, appealing for recognition of Vietnam's independence. On the 25th, under pressure from the Vietminh, he formally abdicated, declaring himself "happy to be a free citizen in an independent country". A few days later, as "citizen Vinh Thuy", he was named "Supreme Adviser" of the provisional Vietminh government—that is, Ho Chi Minh's closest collaborator. It did not take Bao Dai long to realise that the Vietminh was under communist control and that the only future possible for nationalists, including himself, under the new Vietnamese republic, lay in collaboration with the communists. Failing that, the alternatives were liquidation or flight. Bao Dai chose flight. On March 18th, he left Hanoi for Chungking at the head of a special mission to Chiang Kai-shek's government; but instead of returning, he went on to voluntary exile in Hong Kong.

It was there, but not until December, 1947, that the French, belatedly despairing of ever reaching agreement with the Vietminh, at last sought him out as an alternative leader. It was the beginning of Bao Dai's third period of frustration. We have seen in Part II in what spirit the French made their approach to the ex-Emperor. When he finally returned to Vietnam as Chief of State in April, 1949, he soon discovered the limitations of the agreements he had just signed with the French Government, under which the unity and independence of Vietnam had at last been recognised. It was 1932 all over again, with the French High Commissioner and Commander-in-Chief as the real rulers of

Vietnam, and French officials duplicating—and superseding—the functions of the Vietnamese ministers. Bao Dai took over the Prime Ministership on July 1st, 1949, and gave it up on January 21st, 1950, retiring to his hunting-lodge forty-five miles from Ban Methuot in the heart of the Annamese jungle. Contrary to the general impression, however, he did not disinterest himself in the affairs of state. With the able assistance of his Directeur de Cabinet, Mr. Nguyen Dé, he knew everything that went on, corrected or redrafted bills, frequently infuriated the French with delaying tactics, and received a stream of visitors, to each of whom he gave, with rare lucidity, an exposé of the situation. It was there, as one of his visitors, that I first met him.

This was not, of course, leadership. In the hothouse atmosphere of Saigon, a police state waxed in the midst of private and official corruption. Bao Dai, who was, like so many others—and with perfect legality—transferring money to France at a profitable rate of exchange, seemed to take less and less interest in developments. His visits to France became more frequent and more prolonged until, in 1953, he settled there, apparently in permanent exile. But again the detachment was apparent rather than real. His efficient intelligence service kept him abreast both of international moves and of Vietnamese intrigue and counter-intrigue. Incapable of direct action, he seemed to be waiting for French policy in Indo-China to collapse under the weight of its own mistakes and contradictions. Then, he may have thought, would come the reward of his own inertia: both sides—nationalists and communists—would seek him out as the one man who could make and preserve the unity of Vietnam.

But in politics the reward of inertia is oblivion. Bao Dai was merely heading for his fourth, and surely last, period of frustration. In mid-June, 1954, he appointed his former Minister of the Interior, Ngo Dinh Diem, as Prime Minister. In north Vietnam, the French Union Army had been disastrously defeated at Dien Bien Phu; in France, M. Mendès-France had come to power on a pledge to end the war in thirty days or quit; in Geneva, the outgoing French Foreign Minister, M. Bidault, had lost his attempt to turn defeat in the field into victory over the conference table. For Mr. Diem, the situation looked desperate; but he had an asset which no previous Vietnamese Prime Minister had enjoyed for more than eighty years: under agreements negotiated by Bao Dai's previous Prime Minister, Prince Buu Loc, France had finally recognised the full independence of Vietnam, this time without visible strings. There is no need to follow Bao Dai's long-distance struggle with his new Prime Minister to its humiliating but inevitable end. But it is worth observing that Bao Dai, for all his intelligence, had built himself into a dilemma from which there was no answer but escape. On the one hand, he had handed over power to a man who accepted it only on condition that Bao Dai should stay out of Vietnam; on the other hand, he dare not dismiss Diem because the American government had publicly adopted the policy of making its programme of economic and military aid to south Vietnam conditional on Mr. Diem's continuance in office. A man of action would have dismissed the defiant Premier, returned to Vietnam and dared the Americans to do their worst. Bao Dai tried to bring down Ngo Dinh Diem by various stratagems, and in the end was himself deposed.

Let us freely admit, then, that from start to finish, Bao Dai lacked the character and the gifts of leadership, and that the Bao Dai experiment was a failure. But would the experiment have failed had it been conducted by the French in a different spirit and with different aims in view? All observers are agreed that he had his idealism and his belief in progress and modernisation; would his character have deteriorated as it did, had the French treated him with good faith and allowed him freedom to act? I should answer "No" to both questions. It might still, however, be objected that even if the French had played fairly with the Vietnamese nationalists under Bao Dai, the ex-Emperor would have lacked the dynamic leadership which alone could have won the mass of the Vietnamese people away from Ho Chi Minh. The circumstances were favourable to an experiment conducted in that spirit. Bao Dai himself had a considerable following and great prestige as the Emperor or former Emperor. During the second world war, the French had tacitly recognised these facts by forbidding Bao Dai to visit Cochin-China, for fear that he would rally nationalist opinion in a colony which the French considered irrevocably their own. The Vietminh, likewise, recognised the value of Bao Dai's support; otherwise, Ho Chi Minh would not have invited Bao Dai to become his "Supreme Adviser". Ideally, given Bao Dai's hereditary position and his natural indolence, the Bao Dai experiment would have been a complete success only if the French had turned, not to him alone, but to him *and* a dynamic nationalist leader who would have been Prime Minister to Bao Dai's Chief of State. Of the many Vietnamese politicians I have met, only two—outside the communists—impressed me as having the necessary qualities: the late Nguyen Huu Tri, former governor of Tonking, and Ngo Dinh Diem himself. For various reasons, Tri was never really in the running, but Diem always was, and it happens that at the time the Bao Dai experiment was initiated, Diem was both available and willing to serve. That he was not appointed was one of the missed opportunities of contemporary history.

It must be admitted that the opportunity was missed by Bao Dai himself as well as by the French. Intransigent as ever, Diem had refused to collaborate with the Vietminh, which killed one of his numerous brothers and interned him. Later, having regained his liberty, he was one of the nationalist leaders who commuted between Saigon and Hong Kong to exert whatever influence they could on Bao Dai. On September 18th, 1947, the ex-Emperor had declared himself ready to negotiate with the French. On December 6th, aboard a chartered Catalina flying-boat, he "landed" in the Bay of Along, where he met the French High Commissioner, Emile Bollaert. Two days later, he initialled a secret protocol which was to serve as a basis for future negotiations. This document used the word "independence", but hedged it around with restrictions. When Bao Dai triumphantly produced it before his advisers, they were dejected. Crestfallen, he summoned the leading nationalists, including Diem, to Hong Kong, to ask their advice. For Diem, nothing short of "dominion status" would suffice. Without committing himself, Bao Dai left for France, to observe French power at source. During his stay in Europe, Bao Dai had further meetings with Bollaert, but in Geneva. The High Commissioner had proposed the convocation of an assembly, or congress, which would give Bao Dai a "mandate" to negotiate in the name of the Vietnamese people. Both Bao Dai and Diem saw through this proposal: the congress, having "mandated" Bao Dai, would dissolve itself, leaving Bao Dai with the unsatisfactory protocol and negotiating in the name of Vietnam. In Saigon, Diem and another nationalist leader, Phan Huy Dan, called together nationalists of all shades, who resolved that any congress or assembly should nominate its best qualified representative—not necessarily Bao Dai—to form a government and negotiate with France. This was not at all what Bollaert or M. Robert Schuman's government in Paris was after, and the "congress" idea was dropped.

It was at this moment that the opportunity of a Bao Dai-Diem solution came and went. By the time Bao Dai had returned to Hong Kong, in March, 1948, Diem had decided that he was willing to form a government, providing Bollaert was prepared to take the first steps towards dominion status. He flew to Saigon, where the High Commissioner received him on March 22nd. It was a disappointing meeting. M. Bollaert told Mr. Diem that he was willing to interpret the protocol liberally, but not to change its wording; and dominion status was out of the question.

Mr. Diem made a final attempt to direct the Bao Dao experiment along nationalistic lines. He proposed the formation of a study committee, which would be composed of various elements including the Vietminh, and would be charged with drawing up a list of demands which Bao Dai could use as a basis for negotiations with the French. It was then that Bao Dai himself missed the opportunity which the French had already passed over. He chose to listen to Dr. Phan Huy Dan rather than to Mr. Diem. Dan—who had joined Mr. Diem in summoning the nationalists in Saigon—now proposed the immediate formation of a provisional government. He argued that this government could at least bring about the "unity" of the country (including Cochin-China); independence could come later. Bao Dai agreed, but Diem withdrew his candidature for the premiership; the opportunity had passed. (It is ironical to recall these events; six years later, Bao Dai handed over power to Ngo Dinh Diem, and a few months after that, Phan Huy Dan returned from a long exile to organise an opposition to the Diem régime.)

It is plain that the French Governments of those days—M. Ramadier's, which initiated the Bao Dai experiment, and M. Schuman's, which implemented it—had not made the mental adjustment to the realities of Asian nationalism which the situation demanded. By approaching Bao Dai as a means of preserving French power, not as a means of coming to terms with Vietnamese nationalism, they invited a long and losing struggle with the Vietminh.

There remains another question: could the Indo-China war have been avoided altogether? Clearly, it could have, but only at the price of conceding to Ho Chi Minh, in 1946, the demands that were grudgingly, and with bad faith, granted to Bao Dai three years later: the unity and independence of Vietnam. From the first, therefore, the choice before the French was not between keeping Vietnam and losing it, but between losing it to the communists and losing it to the nationalists; in the end, it was lost to both: Ho in the north, and Diem in the south. The immediate reality the French faced after Japan's collapse was a nationalist movement led by the communists under Ho Chi Minh. M. Sainteny, as I have mentioned elsewhere, believed it to be both possible and desirable to reach agreement with Ho on the basis of an independent Vietnam associated with France. It was a belief to which he clung even after the Geneva conference of 1954 and the French recognition of Mr. Diem's régime in the south. He returned to Hanoi as French "Delegate-General", charged with safeguarding the remaining French cultural and business interests, but with a private hope that somehow the Vietminh leaders could be persuaded to opt for association with France rather than with communist Russia and China. It was a forlorn hope, if only because of the United States policy of support for the Diem régime. But I hope I have made it clear, elsewhere in this book, that it was a forlorn hope even in 1946. Ho Chi Minh was no Tito.

If the "alternative leader" policy failed in Vietnam—where, in reality, it was never honestly pursued—it succeeded brilliantly in Malaya. Chance, it is true, provided an unpretentious but natural leader of men in Tunku Abdul Rahman, Prince of Kedah. But the British, to their credit, seized the chance and entrusted power to the Tunku.

A comparison between Tunku Abdul Rahman and Emperor Bao Dai is less fanciful than it might seem. Both men were of royal blood; both were alternative candidates for leadership in countries gripped by communist insurrection; and both were men of easy-going natures who had been known as "playboys". For the Tunku had given no indication of his real capabilities until his mid-forties. As Harry Miller put it in his biography, *Prince and Premier*:

> He gained a Bachelor of Arts degree at Cambridge University after earning the lowest possible marks for a pass. He failed his Bar examinations because he preferred horse-racing, the "dogs", and dancing. He finally passed them when he was forty-five years of age, and he chuckled because it had taken him twenty-five years to become a lawyer.

The Tunku came suddenly into prominence on August 26th, 1951, when he was elected president of the United Malays' National Organisation. The outgoing president, Dato Onn bin Ja'afar, who had founded the UMNO, had resigned to form a non-communal party, the Independence of Malaya Party (IMP). This, as events showed, was Dato Onn's political suicide. His idea had been admirable but premature; Malaya was not ready for a non-communal party. What it was ready for was an electoral alliance between existing communal parties. It was just such an alliance, between the UMNO and the Malayan Chinese Association, that dominated Malayan politics from the time of its victory in Malaya's first municipal elections in Kuala Lumpur in February, 1952. At that time, the combined party was known as the UMNO-MCA

Alliance; later, the two parties were joined by the Malayan Indian Congress and the resulting body was simply known as the Alliance, though its component groups kept their separate identities.

From the first, the British, both in Malaya and in Whitehall, encouraged and supported Tunku Abdul Rahman, and though their relationship was not always smooth, it was in the end extraordinarily fruitful. When the Tunku was elected leader of UMNO, he was Deputy Public Prosecutor, an appointment which was likely to hamper his political activities. The then High Commissioner, Sir Henry Gurney, was anxious to ensure that a sound Malay leader should not labour under handicaps either of money or of duties. Harry Miller records that Sir Henry arranged for the Tunku to go on leave prior to retirement with a pension two years before the normal minimum retiring age. The High Commissioner also decided that as the leader of a major party, Tunku Abdul Rahman should be a member of the Federal Legislative Council at about £60 a month.

Gurney's successor, General Templer, made Abdul Rahman a member of the Executive Council, the highest policy-making body in the Federation of Malaya. In August, 1953, however, when Templer offered him a portfolio in the government, the Tunku refused. He had been agitating, in public speeches, for national elections in 1954, and attacking the government—without justification—for perversely delaying them; he did not feel he could continue to attack the government if he joined it. But though he declined the High Commissioner's offer, he was aware of the advantages of acquiring administrative experience for the Alliance, against the day when it would come to power; so he persuaded two other members of the Alliance to become ministers in his place.

The low-water mark in Abdul Rahman's relations with the British was reached in 1954. The Tunku continued to agitate for elections that year, in the face of official explanations that the pace could not be so rapid because State and Settlement elections would have to be held before national elections, and months of work lay ahead to pass the necessary legislation, determine the constituencies and register the voters. Abdul Rahman, though himself a member of the royal house of Kedah, had underestimated another difficulty: Britain's treaty obligations to the Malay rulers. The Alliance had decided to insist, not only on elections in November, 1954, but also on a three-fifths elected majority in the Legislative Council—a giant step towards independence. The second demand, even more than the first, almost wrecked all prospect of collaboration between the Alliance and the British authorities. The rulers, who felt their positions threatened, were against an elected majority, but if there was to be one, they wished to keep it as small as possible.

At the beginning of April, Tunku Abdul Rahman sent a telegram to the Colonial Secretary, then Mr. Oliver Lyttelton, asking him to meet a delegation from the Alliance in London before making his decision on Federal elections. Mr. Lyttelton declined to meet the Alliance on the ground that he would then have to meet other delegations. The Alliance decided to go to London anyway, if only to lobby MPs. In fact, Mr. Lyttelton, who was about to visit Uganda, later relented and agreed to meet the Tunku and his followers. On April 27th, however, while Mr. Lyttelton was away, the Colonial Office announced that agreement had been reached between the High Commissioner and the Malay Rulers, on a Legislative Council of 52 elected and 46 nominated members, with a reserve of seven seats which the High Commissioner could fill at his discretion. Though the Colonial Office rightly pointed out that it was unusual for a territory to jump from a wholly nominated Legislative Council to one with an elected majority, the Tunku was not satisfied. But when he met Mr. Lyttelton, on May 14th, he was unable to persuade the Colonial Secretary to change his mind. The agreement with the rulers was considered binding.

The Alliance returned to Malaya in a fighting mood. Ever courteous, the Tunku remained on good terms with Sir Gerald Templer, to whom he gave a farewell party on his recall to Britain. But Templer's successor, Sir Donald MacGillivray, was informed that the Alliance had decided to withdraw all its members from every official council. This decision was widely criticised, both in London, where the Labour Opposition decided not to support the Alliance on this issue, and in Malaya itself, where a number of Alliance members rebelled against it.

The crisis, however, lasted only six weeks. On July 2nd, Tunku Abdul Rahman met Sir Donald MacGillivray aboard the Royal Navy frigate *Alert*. The High Commissioner convinced him that he would act in agreement with the leader of the elected majority in filling the seven reserved seats, and that he would reinstate the Alliance's Legislative Councillors who were boycotting the Council. It was the Tunku who had climbed down, but it was a victory for trust and common sense. A year later, the Alliance won 51 of the 52 elected seats in Malaya's first general election, and Tunku Abdul Rahman was appointed Chief Minister. And on August 31st, 1957, with the inevitability of a Greek tragedy in reverse, he became the first Prime Minister of an independent Malaya within the Commonwealth. Chin Peng, the Malayan communist leader, was still in the jungle.

The alternative leader policy had thus been successful beyond all hopes; and unlike Dr. Nkrumah of Ghana or Pandit Nehru of India, the Tunku had achieved independence without the traditional spell of detention. To be sure, Abdul Rahman had shown admirable qualities of leadership and political sanity. One may doubt that Bao Dai had the first of these qualities in reserve, though he undoubtedly had the second. But one may also legitimately wonder whether the Tunku, if three successive High Commissioners and two Colonial Secretaries had failed to encourage and support him, would have become anything more than the playboy he once was.

2

Better than Cure

IF asked to name examples of political settlements that probably prevented major insurrections, one tends to mention India, Burma and Ceylon. They are perfectly legitimate examples, but too well known to justify further comment. It would be wrong, however, to overlook the Tunisian and Moroccan settlements, which showed that enlightened French Governments—those of MM. Mendès-France and Edgar Faure—were capable of avoiding the monumental errors and obstinacies of previous and succeeding administrations.

When M. Mendès-France had won his dramatic bet with the clock at Geneva, bringing peace to Indo-China within thirty days of assuming office, he turned his attention to North Africa. Both Morocco and Tunisia were in the grip of terrorism and general insecurity. The Sultan of Morocco had been deported and replaced by an obedient figurehead, Moulay Arafa, with the blessing of El Glaoui, the powerful Pasha of Marrakesh; Habib Bourguiba, leader of the Tunisian nationalist party, the Neo Destour, was under detention in France. M. Mendès-France was a believer in tackling one job at a time; having disposed of Indo-China, he set himself to solving the Tunisian problem, but not, for the time being, the Moroccan one. With his usual sense of drama, he flew to Tunis bearing a plan for home rule and accompanied—a stroke of political genius—by Marshal Juin, a tough, right-wing soldier regarded by the French settlers as their "champion". His formula was the intelligent one of combining "pacification" with political concessions; the combination was calculated to restore the confidence of the settlers while giving hope to the Tunisian nationalists. His home rule plan provided for a Tunisian cabinet with French advisers, for an elected assembly and for Franco-Tunisian conventions under which Frenchmen could continue to live in Tunisia in confidence and security. At this stage, M.

Mendès-France was not yet ready to free Bourguiba, but from his exile, the Neo Destour leader recommended the cessation of terrorism. The moderate Tunisian leader, Tahar ben Ammar, a wealthy landowner, formed a cabinet which included Neo Destour members. (By one of those reversals of fortune that are so common in the politics of newly independent countries, Mr. Bourguiba, when firmly in power as President of an independent Tunisia, brought Mr. Tahar ben Ammar to trial.)

M. Mendès-France had, within a few days, set Tunisia firmly on the path of the independence which it had lost to France under the Treaty of 1881. But it was left to his successor, M. Edgar Faure, to round off the job. On March 20th, 1956, M. Pineau, the French Foreign Minister, and Mr. Tahar ben Ammar met in Paris to sign a protocol under which France recognised Tunisia's independence. And on April 15th, Mr. Bourguiba, freed by the French and triumphantly welcomed home in Tunis, formed his first cabinet.

One of M. Mendès-France's contributions to a solution of North African problems had been the creation of a Ministry for Tunisia and Morocco—an act which, in itself, gratified the nationalists of both countries. M. Faure was willing to draw the logical conclusions dictated by Tunisian developments, but the legacy of the Laniel government made the circumstances unpropitious. Terrorism by Moroccan nationalists, and counterterrorism by French settlers, grew steadily worse during the first nine months of 1956. One of the main difficulties, for the French, was to persuade their puppet Sultan, Moulay Arafa, to go quietly; but this he was willing to do only in his own time and without loss of dignity. On October 1st, he left Rabat, the capital, for Tangier; and on October 30th, he formally abdicated in a letter to President Coty of France. That day, the deposed Sultan, Mohammed ben Yussef, left Madagascar—his place of detention —by air for Paris. The French Foreign Minister, M. Pineau, had interrupted his work at the Big Four foreign ministers' conference in Geneva, to greet the Sultan in Paris. On November 6th, still in Paris, Mohammed ben Yussef was reinstated *de jure* sovereign of

Morocco; and two days later the aged Pasha of Marrakesh prostrated himself before the Sultan to beg his forgiveness, which the Sultan granted. On the 16th, like Mr. Bourguiba in Tunisia, the Sultan returned to Morocco, where a fervent welcome awaited him.

Morocco had caught up with Tunisia and, indeed, drawn slightly ahead in the race to independence. A joint declaration signed in Paris by M. Pineau, the Foreign Minister, and Si Bekkai, the Moroccan Prime Minister, in the presence of Sultan Mohammed, recognised the independence, sovereignty and integrity of Morocco. Thus ended a phase which had begun on March 30th, 1912, when France assumed protectorate rights in the country under treaty with the then Sultan, Moulay Hafid.

* * *

There is no doubt that, without the Moroccan and Tunisian settlements, the whole of French North Africa—and not merely Algeria—would have been ablaze by 1956. This probability must be remembered by those who criticise the two settlements on various grounds: for instance, because each provided for "interdependence" with France as well as independence, but left the term undefined, so that the independence of each was ambiguous; or, to look at another aspect, because by repressing a nationalist uprising in Algeria, France soured its relations with Morocco and Tunisia, since neither, for the deepest reasons of affinity, could withhold aid and comfort to the Algerian rebels. These criticisms are perfectly valid. There were three possible courses open to the French in North Africa: repression everywhere, which would have meant the rapid and total loss of all three territories; accommodation everywhere, which might have "kept" all three in the sense of friendship and deeper links with France; and the course which France, in the event chose—cutting its losses in Morocco and Tunisia, the better to hold Algeria.

But was it, in fact, possible for a French government in 1954–56 to reach a settlement with Algerian Moslem nationalism? For that matter, was it possible for the British Government of the day to reach a settlement with the Greek Cypriots? Or to avoid the troubles in Kenya? In quite another context, could the communist rebellions of 1948 have been avoided? Could Fulgencio Batista have taken the kind of action that would have made Fidel Castro's uprising irrelevant?

We are once again, but not unprofitably, in the realm of the hypothetical. In politics every solution has its price and the price will vary according to the condition of the market; moreover, conversely, the buyer's willingness to pay is inconstant, particularly in a democratic society. In 1945, the government of General de Gaulle was offering Algerian Moslems peaceful evolution towards equality; the followers of Messali Hadj answered with the riots and massacres of Sétif. In 1947, the same commodity was on offer in the Statute of Algeria; many of the Moslems were ready to buy, but the European settlers ensured that the contents of the packet were different from those shown on the label, and so there was no sale. In 1958 the settlers, egged on by M. Soustelle, were offering "integration", the magic formula which Ferhat Abbas would have rushed to buy ten years earlier had it been on offer then. By that time and for several years past, the main body of Algerian nationalists, including Mr. Abbas, were in the market only for "independence" which, a year after General de Gaulle's return to power, was still not for sale. In commerce, including the retail trade, a sale takes place when the buyer's desire for a commodity and his ability to pay for it coincide with the price demanded. In politics, too.

It is, I suggest, axiomatic that no government will willingly buy a settlement at a price that drives it out of office. The price of tranquillity among the Algerian Moslems in 1954 was independence, and no French government that showed itself willing to pay it would have lasted more than twenty-four hours. Besides, even if the price had been paid and the government had—miraculously—won the inevitable vote of confidence, it would have had a civil war instead of a rebellion on its hands in Algeria. Similarly, no Conservative government in Britain in 1954–55 would willingly have paid the price for tranquillising the Greek

Cypriots, which was the immediate application of the principle of self-determination. To have done so in 1954 would certainly have divided the Conservative Party or, rather, deepened the existing division that had been caused by the abandonment of Palestine and the Suez Canal base. This division would probably not have forced the Conservatives out of office, although their majority in 1954 was much smaller than it became the following year; but it would have seriously weakened their hold on power. Nor were the further consequences necessarily desirable, even in absolute terms. Self-determination would have led to the union of Greece and Cyprus—a solution which, if only because of the distance of Cyprus from Greece and its proximity to Turkey, would have been built on sand. True, in 1954 the Turks were phlegmatic in Cyprus and indifferent on the mainland; but they would not necessarily have remained calm for long, even if the Macmillan government had not—to their amazement—thrown the Cyprus problem into their laps. To have refrained from meeting the wishes of the enosists on these grounds would have been commendably statesmanlike. But the Churchill and Eden governments could scarcely argue that they decided to ignore the wishes of Eoka and its supporters because they hoped eventually to achieve the sane settlement which the Macmillan government approved in 1959, for there was no thought of a political solution for Cyprus from 1954 to 1957. The official reason for preferring pure repression to the search for a political solution was that Cyprus was an indispensable base for the defence of Britain's Middle Eastern interests. It is quite likely that many of the politicians who supported this proposition believed it to be true; but the real reasons were a general reluctance to abandon yet another imperial position and a fear of the political consequences of so doing. In these terms, the price of tranquillity was considered too high.

In Kenya, to an even greater degree than in Cyprus, the government was faced by the demands of a group of extremists, among whom the primitive and the insane competed for leadership. There, as in Algeria, the problem was immensely complicated by the presence of European settlers, who would not have accepted a solution that appeared to consist of appeasing the black population. In 1952, no British government—whether Conservative or Labour—could have paid the price of tranquillity. Nor, in 1948, could the governments of Malaya, Burma, Indonesia and the Philippines have given in to the demands of their local communist parties. Governments are at least as reluctant as public companies to go into voluntary liquidation. And dictators are more reluctant still: Batista could scarcely have been expected to stand down in Castro's favour in 1956; nor could he cleanse Cuba of the corruption which the *Fidelistas* complained of without losing the support of the very elements who kept him in power.

The date is all: in the year of rebellion no solution is politically possible (that, indeed, is why there is a rebellion); but earlier it might have been. The element of doubt is inevitably strong, for governments are composed of more or less rational human beings; and even if they have the intelligence to discern a possible solution and the foresight to prepare for it in what appears to be good time, their tenure of office depends, in the final analysis, on the support of many more human beings, who tend, in the mass, to be even less rational than they might be as individuals. And mass emotions and prejudices are political factors in their own right. Can one legislate against a colour bar in Kenya or Southern Rhodesia? Or against the *tutoiement* of Algerian Moslems by their European betters? Or against the Hellenism of a Greek Cypriot?

But if one cannot reasonably ask of a government that it should forget self-interest (since if it did, it would no longer be a government), one may reasonably require that its self-interest be enlightened. And this in turn demands foresight and honesty—at least with itself. The Cypriot problem of the 'fifties was inherent in the views of the Cypriots at the time of British annexation during the first world war. After the violent warning of 1931, the British Government (which, it is true, was more worried about the great depression) ought to have started thinking of ways to avoid trouble later. Since no British government has ever approved of *enosis* as a deliberate aim, it ought to have occurred to one of them that the best way of denying a popular demand is not necessarily by denying it a political outlet. Independence—within or outside the British Commonwealth—was always a possible solution to the problem of Cyprus. Successive British governments always argued: independence equals self-determination equals *enosis*. But there was always a fallacy in this reasoning: given a rapid evolution towards self-government, followed by actual self-government for a fairly long but stated period, the Cypriots might well have found that the practical advantages of running their own affairs, and of the Commonwealth connection, outweighed the emotional appeal of being ruled by a poor and distant motherland. Archbishop Makarios was well aware of this, as the captured minutes of the Ethnarchy Council clearly showed: he overruled the arguments of those who thought that the Greeks should settle for self-government for a stated number of years, followed by self-determination, on the ground that by that time the Greek Cypriots would no longer want *enosis*. If there was a solution to the Cypriot problem, it surely lay along those lines.

The Cypriot problem was, of course, unique. But that of Kenya was not. In the wider sense, it was part of the general problem of the surge towards independence in the Asian and African dependencies of the European powers; and in the narrower sense, it was similar to the particular problem of all territories with large settler populations (which include not only Algeria and Southern Rhodesia, but also, in a different racial setting, Malaya and Fiji). The Asian independence movement in the 'forties ought to have pointed to a similar movement in the 'fifties. And to be sure, many people correctly read the warning; but relatively few foresaw the rapidity with which the anti-colonial movement in Africa was to catch up and merge with the Asian movement. In consequence, the Afro-Asian Conference at Bandung in April, 1955, came as a surprise and a shock. In west Africa, where there was no settler population of consequence, the British saw the warning and acted by swiftly leading the Gold Coast and Nigeria towards independence. In east and central Africa, where strong settler communities acted as a brake on initiative, British colonial policy was much less farsighted.

It is not, of course, in the British tradition to try to find a political solution by logical analysis. But it cannot have escaped many officials that the number of courses open to the rulers of plural societies is, by the nature of the problem, strictly limited. One may legislate for segregation and the permanent domination of one community, as the Nationalist government of the Union of South Africa has been doing with its probably tragic experiment of *apartheid*. At the other extreme, one may deliberately encourage miscegenation—though where a prejudice already exists legislating *for* miscegenation must be even more difficult than legislating *against* a colour bar. (An impartial observer cannot help noticing that societies that have encouraged racial mixtures— like Brazil, the Philippines or Hawaii—appear to be a good deal happier than those that have rigorously resisted them. And it may not be entirely by coincidence that the Portuguese, who neither maintain a colour bar nor frown on mixed unions, appear to have had no trouble in their African colonies in the first half of 1959, when there had been violent unrest in the Belgian Congo and in the British territories of Nyasaland and Uganda.) It is perhaps typical of the British leaning towards compromise that the Colonial Office, shunning both extremes, fostered instead the ideal of "partnership" in east and central Africa. However, it takes two to make partners, as it does to make a quarrel; for having resisted partnership in earlier years, the white settlers of Kenya found themselves in mid-1959—when these words were written —nearer the prospect of an African state than they would have liked to admit.

But these are not, of course, problems for the white man alone. After independence, Burma and Indonesia faced it, too. For the dominant element—the Burmese in Burma and the Javanese in Indonesia—there existed, from the start, the problem of reaching accommodation with minority peoples within the state. We have measured the extent of their failure.

But it is more difficult to measure, in hypothetical terms, the possible effects of the actions the Burmese and Indonesian *failed* to take. Who knows what troubles Aung San would have avoided for his successor if he had paid as much attention to the fears and aspirations of the Karens at the Panglong conference of 1947, as he did to those of the Kachins, whose fighting qualities he wished to enlist on his side? We cannot answer because Aung San did not try to reduce the suspicions of Karens. But we may safely say that the attempt would have been worth making. It is no answer to say that in the general lawlessness and scramble for power of the post-war period, and in the face of the communist challenge, any such attempt would have been doomed to failure. It is pre cisely *because* the circumstances were so unfavourable that the attempt ought to have been made, for nothing that might have improved the conditions of Burma's assumption of sovereignty should have been left undone.

Similarly, President Sukarno of Indonesia bears a heavy responsibility before his countrymen: for failing to rise above party and for tolerating the misgovernment of the party he had founded (the nationalist PNI); for failing to realise the danger to Indonesia's independence which the rapid growth of the Communist Party (PKI) presented during the 'fifties; for venting his anti-colonial wrath on thousands of "Dutchmen", many of whom had never set foot in the Netherlands; for failing to see that Indonesia was not viable under a unitary constitution; and, in the last analysis, for failing to understand that he himself was the greatest obstacle to Indonesia's unity. The 1958 rebellion was quite the most avoidable of the disturbances considered in this book. But the will to avoid it would have taken a statesman at the helm; and the man in charge had neither the will nor the capacity which a complex situation demanded.

When one turns to the rebellions against totalitarian or dictatorial rule, one wonders whether our exercise in hypothesis is worth continuing. Of course Batista could have seized the land and shared it out among the needy peasants, of course he could have closed the brothels and gambling houses, dispersed the secret police, called free elections. But if he had done these things, he would not have been Batista. Similarly, the communist rulers of Hungary could have allowed freedom of expression, refrained from torturing the opposition and explained to the Russians that oppression was dangerous. But if they had done these things, they would not have been communists. We have reached the no-man's land of inverted Marxist logic, where mere reason cannot hope to survive.

*   *   *

By writing all this chapter so far, and indeed most of this book, from the point of view of rebels against authority, I may have given the impression that I hold all authority to be wrong and every rebel to be right. This is far from being my opinion. I have merely tried to show that rebellion is usually a symptom of misgovernment; that it is better for governments to seek political solutions than military ones; and that there is nothing inviolable about the legitimacy of power. At one time, the accredited representatives of foreign powers in countries like Tunisia and the Gold Coast were mere consuls or consuls-general; a few years later, they were ministers and ambassadors, for in the meantime sovereignty had changed hands.

But in achieving this goal of sovereignty—however untempting it often seems to the uncommitted observer—some rebels have undeniably been more successful than others. And the failures, relative or absolute, have not, by any means, always been due to the strength and determination of the authorities. Rebels, like officials, have their shortcomings. It was foolish of the Indonesian rebels to proclaim a government in February, 1958, when, manifestly, they lacked the strength and popular support— particularly in Java—that would have ensured success. And we have seen in our chapters on terrorism how fallible and unsatisfactory is that unpleasant method of rebellion.

True, the incomprehension or ham-handedness of governments often invites the terrorist response. Denied constitutional outlets for opposition, the more impatient or coarser-grained rebels are nearly always tempted by terrorism. Yet they can hardly pretend that alternative courses have been left untried. Mahatma Gandhi's teachings of non-violence and *Satyagraha* ("soul force") played a major part in gaining "India for the Indians". Admittedly, however, "a major part" does not amount to the full credit, though it would make things easier for the contemporary historian if it did. The teachings of Gandhi did at least influence the Indian National Congress in the fundamental sense of persuading it to decide in favour of civil disobedience instead of armed rebellion. But disobedience to Gandhi's teaching was often as conspicuous as disobedience to the British Raj. Three times, between 1919 and 1922, Gandhi called off the movement of civil disobedience, because it had degenerated into popular violence. In 1923, when he was in prison, the Bengal Revolutionary Council, many of whose members also belonged to the Congress Party, started a widespread programme of assassination. Checked in Bengal, the terrorists moved to the Punjab and the United Provinces. In April, 1929, they threw bombs into the Legislative Assembly in Delhi, and in December they tried to derail the Viceroy's train. Between July, 1937, and September, 1939, when the then Viceroy, Lord Linlithgow, had allowed the Congress Party to form ministries, communal violence was on the increase in Bihar and the United Provinces. Indeed, throughout the years of Gandhi's political activity his teaching consistently failed to prevent violence between the Hindus and Moslems—until the final bloodbath that followed the partition of the Indian sub-continent in August, 1947.

It would be misleading, in the light of this dismal catalogue, to look to India as an example of non-violent rebellion. But it is perfectly fair to say that the Indian nationalists won independence without resorting to armed insurrection. And it is equally fair to point out that it took them thirty-two years to do it, starting from Gandhi's first campaign of civil disobedience in 1915. Few rebels are prepared to wait that long.

* * *

There is then, it seems, no perfect recipe for rebellion, as indeed there is none for ruling over those who would prefer to rule

Index